THE NORFOLK LIBRARY

NO HALT AT SUNSET

The Diary of a Country Housewife

NO HALT AT SUNSET

THE DIARY OF A COUNTRY HOUSEWIFE

ELIZABETH M. HARLAND

A man's work ends at set of sun
A woman's work is never done

THE BOYDELL PRESS · IPSWICH

Published by the Boydell Press
PO Box 24 · Ipswich IP1 1JJ

First published 1951
Reissued 1974

ISBN 0 85115 032 2

Printed and bound in Great Britain by
REDWOOD BURN LIMITED
Trowbridge & Esher

CONTENTS

v

NOTE

The greater portion of the entries in this "House-wife's Journal" were originally published in the *Eastern Daily Press* of Norwich, by whose kind permission they are now reprinted.

I

MAY 2 Wake to dull, cold, damp morning. But weather completely fails to exert its usual subduing effect when I
remember that after nearly four years of hunting for sizeable
house with small acreage of land, we have now found same, and
are only waiting for repairs to be done by landlord to move in.
Hymn my joy for the two -hundredth -and -fiftieth time in last six
days, and end up by demanding happily of Adam where he thinks
we'll be two months from to-day.

Exactly where we are to-day, he answers morosely, not sharing
my simple faith in builders' promises. If I ask him, we were much
too hasty in cancelling our 'plane reservations, hotel accommoda-
tion, and Dublin drive-yourself car for proposed motoring trip
through Eire at the end of July. And if we get to Hillingsett before
next Christmas, he'll be uncommonly surprised.

MAY 3 Could spend hours dawdling through Norwich Market
Place, with its colourful stalls and friendly stall-holders.
Highly entertained this morning by patter of vocal vendor of
hosiery who at one point offers to sell first six lady clients one pair
of silk stockings each for threepence. Long to advance through
throng brandishing threepenny pieces, but do not really care for
shade (or texture) of stockings, so tear myself away to buy lemons
at another stall. Then home to make lemon curd.

Have three recipes for this, two from grandmother's day, one
recently given me by Kate, all good. No. 1 demands 1 lb. sugar,
½ lb. butter, 4 eggs, grated rind and juice of 2 lemons. No. 2
requires ½ lb. sugar, 2 oz. butter, 2 lemons, 3 eggs. No. 3 takes
¼ lb. sugar, 1 oz. butter, 2 eggs, 2 lemons. Plump for No. 1 with
margarine substituted for butter, and an extra lemon as we like
ours tart in flavour. Then proceed to melt margarine in saucepan,

11

add sugar, grated rind of lemons (yellow only) and juice, lastly the well-beaten eggs, and stir continually until mixture thickness of cream. Success, of course, as with egg-custard, depends in removing saucepan from stove just before it reaches the required consistency (approximately 4–5 minutes).

MAY 5   Have always felt that women should sit on housing committees, and look over architects' shoulders in an advisory capacity. Are they doing more of this than they did? Was certainly refreshingly surprised by interior layout of new council "housen" now being built at GUIST, when shown over one this afternoon. A roomy hall, with space for a pram underneath the stairs; a pleasant sitting-room with a fireplace easy on fuel: kitchen-living-room big enough to allow the housewife to keep toddlers under her eye (instead of being forced to choose between risk of their pulling a boiling saucepan off the stove in the kitchenette, or efficiently wrecking the living-room whilst she cooks) and equipped with cupboards and a stove for cooking and water-heating: a light airy scullery with electric cooker, built-in dresser, sink with hot and cold water placed below a window and set at a reasonable height instead of one only suitable for dwarfs: adjoining pantries: three bedrooms with built-in cupboards: a bathroom: and space for magpie hoards in the roof. If we weren't already suited, should have been tempted to put my name down for one right away!

MAY 6   "The public is getting tired of the same old cod," said an official at a Fishmongers' Conference recently. Couldn't agree with him more, though I gather he's chiefly concerned with display on shop slabs. Own contribution to brighter cod movement include stewing it in cider and serving with a white sauce enlivened with a teaspoon of tarragon vinegar, dash of lemon juice, and chopped parsley: and placing our portions in fireproof dish, covering with canned tomato juice, adding pepper, salt, and chopped onion to taste, and baking in medium oven for about twenty minutes.

MAY 7   In Norwich twice during week, but no time to fit in visit to hairdresser's, so once again wash and set locks myself. This is usual immense non-success, much care and labour producing result resembling house-sparrow's nest, and such a flow of wit from Adam that ask him sourly if he's been in the knifebox. Wish for the *n*th time had naturally curly hair like my offspring Eve, and wonder why some enterprising person doesn't start a travelling hairdressing saloon. Mobile canteens, cake shops, fish-and-chip vans abound. Why not a mobile hairdresser's? Am convinced this would be a boon to country housewives. And if anyone will start a round, will gladly be first client.

MAY 8 Pay surreptitious visit to blackbird's nest discovered in ivy on garden wall a week ago, and find three eggs in it. Retailing this to Rosemary (born a "townee") at tea, she enquires blankly how I knew it was a blackbird's the first time if there weren't any eggs?

Any country bumpkin, myself included, can answer that, I tell her promptly. Blackbirds always build their nests of dried grass, about six inches in diameter, and three or so deep, and reinforce it with a mud lining, which in turn is lined with more dried grass. Thrushes commence in the same way, but stop when the mud wall is completed. The chaffinch's nest, perhaps one-quarter the size, is made of lichen and moss, horsehair and sheepswool, blended by the most superb craftsmanship into one enchanting whole. Wrens favour moss with a warm, preferably horsehair, lining, and are one of the few species to add a roof, the entrance being a round hole in the nest side. Swans build a solitary sedge pile on river banks or in willow belts. Herons, contrary to what one might expect, build their yard-wide stick-and-grass nests in trees, and dwell in colonies, like rooks. Sandmartins, also colonists, have miniature rabbit burrows in sand and gravel pits, with a few shreds of grass at the end of them. Kingfishers, individualists like the swans, choose earth, clay, or sandy banks near rivers, emulate the sandmartins by using tunnels, but make the actual nest by the simple but unlovable method of regurgitating the bones of the fish they swallow. Housemartins and swallows both use mud-scales lined with feathers, the latter favouring saucer-shaped nests, the former preferring a style somewhat like the wrens. House-sparrows are untidy as the martins are houseproud, a jumbled bundle of feathers and straw passing for a nest unless they dispossess the housemartins, as they not infrequently do.

Am quite prepared to enlarge on the architectural habits of woodpeckers, moorhens, wild ducks, robins, "yellow-hammers" and blue-tits, "pee-wits" and skylarks, turtle-doves and pigeons, the warbler tribe and anything else she fancies. But deduce from Rosemary's dazed expression that it's time to change the subject, so hastily enquire after health of other occupants of married quarters at R.A.F. Station, Eastmere, instead.

MAY 10   Variety not only spice of life, but definitely soul of salad dressings. The simple oil (3 parts), vinegar (1 part), with pepper and salt to taste, lends itself to endless variations, lemon juice substituting for vinegar, top-of-milk for oil, with added pinches of sugar, minced parsley, chervil, mint, chives, thyme, and so on.

White sauce makes a useful foundation to cream-type dressings. One that keeps well can be produced by adding to white sauce that takes one pint milk the following, well mixed: 1 beaten egg, 2 teaspoons each salt, sugar, mustard, pinch of pepper. Cook, preferably in double saucepan until thickened, gradually stirring in one cup of vinegar. Incline to wine vinegar myself. Adam prefers malt. Lise, in Denmark, sometimes uses spiced vinegar made as follows: Boil 2 pints vinegar until reduced by half, pour into bowl containing three minced shallots, a sprig of thyme, 2 bay leaves, $\frac{1}{2}$ teaspoon salt, a few crushed peppercorns. Cover, leave one hour, then strain.

For an easy mayonnaise, add salt, pepper (pinch cayenne and mustard optional), 1 tablespoon vinegar, to 2 egg yolks. Then, beating vigorously, add $1\frac{1}{2}$ cups of oil (salad or olive), first drop by drop, then in increasing quantities. If you're unlucky or careless, and it curdles, either fold in an extra egg yolk a little at a time, or put a dessertspoon of boiling water into a second bowl, and add the mayonnaise drop by drop, stirring all the time.

MAY 12   Our Vicar having called round yesterday and let fall that when in Lincolnshire last week he bought sixty tulips for three-and-sixpence from wayside stall, impress on Adam that if he returns from Wisbech area to-day without a large bunch for me, he'll find out why wives leave home. He'll certainly do his best, replies Adam, but cannot promise anything, as Tulip Sunday was the one before last, when those parts sported almost as many sightseers as tulips, some of them from as far away as Glasgow. Since when he's seen acres beheaded, so that the sap goes back to the bulb. But never a wayside stall, either then or earlier, or I should have had some tulips before.

Purr at this. And purr louder still when Adam returns with immense sheaf of plain, frilled, and parrot tulips, in every shade of colour imaginable, bought from bulb farm which doesn't usually sell flowers, but has succumbed in this instance to Adam's manly charm. Blooms have had to stay in car waterless all day, however, and are now somewhat jaded, so leave them in tall jug with cold water right up to their necks. And also drop penny in jug. These remedies suggested by old London flower-seller, and equally good for daffodils, etc.: though her considered opinion is that tulips prefer teaspoon of sugar to copper coin. (Not in these days, in my vases, I fear!) She recommended aspirin for almost any fainting flower, especially wild ones: warm water for mimosa, the splitting of carnation stems, and the beating of chrysanthemum stalks. Whilst to ensure the rest of the blooms coming out simultaneously, she alway snipped out the top from gladioli spikes.

MAY 13   Round W.I. Exhibition at St. Andrew's Hall, which brings out all the squirrel in me, and makes me long to decamp with everything in show. How Dickens . . . and Parson Woodforde . . . would have revelled in the display of food. Such sweets and mixed biscuits; such rich fruit cakes, in spite of rationing; such crusty loaves; such jars of jams, jellies, marmalades, and honey; such bottles of fruit, vegetables, salad creams, and dried herbs; not to mention ready-to-eat two-course meals, and a table of uncooked hams. "She doesn't use black treacle for hers. Golden syrup and Demerara sugar," observed one onlooker to another, intent on these last.

Watch one demonstrator filling grape-fruit skins with potato salad. Long to be able to arrange flowers with skill of another performing miracles at bottom of hall, and wish Eve could be here to see the combination of lilac and guelder rose in one corner. Pause to admire patchwork articles, and silently echo comment of bystander who says, "They must have the patience of Job". Break tenth commandment again and again looking at knitted garments. And lingering by Dereham's perfect co-operative cot, imagine a brother for Eve, and wonder how many more cot-gazers have turned wistfully away.

MAY 14   Sandwich lunch in prospect, with usual problems . . . how many and what? Too few a great mistake, but too many worse in view of paucity of butter and unattractiveness of left-overs: though dipping these last in batter and serving them fried does help, always supposing one can spare the fat. For fillings decide on (*a*) grated cheese mixed with equal quantity of margarine and some shelled walnuts (crushed with rolling pin) plus shredded lettuce; (*b*) corned beef and sliced tomato. N.B.— former much improved by few days in refrigerator, which also makes it easier to cut thinly; (*c*) cheese mixture as in (*a*), minus the walnuts, but plus dash of Worcester sauce, radishes (grated) from the garden, and watercress (chopped) for which I have paddled into the mill-pool. Whilst sponge sandwich filling is made by creaming 4 oz. icing sugar with 2 oz. margarine, and adding remaining crushed walnuts.

Morning has started blanketed with fog, but this now lifts, out comes the sun, and off we go to Fakenham Steeplechases. Purposely arrive early to secure place in members' car park just behind winning-post, as this means we needn't bother to go up on the stand, though Adam mentions firmly that it's no good thinking I can stand on car roof, it's in a poor enough condition now. Have plenty of time before first race due to start, so walk round course inspecting jumps, and do some jumping on own account as small aircraft suddenly looms overhead, obviously about to land. When it does, well away from everyone, usual miracle occurs, small boys materialising out of space and surrounding it within ten seconds. Racing grand, with remarkably few "spills." At one moment saw clouds of spray in distance, and feared had missed chance of realising life-long ambition to see someone land in middle of water-jump, but nobody has. As usual, do not "spot" a single winner, but this only means transferring the sum of sixpence from my purse to Adam's, for discovered years ago that horse does not exist strong enough to carry added weight of my most modest bet, whilst to stake the smallest coin on the family 'chaser was tantamount to calling out the ambulance for brother John, his jockey. And, anyway, have had a lovely day.

But do dogs really enjoy race-meetings? On a lead a dog's-eye view is apt to be little more than a forest of legs. Off it, they are a lurking menace. Have vivid recollection of one pre-war point-to-point when over twenty runners paraded at the start, which was also the home side of the last fence. "They're off!" Up the straight they came, between the crowds, towards the first fence. Yap! Yelp! Yap! Right in front of them somebody's pet streaked across the course and, baulked in take-off, down came more than one horse and rider. We were spared any such incident to-day, though the small but active minority of spectators who evidently feel it a point of honour to bolt from one side to the other just after the hunt servants have cleared the course were well in evidence, as usual.

MAY 16   Downstairs to find Aga cooker out, of own accord. This has never happened before, and no apparent reason for disaster now. Had thought of making childhood favourite Queen Gertrude pudding for lunch . . . 2 oz. breadcrumbs, 6 oz. sugar, 1 oz. butter (marg.) melted, grated rind 1 lemon, 1 pint milk, well-beaten yolks 2 eggs, mixed together, baked in moderate oven, when nearly cold spread with layer of raspberry jam, then topped with well-whisked whites of eggs to which little sugar added, and put in cool oven until meringue is light brown. Abandon this forthwith for unadorned bottled strawberries, and help Adam wrestle with Aga, armed with brushes, newspapers, charcoal, and pious hopes.

MAY 18   Being keen members of Soil Association, with strong views on conserving soil fertility, have lost no time in replying to recent R.D.C. advertisement re sewage sludge for composting, my parent is willing to loan site for heaps as we have no room where we are and Hillingsett outside R.D.C.'s juris-diction, and have promptly ordered 15 tons of straw. Set off for site at crack of dawn this morning to superintend unloading of straw, and setting out in adequate bases, when horrified to dis-cover exactly how much 15 tons is. Efforts to find out beforehand how much unbaled straw goes to wagon-load has signally failed, and in our ignorance we seem to have acquired equivalent of three stacks! Can only be thankful that prices decided us against ordering 40 tons, which was our first estimate!

MAY 19   Adam, on spur of moment, decides to have four teeth out. Feel I should have had quite fortnight's warning, to hunt up invalid food. Luckily fish man calls late in afternoon, so welcome back sufferer with soup . . . half-pint of milk in which sprig of mint, spring onion, teaspoon of marmite, pinch of salt and pepper have been simmering for fifteen minutes. Next course fillet of plaice (William Cat watches preparation of this with much interest), cooked by wrapping in greased paper, baking in oven ten minutes, served with bottled tomatoes and lemon slices. Caramel custard to follow, made by putting 2 oz. loaf sugar into saucepan with $\frac{1}{4}$ pint cold water, boiling quickly with lid off and without stirring until pale coffee colour, then pouring mixture round insides of small dry moulds, where it immediately hardens. Custard mixture, comprised of 2 well-beaten eggs, $\frac{1}{2}$ pint milk, $\frac{1}{2}$ teaspoon sugar, then added, tins covered with greaseproof paper, and puddings steamed gently until set.

MAY 20   Enquire anxiously how does mouth feel, and what can victim eat? Anything, says Adam. This new technique whereby false teeth inserted immediately own ditto removed, seems very successful. (Query, is it so new? As seem to remember tales of good old days when master's teeth extracted, and servant's, yanked out at same time, thrust into former's gaping gums. Though bound to add this long before Lister, and results usually unfortunate.) Anything? Salad, for instance? Certainly, answers Adam promptly. Have only lettuce and rest of bottled tomatoes on hand, but supplement these with watercress from mill-pool, parsley (said to be excellent for nerves), and dandelion (which Culpepper recommends for liver and insomnia) from garden. Radishes finished last week, when put in more seed. Site on following day looked like floor of birds' ballroom after gala event. But much relieved this morning to see neat row of seedling plants.

MAY 23   Hillingsett Lodge being blessed with small poultry food allocation, pay morning visit to neighbouring poultry farmer to acquire details of latest methods of feeding fowls, as own experience belongs to halcyon days when rang up merchants and ordered five tons of laying meal without a second thought. Return home with much information and fragment of probable Roman pot unearthed when drains being dug out on meadow. Reflect that in days to come somebody may be poring over relics from our dustbin, and can't imagine what they'll make of them. No time to pursue this train of thought, however, as Freda rings up and proposes herself for tea. Days when fruit cakes stowed away in tins in pantry against just such emergencies as remote as those of abundant poultry food. Can muster 8 oz. sugar, 8 oz. flour, 6 oz. margarine, 1 egg, a few currants, and a lemon, so get down to biscuits. Mix sugar and flour, rub in fat, mix with egg, flavour with lemon juice. Half result, adding currants to one portion. Roll out wafer thin, cut in rounds, etc., and bake in medium oven for about ten minutes.

MAY 24 Overnight several potatoes reft from basket under sink, bitten and left lying about scullery floor. Samuel Whiskers and family have evidently paid another call when William Cat otherwise engaged.

"It's the penalty of living near water," Guy informs us, when he drops in. "You always get rats where there's water. And if you keep fowls, it's worse." We don't, yet, we point out. Guy hasn't said we do, he's merely stating fact. Anyway, Brandy has oats. Kept in a tin, we hasten to assure him. And, at the moment, with Eve away, he's elsewhere. What about those bullocks in the yard behind your buildings, enquires Guy. Well, then . . . "Though you'd get them just the same, bullocks or no, because of the river. The thing to do is find their runs and keep a trap set." Rats, according to Guy, have regular habits. In summer they take to fields and fences. As winter approaches, they make for buildings and warmer quarters. Arrived at latter, the first thing they do is to undertake tour of inspection. When he took his first farm this alive with rats, enlarges Guy, so he went on tour of own. A spot where one outside wall ended and another began, a foot or so below, struck him as likely place for trap, since rats favour promenades along coping of walls; and night after night he caught one there. Then a day passed without one . . . a week . . . two . . . "Find their run, keep a trap there, and soon you won't have a rat on the place."

We know whereabouts of several of the Whiskers' runs, some ·of which are obviously in walls of house. But the Whiskers evidently a family apart. Not only are they exceptions to Guy's ruling of summer holiday, but they have ways of dealing with traps. Have already set several, only to find next morning no sign of bait or corpses. When, following weird and wonderful arrangement, by Adam, of mouse and rat traps designed to confuse marauders, something did go off, no rat in it, though youthful victim nearby apparently expired from shock. Have been no luckier with sundry "infallible" recipes for poisoning, since these naturally depend for success on intruders sampling them, and so far Whiskers family have left all such offerings alone.

"Look at that!" exclaims Adam suddenly, glimpsing through

window three of Whiskers tribe approaching kitchen door from direction of rain-water tank. Master Whiskers pauses to nibble at my newly planted wistaria. His parents stand on hind-legs, and scratch at kitchen and scullery doors. Adam darts into the hall for the 4.10, and a second later is out of front door and creeping down drive to corner of house. Bang! Mrs. Whiskers (we hope) is no more. But, undeterred, her relations are back again within ten minutes. Have been bemoaning that Hillingsett House nowhere near river. But foresee certain compensations in this.

MAY 26   Wake to sound of steady, persistent swish—swish—swish. Outside drive is full of small lakes, and young torrent cascading off roof of old mill adjoining the house and merrily overflowing tank outside scullery door. Inspect rain-gauge in due course, tipping out another ten points, making one hundred and eighteen for past three days, not to mention shower of hailstones yesterday that temporarily made premises look as if a celestial grocer had suddenly discarded truck of loaf sugar. Know that "Rain in May means long hay", and that we are badly behind on our rain schedule. But as rain continues, wish that clerk of weather not so all-or-nothing by temperament, as had planned to spend morning weeding garden. Get down to sundry overdue household chores instead, and deal with distinctly off-white pair of wash-leather gloves, using best soap-flakes and warm water, washing on hands, and scrubbing fingers with nail brush. Rinse well in fresh soapy water, put back on hands, dry on towel, remove gloves, blow into fingers, and hang up to finish drying at a safe distance from direct heat.

MAY 28   Recklessly sacrifice some of small sugar hoard for fudge. Put 1 lb. granulated sugar, 2 tablespoons cocoa, 1 gill milk, 2 oz. margarine (butter is better, of course!) into saucepan, stirring until sugar dissolved, boiling approximately eight minutes. Then turn into bowl, add 1 oz. chopped nuts, few chopped glacé cherries, teaspoon vanilla essence, beating briskly until mixture thickens and begins to coat sides of bowl. Turn into margarined (buttered) tin, cutting into squares when cold.

MAY 30   Meet Horticultural Officer at Hillingsett by appointment this morning, when he takes dim view of black-currant bushes already there, and says all those in kitchen

garden and plot over west fence of same must come up this year,
there's a lot of big bud and reversion in the others, and he'll give
those another look next month. Next, pounce on builder's foreman for firm moving date. Can I book furniture people for 30th
June? On no account, says he. There's a lot of work to be done,
only £100 worth can be done without licence, and latter hasn't
yet come through. He thinks he's safe in saying they'll have
finished inside the house by the end of July. But will I ask him
again in three weeks' time?

MAY 31   Having eaten rhubarb stewed, rhubarb in pies,
         rhubarb shape (set with cornflour), rhubarb with
custard, and rhubarb without, decide time has come to bottle
some stalks. Use scissors to cut these into appropriate lengths
(N.B.—Scissors one of most useful kitchen tools, far better than
knife for dealing with bacon-rinds, fish fins, etc.) Pack into
bottles, fill with cold water as cannot spare sugar at moment, and
sterilise. If strawberry crop is short, as some growers fear it may
be after recent frosts, must not forget that bottling strawberries
and rhubarb together, in syrup, a distinct idea, as the rhubarb
acquires the flavour of the strawberries.

JUNE 2   Canned several tins of peaches last August, first batch
         with borrowed machine, second with new canner given
me by Adam. All latter appeared perfectly sealed, but presently
one after another developed a leak, contents of several cans had
to be relegated to compost heap, and carefully memorised doctor's
telephone number before venturing on others. Decided disaster
must be due to my unfamiliarity with canner, so sought help
from Norfolk Education Committee. To-day their instructress
called, when I have boiler, kettle, saucepan, sugar, cans and
rhubarb in readiness. But first we seal a fruitless can or two, then
test in a bowl of hot water. Cans promptly blow off bubbles in
manner reminiscent of a spouting whale. Fault evidently lies
with canner, so operation rhubarb abandoned forthwith. Later,
open remaining can of first peaches. Invariably keep in a tin a
store of pastry tartlet cases, made with ½ lb. fat, ½ lb. self-raising
flour, gill water, teaspoon sugar, and now slice half the peaches
lengthways in strips, thicken half the juice with dessertspoon
cornflour and add cherry-red colouring, balance two slices of
peach on rims of dozen tartlet cases, and dump spoonful of

thickened juice into centre of each. Cut up rest of fruit into small squares, fill up another eighteen tartlets, and edge these with mock cream made by creaming 3 oz. sugar and drop of lemon juice into 1½ oz. margarine. Can used neat wouldn't have gone half as far.

JUNE 5   To Norfolk and Norwich Hospital on blood-donor excursion, my fourth. Several people have suggested I have enough to do as it is, and say they can't understand why I take on this particular job. Feel there is only one answer to this. None of us can be certain that no accident will ever befall us or ours. Suppose it does, and a blood transfusion is necessary? If victim is Adam or Eve, should be willing to give every drop. But I might not be there. And Eve and self are in different blood groups anyway. Consider that if I'm willing to profit by generosity of other donors, the least I can do is to give own services. It's the simplest operation, takes only a few minutes, and happens only once or twice a year.

JUNE 6   "Always reckon on guseberry pie at Whitsun," remarks Sam. Adam no gooseberry lover, so have put none in garden. But one solitary bush, smothered in ivy, droops over parapet of mill-pool. Risk a ducking and retrieve half-a-pint of smallish gooseberries. Look longingly at pre-war recipe for gooseberry soufflé, which requires exactly this amount. But recipe continues, "stew, rub through hair sieve. Then cream 2 egg yolks and 2 oz. sugar over pan of hot water. Take basin from water, stir in one by one gooseberry pulp; gill of cream, whipped; the egg whites, whipped stiffly; ½ oz. gelatine dissolved. Stand on ice, stir occasionally until beginning to set, pour into soufflé dish, stand on ice or in frig. till firm, serve with whipped cream." Idle to think about cream these days, so make custard instead from half-pint milk brought to boil with piece of lemon peel in it, 2 well-beaten eggs and 3 saccharin tablets, and add to sweetened pulp for gooseberry fool.

JUNE 7   Return from flying visit to Hillingsett to see how builders are getting on, and am asked by Adam how many men on the job this time? Answer carelessly "Several", and am immediately taken to task. If that isn't Norfolk all over, says he. Instances Guy one day last winter, who when asked how many people at Carrow Ground watching football match preceding Saturday, made same answer, and Adam subsequently discovered attendance over twenty-seven thousand. Whilst tyre distributor has told him of customer who sent in order for "several" tyres, he forwarded fifty, and received an indignant letter by return saying "I said several, not a few". To which I answer meekly I think there must have been ten or twelve at Hillingsett.

2

JUNE 9   Archaeological Society excursion this afternoon include wonderful display of needlework at Fakenham Rectory. Tapestries and needlework pictures cover wall after wall, and there is scarcely a chair, sofa or screen that is not equally a monument to patience, industry and the leisure of a vanished age. Recall guiltily the small and inferior strip of canvas that for the past four years has been lying, half-worked, at bottom of oak chest at home, and wonder when, if ever, I shall finish it. And long to decamp with at least half-a-dozen of the superior creations around me. Should also like to know answer to query audibly expressed by another admiring onlooker, "However do they keep the moths off? '

JUNE 11   Milk being plentiful just now, decide to make milk cheese. Warm one gallon new milk to blood heat, add cheese rennet at rate of one teaspoon to five gallons, and stir for about two minutes. Keep bowl warm on side of Aga until junket results (one to two hours). Then ladle curd into cheesecloth, and hang up to drain, keeping warm and out of draught. In twenty-four hours it will have shrunk by nearly two-thirds, when shall put it, cloth and all, into small cheese press (ordinary china bowl inverted over cake stand, or for two gallons or over, upper half of steamer saucepan, make admirable substitutes for press, curds being ladled in at intervals if it won't all go in at once.) Twenty-four hours after that, shall remove from cloth, rub surface with salt, when cheese, weighing about $1\frac{1}{2}$ lb., will be ready to eat. In Poland chopped spring onions are added to curd in early stages.

JUNE 13   Beth, who contemplates matrimony in autumn, writes to ask if I can produce good recipe for wedding cake. If I have any currants and such to spare . . . she hints

24

delicately in a postscript. And who first thought of wedding cakes, anyway? The patrician Roman bride had one of sorts, I tell her, which was broken over her head at the wedding feast as a symbol of plenty, and each guest was given a piece to ensure plenty for themselves. But our own credited with following origin. Immense baskets of crackers were used by early Anglo-Saxons. Later these replaced by small, highly-spiced buns brought by guests and placed in huge pile across which groom must be able to kiss bride to ensure future happiness. Then a French chef, travelling in England, attended a local wedding, thought how awkward, not to say unsafe, the mound of little cakes appeared, and enquired pertinently, "Why not one large cake instead?"

Recipe can recommend personally is: $3\frac{1}{2}$ lb. butter (or margarine), $4\frac{1}{2}$ lb. each flour and sugar, 4 lb. each currants and sultanas, 2 lb. each glacé cherries and peel, $\frac{1}{2}$ lb. chopped almonds, thirty-five eggs, juice of two lemons, few drops almond essence, $\frac{1}{2}$ pint brandy. Bake in cool oven from six to seven hours. Cake should be made some months beforehand. Just ahead of great day cover first with almond icing made from $1\frac{1}{2}$ lb. ground almonds, 2 lb. icing sugar, few drops almond essence, whites of egg, and repeat if this not enough to cover required area. Then two layers of royal icing, made from four egg whites, 3 lb. icing sugar, juice of two lemons (again repeating if necessary), and decorate. End with pious hope that she has enough of the right sort of friends for all this, if not let me know, and will work out austerity model. Then post off letter with small parcel, and trust that October will suit own existing wedding garments.

JUNE 15   To furniture sale at Carrow, itch to possess having been thoroughly aroused on view day, but determined to bid only for carpet we really need for Hillingsett Lodge drawing-room, and not for numerous things I should merely love to own. Struck, as usual, by forlorn appearance of the various "effects", which, like words removed from their context, have temporarily lost much of their stature and meaning. Lot 467 draws near . . . nearer . . . is cast upon the table, and I promptly join the bidders. Have previously agreed with Adam on what seems to us stupendous-colossal price. But with horrid rapidity the bidding gallops to our limit, hesitates a fraction, like a horse in two minds about refusing a fence, then is over and away, leaving me very much an also-ran. Before setting out, have made most elaborate plans for triumphal homecoming with carpet, measuring up back of car, wondering if I shall take trailer, or entrust precious purchase to furniture removers at sale. Cannot help recalling, as go home empty-handed, historic occasion when male parent departed on salmon-fishing jaunt loaded with frail baskets and full of instructions to us to be on lookout for every parcel post, only to return at end of holiday with baskets full of rock-plants.

JUNE 16   See the W.I. Conference is all in favour of water taps for every home. Contemplating our new pump, which, with infinite labour, only averages half-a-pint per swing, whereas outworn one gave half-a-gallon for quarter effort, felt I couldn't agree with them more. Hope, however, that they will undertake equally necessary campaign to combat waste when taps are installed, and think of James's remarks when last I was in London, and Enborne Valley Scheme under discussion. If every user in Greater London saved just one gallon a year, the scheme would be absolutely unnecessary, is considered opinion of one who knows. Recall summer of two years ago, when our bath was repainted, and well gave out before bath was filled with cold water as advocated by painter. Can think of numberless friends (with taps) who had to ration baths at same period, and to cart water from river, and foresee taps without water and highly unpopular plans for local Enborne Valley in future, if strictest economy is not practised, and water is not recognised for the precious thing it is. Own supply at moment is adequate, as we carefully stagger demands on pump, and have baths out whenever opportunity occurs. Have hideous suspicion, however, that the Whiskers family have recently been tunnelling between well and river, and one of them fallen into former, for cup of hot water that precedes our early morning tea has suddenly acquired distinctly gamy flavour. Combat this by boiling thoroughly, and adding equal quantity of lemonade made as follows. Put juice and thinly-pared rind (no pith) of 2 lemons into basin, add $\frac{1}{4}$ lb. brown sugar (ordinary sugar, or 10 saccharin tablets, will do), then pour on $1\frac{1}{2}$ pints boiling water, and stir well.

JUNE 18   Presented with large basket of gooseberries, so decide to make jam by Norwegian method so successfully followed by Rosemary, which can be used for all fruits, saves wastage of both fruit and fuel, and produces jam of excellent quality and flavour. One pound sugar to 1 lb. fruit essential. Put fruit into pan, bring to boil, and boil rapidly until cooked, but not overcooked. Remove from heat, add sugar, and stir continuously in one direction until cool (approximately twenty minutes). Pour into sterilised jars, and tie down. Keep in cool place, though this doesn't seem to matter unduly, as Rosemary usually keeps hers on top shelf of hot kitchen in current R.A.F. married quarters, not to mention moving it round with her every time Tim's posted. Incidentally gooseberry sauce is to mackerel as red-currant jelly to mutton and hare, so portion left over from filling jars comes in beautifully for fried mackerel course at next meal.

JUNE 20   In further pursuit of drawing-room carpet, call at offices of auctioneer advertising furniture sale at Fendham House next week, and ask for catalogue. No catalogues, says clerk. But can have order to view. So as Fendham get-at-able by slight diversion on journey home, decide to look at carpets right away. Recall passing through Fendham early in 1939, when was pleasant little parish in usual style, with full quota of fields and farmhouses, lanes, woods and pastures. Now all remembered landmarks obliterated by abandoned aerodrome, and soon haven't least idea where I am. Elderly rat-poisoner at work on fences a mile back has suggested I follow yellow arrows on tarmac of perimeter track, but this somehow contrives to bring me back where I came in. Second attempt, ignoring arrows, brings me within sight of Fendham church, now marooned in a network of runways. Am still trying to remember whereabouts of Fendham House in relation to church, and which of three ways in front of me will take me there, when farm-tractor and trailer bounce out of adjacent hangar, driver says he's going past gate, and all I need do is follow him. This eventually results in arrival at destination, where carpets prove unsuitable. But must confess am not wholly sorry for this, as am sure should never find premises again without a pilot. And find this particular aftermath of war as depressing to contemplate as a blitzed city section.

JUNE 23   Entranced by visit to kitchen at Pynkney, where lengthy brick dresser affair of unknown origin and purpose has recently been diagnosed as part of Tudor cooking arrangements. Front consists chiefly of five arched recesses on lines of dairy or wine cellar, whilst top has similar number of small iron-lined apertures with grills set about five inches down. The whole runs below the windows, since it belongs to an era when chimneys were few, or non-existent, and smoke from the roaring wood fires perforce escaped through windows, or remained inside to harden the house timbers, and, in the opinion of some of the inmates, keep the household free from "rheumes, catarrhs, and poses". Marvel with hostess at amount of food our forebears ate each day, and wish we could lay our hands on some of it at present time. Cheered on reaching home, however, to find gift of brace of "conies." And "rheumes" or no, must confess I prefer modern cookers. Make one rabbit into pie with slices of bacon, two sliced hard-boiled eggs, seasoning, half-pint stock, and pastry to cover, and bake $1\frac{3}{4}$ hours. Joint second rabbit, put pieces into saucepan with just enough water to cover, salt, pepper, spring onion, and simmer until tender . . . about $1\frac{1}{4}$ hours. When cool enough to handle, remove meat from bones, mince, shape into portions on lines of rissoles. Then make good white sauce from two tablespoons flour, 2 oz. margarine, yolk of one egg, three-quarters pint milk, pepper, salt. Coat mounds with sauce. When cold decorate with tarragon leaves from garden (cress will do just as well) and "roses" made from margarine coloured with drop of cochineal, and squeezed through forcing bag and tube used for cake icing. Have often used this second rabbit recipe at buffet-supper parties, when guests invariably thought it was chicken.

JUNE 24   To Hillingsett, to meet Horticultural Officer, who says currants won't be fit to pick before mid-July. At same time tackle builder's foreman on date we are likely to be able to move in. Hopes of doing this when Eve on leave receding rapidly. But foreman thinks he can safely say they'll be out of house by Saturday, August 13th. Then on to Norwich, as I have some shopping to do. Approaching, nearly overturn car, as whole attention taken up by what looks like sheet of water spangled with dark green reed clumps, over fence on left in distance. Cannot imagine what it is, unless is mirage of type that appears to travellers in desert, as have had spell of dry weather, and any-way field so high above nearby meadows and river that floods impossible there unless all Norfolk inundated to height of cathedral roof. Presently am near enough to discover it's a field of flax in bloom, the "reed" clumps being stalks of that unlovable and irrepressible weed, "fat hen". Later leaving city via Earlham Road, turn right by cemetery, and catch sight of flax again, now by turns a sheet of glass and young lake. Quite unbelievable unless one's actually seen it.

JUNE 25   This week's meat (steak) as usual tough and tasteless. (Query: What happens to our prime Norfolk beef these days?) Disinclined to bury it in garden for weekend, as suggested by Guy, as distrust activities of local dogs and William Cat. Cannot follow Jamaican method and wrap in pawpaw leaves for obvious reasons. So deal with one-half in Barbara's way by beating and sticking it well with fork, then soaking in pepper, salt, and a little Worcester sauce for half a day before grilling. Shall treat the remainder by coating both sides with made mustard two hours or so before cooking. This is a great improvement, and doesn't taste mustardy, either.

JUNE 27   Had finished preserving gooseberries, but start again with some from Hillingsett to try out newly acquired Canadian recipe for jam which has distinct flavour of muscat grapes. And whilst I'm on job, what about chutney asks Adam. He likes that, gooseberry or otherwise.

Jam needs 6 lb. sugar, 6 lb. gooseberries, 2 lb. elder flowers (of which hedges are now full), two pints water. (My sugar store being low, I use only half quantities.) Cook gooseberries slowly in water until reduced to pulp (about half-an-hour) with elder flowers in large loose muslin bag resting on top. When done, stir bag round in pulp for moment, then suspend over pan and allow to drip until cool enough to squeeze out. Add sugar. Boil to setting point, pot, and tie down. For chutney, use 3 lb. gooseberries, $\frac{1}{2}$ lb. chopped onion, $\frac{1}{2}$ lb. sultanas, $\frac{3}{4}$ lb. brown sugar, $\frac{1}{2}$ teaspoon cayenne pepper, 1 oz. each mixed spice, crushed mustard seeds, salt, and 1 pint vinegar. Put all ingredients into saucepan, simmer until tender (about one hour), pot, and remember to keep at least three months before using.

JUNE 29   If there isn't a saying "Fickle as our English weather" feel there should be, especially when faced with to-day's cold, cloudy morning after yesterday's heat. Question now arises, "Will day get out?" as we are leaving early for

Norfolk Show, and must decide at once on how to dress and what food to take. Ham, fruit of hundredweights of boiled potatoes, scraps and effort expended last autumn on Scott and Whaley, our two pigs, has already been cooked by swathing it in flour-and-water pastry case (barley meal is better, but doesn't come our way), and baking in oven 5–6 hours. Some tomatoes have been stuffed with scrambled egg, a much quicker and better-looking filling than hard-boiled. But do we take plain strawberries, or Thermos full of strawberry ice cream? Made mixture for latter last night, using one pint sieved strawberry pulp, 3 oz. sugar, juice of one lemon, one pint custard (whipped cream better, of course, than this last, but custard made from approximately $\frac{3}{4}$ pint milk, 2 eggs, 2 oz. sugar, a good substitute), and have risen at crack of dawn to freeze this, remembering to whisk mixture once or twice during freezing process. But atmosphere remains wintry, so we leave ice cream in frig., and after several quick-change acts I finally set out for Show in tweed suit and brimless felt hat.

Run into Freda in members' car park. She also "suited," but has had forethought to bring linen frock in car to change into if it gets really hot. Only wish I had had brains enough to do same, not to mention pop in second hat as well, as sun now out in full force. Before we're on the showground half-an-hour, however, sun has gone in again, so am able to concentrate on exhibits.

These, as always, enthralling, whatever one's main interest in life, and feel that any "townee" who doesn't contrive to visit at least one agriculture show in his or her life has missed a most illuminating not to say exhilarating experience. This one, of course, different from all others for us, as first time we are able to look around with actual holding in view, as against dream acres in sky. Visit stand after stand of poultry and garden equipment, fruit and vegetable packing displays, walking tractors (where we're nearly deafened by roar of vast assembly of agricultural machinery with engines running full blast), and rural industry exhibits, several of which we lose our hearts to, but cannot at present afford to buy. Adam then chiefly concerned with pig section, from which he can hardly be torn away to accompany me to Electricity marquee, where I am at present interested in washing-machines as the lady who obliges us is, in farming parlance, about to decline washing. A good thing he's brought a young suitcase along for all the leaflets we're picking up, remarks

Adam at one point, and adds that at the rate I'm going, I shan't want any library books to read for months. Acquire several more before lunch, however, so just as well we're having meal in car, instead of having to stand, grasping weighty suitcase, in queue for members' luncheon.

First stop in afternoon is Flower Show, where we add to our store of catalogues, though suspect display on hand to-day less result of any particular seeds and bushes than what somebody once gave as definition of genius, i.e. an infinite capacity for taking pains. And since this must include time in which to take said pains, and as we are already trying to cram forty-eight hours' work into twenty-four-hour day, cannot see where extra time is coming from. Refuse to be cowed by mathematics at this stage, however, and repair to grandstand, where for next two or three hours we propose to rest our legs, and watch the parade of heavy horses, the musical ride, and some of the jumping at same time. These all grand, and though no good at dealing with horses personally . . . am quite frankly terrified of them, to Eve's scorn and amusement . . . feel it will be a bad day if life ever completely mechanised.

JUNE 30   Eve's birthday three days away, and she stationed in vicinity of Portsmouth, too far off to make week-end leave for the occasion practicable, so pack up parcel containing various eatables, including coffee birthday cake, a taste for which she evidently inherits from her grandfather. Cake takes four eggs, half-pound each flour, sugar, and margarine (butter not being available), and two tablespoons coffee essence. Usually bake this in round tin in moderate-to-good oven about 1½ hours, icing when cool with 6 oz. icing sugar creamed with 4 oz. margarine, plus coffee essence to taste, and decorating with "hundreds and thousands" when available. This time, for easy packing, have put mixture into two oblong tins, baked them about forty minutes, and, when cool, cut cakes in halves lengthways, and used icing mixture as filling. Post this off on way to Hillingsett, where blackcurrants already ripe in spite of Horticultural Officer, and picking, of which I am in charge, starts this morning.

JULY 1   Hillingsett twenty minutes' fastish drive from present domicile, Norwich best part of hour's run from both. Attempts to reconcile claims of blackcurrants, dental appointment, visit to fruit farm (in different direction) from which we are buying more currant bushes in due course, and other diversions consonant with Adam on holiday, result in our reaching home late, tea-less and exhausted, our one thought a meal and a moment to relax. As car stops outside front door, can hear telephone shrilling, race indoors, and snatch up receiver just before it stops. Is local postmistress to say she's been trying to get us ever since four-thirty with telegrams which run: "Have organised long weekend . . . Leaving by air for West Raynham 4 p.m. to-day. Due 5.30. Eve."

It's now well after six, and later still by time I get through to R.A.F. station at West Raynham, when four voices in turn at other end say that station closed down at 5.0, and they really don't know. Fifth admits that aircraft in question landed some time ago, but knows nothing about any Wren, after which he volunteers to look round for her and tell her we are on our way. During this conversation, Adam has grabbed last two ounces of chocolate in house, and turned car round. I jump in, we fly out of the gate, but hundred yards farther pull up with screeching brakes as car driven by Battle of Britain pilot friend swerves round corner, with Eve in passenger's seat. Whole thing a series of lucky chances, as at 2.30 p.m. Eve has had no more idea of homecoming than William Cat. But cycling across airfield has noticed newly landed aircraft, has enquired where it's come from, been told from her home county, that it's off again at four, what a pity she hasn't got a long week-end, why doesn't she ask for one? Which she promptly does. Normal procedure takes about three days, but "Not to worry" says the Navy, and presently she's on her way, and even got her ration card. On landing she's walking along to flying control, when whom should she see but Stephen. And here she is. She has to report back by nine on Monday morning, so must catch two o'clock train from Norwich Sunday. But at least she'll have part of birthday at home. (Though no birthday cake!)

JULY 4   Forgot to soak milk bottle of picnic set, and spots of sour milk that refuse to be dislodged by brush now securely ensconced under shoulders of bottle. Have perfect bottle cleaner on hand, however, in the shot removed from ordinary sporting gun cartridge. Rattle these around in bottle with little water, and every vestige of sour milk soon gone.

JULY 6 Curiosity, an abiding interest in other folks' jobs, and the fact that Adam has business in Wisbech, results in my joining strawberry "pluggers" in warehouse on edge of Brinks. There are perhaps sixty of us to-day, our ages ranging from nineteen to ninety, and surprisingly (for plugging mainly a housewife's part-time job) five are men. The nonagenarian is one of them, plugging slowly and steadily away, the remote expression in his patient pale blue eyes suggesting that he is miles away in both time and space, and, alone among the chatterers all around, he speaks to no one. We sit at trestle tables on boxes or up-ended fruit-trays (mine being of the latter and as tricky a seat for the job as a shooting-stick) accumulating de-stalked berries in large bowls, and heaps of stalks on the table in front of us. My left-hand neighbour, a lady with a figure like Tessie O'Shea's, asks me where I come from, and on hearing, says she used to live in the country too, she daresays it's healthier, and (in answer to a question of mine) plugging usually starts at nine o'clock in the morning and often goes on till half-past nine at night, it all depends how the strawberries come in. My right-hand neighbour, whose white hair makes her look older than she is, or at any rate confesses to being, complains about her feet. Across the table a younger woman tells the lady seated beside her, "When I got married, my mother was a Conservative, and she would have me join. I'm not a Conservative, I said. Still, I didn't want to put her out, so I might as well. I can pay the money myself, I said. So that's how it was." But am destined to overhear no more of this novel method of choosing one's brand of politics, as at that moment a man begins riveting a strawberry cask, somebody turns on a wireless set at full volume, and the forewoman cries loudly, "Come along. More bowls. I'm unemployed."

Twelve pounds is the unit for which each plugger receives a token, the price this year being $1\frac{1}{2}$d. per lb. Then into a cask holding 312 lb. the berries go, presently to be immersed in an acid that preserves them until they are wanted for jam. A few barrels are marked STALKS, and these, unplugged, are intended for the cheaper jam trade, the forewoman tells me, their stalks being picked off as they move along a conveyor belt, just before being jammed. It's possible, forewoman continues, to plug four bowls per hour. But nobody is doing this to-day, for most of berries on small side, and my performance, one bowl in thirty minutes, is about average. Supply is short, too. The afternoon's quota is disposed of in a couple of hours, and no more being expected before six, everyone leaves off at four. Reach home with strawberries bought on journey back. Plug 4 lb. of these with practised hands, crush in preserving pan, add 6 lb. sugar, boil furiously for three minutes stirring hard the while, remove from stove, and stir in proprietary brand of pectin, which produces 10 lb. jam of superlative colour and flavour, which always sets really firm. Always make my strawberry jam this way. Alice uses redcurrant juice or lemons as her setting agent, her jam being made by adding juice of 4 lemons or half-pint redcurrant juice to 4 lb. sugar and 4 lb. fruit, and boils until it sets . . . about half-an-hour.

JULY 8   No currant-picking for last day or two, owing to weather, which continues to be what is politely described as "variable", sometimes conforming to official forecast, and sometimes not. In any case, I can't expect them to be right about Norfolk, where it rains on one side of the fence, but not on the other, protests Tim, the Met. expert, when weather prediction under discussion. Must say I see his point, as can recall afternoon at Silford when a drilling team at work near middle of farm abandoned work and went home soaked to skin, whilst Peachey horse-shoeing four fields away, didn't bother to stop and get coat he had dumped on fence. On another occasion stack was threshed in brilliant sunshine on the Eastaugh Field at top of hill, whilst young cloudburst drenched valley half-mile away. And how many times orders had to be changed during the day! Not sure this fickleness on part of weather hasn't its uses in character-forming, however. If he's to remain in business, the farmer must be capable of making lightning decisions and acting on them . . . a point fully appreciated by general under whom my parent served in World War I, who, enlarging on this theme, ended with remark that he always felt good deal safer if he had several farmers amongst his officers and men.

JULY 11   One's own dried herbs infinitely superior to bought variety, and so easy to do. So once dew is off, gather mint, sage, parsley, and balm, tie up in small loose bunches, and string up in kitchen to dry, thus ensuring winter supply of mint sauce, sage stuffing, and essential additions to soups, stews, etc.

Have lost my tarragon, alas! So must acquire another, and several other herbs I haven't got at the moment, as they make such a difference to food flavours. Make fresh mint sauce later in day, remembering to chop leaves and sugar together, as this make better sauce. Then turn 2 oz. of dull margarine into mint butter by creaming it, adding two teaspoons pounded mint, one teaspoon lemon juice, dash of cayenne, salt. This makes a change in sandwiches, etc., and onion, chive, or any other herbs can be used instead of mint.

JULY 14   Currant-picking at Hillingsett in full swing again. On principle that there's always a better way if one can find it, have recently been joining in picking myself. Own conclusions to date are that adjustable seat and basket-holder would undoubtedly help, the more experienced pickers agree with these suggestions and offer fresh ones, whilst the humorist of the party, commenting on my lament that though next year we hope to have a garden truck to cope with full baskets and trays, it won't arrive in time for this one, says what's the matter with borrowing the church bier? Return home with several pounds of raspberries from kitchen garden, and being temporary grass widow (have always wanted to know why "grass" in any case?), with only own meals to think about, spent rest of evening making jam.

Favourite family recipe takes $\frac{3}{4}$ lb. sugar (warmed in oven) to each 1 lb. of fruit, the latter being first boiled for twenty minutes, when sugar added, and jam boiled for ten minutes, or until set. Personal pet takes more sugar but less time, and needs $1\frac{1}{2}$ lb. sugar to 1 lb. fruit put into pan together, the whole brought to boil, then "galloped" for five minutes, stirring continuously. Make first batch this way, and second by Rosemary's Norwegian method recorded June 18th, so that can later compare the two. Must say the latter quite the most restful to make I've so far met, and peacefully think own thoughts whilst stirring in sugar, and sipping lemon squash to which have added half a score crushed raspberries, a slice of cucumber, and two ice cubes. These "extras" very good in cider, too.

JULY 15   Day spent supervising picking of blackcurrants, picking blackcurrants myself, packing blackcurrants, eating blackcurrants, making entries in account book re blackcurrants, and, on reaching home, making jam with black-currants with recipe that takes 4 lb. of blackcurrants (stalked and washed), simmers them in 2 pints water until well cooked and bulk reduced, then 2 lb. sugar added, and the whole boiled quickly until setting point reached. Am just putting jam into jars and rapidly approaching stage when sight of one more blackcurrant calculated to send me into fit of screaming hysterics, when some-body knocks at back door. Is elderly villager clasping chip full of blackcurrants to say he's just been picking his, he knows we haven't any in garden here, and thought I might like to buy some!

JULY 16   What, demands Barbara, can she do with sour milk? Hers has turned again. Suggest (*a*) she hangs it up in muslin to drain for cheese; (*b*) she eats it like junket, with brown sugar and a sprinkling of breadcrumbs, as they do in Denmark.

JULY 18   More raspberries to hand. Bottle eight 2-lb. jars, washing fruit first, and packing into jars without water, as prefer both these and strawberries bottled in their own juice. Put these into simmering oven of Aga cooker, where they will be safe for the next 3–3½ hours, then decide to can the rest for Eve's benefit. Canner has been shuttlecocked back and forth between self and makers, which last say it is now all right. Only one way to make sure of this, so switch on wash-boiler which provides our bath-water, pack fruit into cans, make syrup with 1 lb. sugar, 1 quart water, which should do six cans, fill them with boiling syrup and seal. Always find it easier to cope with cans by using string net for remaining stages, and Brandy's hay net just the thing for this. Drop net and contents into wash-boiler, it reboils in fifteen minutes, so let it boil a further twelve, then haul out net, dash through house, and drop burden into river, thus securing cold running water mentioned in instructions, with minimum of effort. Rescue them fifteen minutes later, and store temporarily on tray in scullery for observation, trusting that makers of machine are right. Then to cake-making, as guests to tea to-morrow, no cake on premises, and no shops to run to, either.

Operation raspberry has played havoc with hard-won sugar hoard, so try creaming 4 oz. honey with 4 oz. margarine, add 4 oz. self-raising flour, 2 well-beaten eggs, grated rind and teaspoon juice from half a lemon. Put spoonful of mixture into bun tin as precautionary measure, the rest into sandwich tin, and both into medium oven (bun out in fifteen minutes, cake in about thirty). Both emerge looking normal, and bun at least tastes all right, with faint and not unpleasant flavour of honey.

3

July 21   Combination of Archaeological Society excursions, blackcurrants, household chores, correcting galley proofs of last book and making notes for future epic, to say nothing of hurried visits to various friends who have built-in chimney-pieces, as we want to pick out good design for ours, is proving decidedly exhausting. Adam mutters sinisterly that he'll be putting pen to paper any minute now on the trials of an author's husband. Can think of several retorts to this, but no time or energy to utter them, as am too busy wondering if day will get out sufficiently for currant-picking. (Query: What has happened to all the barrage balloons? Feel sure these could be utilised to support canopies over fruit bushes to keep off those irritating little "dags" and "smirrs" of rain that only last a few minutes, but often stop picking for entire day.) Whatever happens, must catch up on excursion and lecture notes, and get these written out in appropriate record books whilst I can still read my rough notes.

Excursion earlier in week includes visit to Burgh Castle, the one-time Roman fort overlooking Breydon Water, which for years have always been going to see, but never before reached. Staggered to find so much wall in situ, as shortage of local building materials usually responsible for total disappearance of interesting relics in our parts. Rather less to be seen of Caister Castle, the fifteenth-century stronghold built by Sir John Fastolf in the neighbourhood of what was probably once another Roman camp (and the moat has inconsiderately gone dry for first time in years). But quite enough to set imagination agog, and make one agree with authority who describes ruins as one of finest pieces of medieval brickwork to be found in country. Scene peaceful to-day, in spite of vast numbers of visiting archaeologists. (Query: Has anyone yet minted appropriate noun of assembly of archaeologists? An antiquity . . . an excavation . . . a foundation?) But something about the walls and tower forcibly recalls some of the incidents of its stormy history. From Sir John it came to the Pastons, in whose Letters are to be found grim accounts of the siege to which it was subjected by the Duke of Norfolk. The Letters also relate the incident of the two women whose husbands were killed there, and who subsequently sued the Pastons for damages: and cannot help feeling that if this principle extended and upheld against present-day governments, it might contribute materially to world peace.

Rather intrigued by Sir John's cooking arrangements, but quite unable to imagine how they worked, as in present state they look exactly like set of brick pigeon-holes. Own meals at present distinctly precarious owing to lack of time either to prepare or eat them, and consist mainly of bread and butter and raspberries. Have suddenly been overwhelmed with latter fruit on all sides, parents' garden, present garden and future garden all contributing their share. Packed in bowls and well sprinkled with sugar, they will keep fresh for two or three days if put in cool place, and have successfully preserved them for whole week this way in refrigerator. So am trying to preserve several pounds for Eve, due on summer leave on Saturday evening. Raspberries in one chip both wet and squashy, so stew these with added water and little sugar, and pass through strainer, resultant syrup making excellent drink either neat or added to lemonade.

JULY 22   Morning fine at least, so currant-pickers can get to work. Rearrange own day to include morning visit to Norwich, as simply must look around sales for replacement towels, etc.: afternoon scheduled for weighing and dispatching currants at Hillingsett, and back to Norwich again to collect Eve from Thorpe station just before midnight (if train is on time), telephone call last night having announced that leave starts 4 p.m. to-day, too late to board aircraft leaving for West Raynham, or to catch better train. Must also find time to deal with 12 lb. of blackcurrants. Should like to make some more jam, and Adam partial to jelly, made by simmering 4 lb. fruit (stalks and all) in $2\frac{1}{2}$ pints water until well cooked, then squash fruit, and strain through muslin or jelly bag. (If thick mixture, i.e. "cheese" required, rub through hair sieve instead.) Add 1 lb. sugar for each pint juice, and boil quickly until setting point reached.

Unfortunately, cannot spare sugar for either, so shall bottle them in water and jam or jelly them later if sugar supply allows. Rosemary is making *syrup* for the children from another 12 lb. by adding one pint water, bringing to boil whilst stirring constantly, boiling hard one minute, pressing out juice, stirring in ¾ lb. sugar to each pint, straining through muslin, then bottling and sterilising in same way as for bottled fruit.

JULY 23   Currants (final edition) duly dealt with, Eve collected, fruit bottled. But regret to say returned from sales without sheets and towels, but possessor of becoming linen frock instead. Wear this on Archaeological Society excursion this morning to Elsing Hall, one-time home of Sir Anthony Browne, Henry VIII's Master of Horse and favourite, and proxy bridegroom to "my Flanders mare", as his sovereign so ungallantly called Anne of Cleves. In bright sunshine house, which in any case was much restored last century, offers no ghostly impressions. And though I linger in drawing-room, ears pricked to catch the sound of furniture being moved by unseen visitants across the hall, which was wont to occur during occupancy of last owner, my psychic sense refuses to function, and all I hear is noise made by comings and goings of fellow-members.

Abandon tour at this point, as Castleacre next stop, have already prowled around this at least eight times, and though no objection to another visit in near future, to-day have pressing engagement with compost heaps in opposite direction. Have also sundry calls to pay, and Eve has to fetch Brandy, so home late. But quick meal available with previously cooked potatoes reheated in little boiling water, fried plaice served with slices of cucumber instead of lemon, and the inevitable raspberries.

JULY 25   Eve anxious to see how Hillingsett progresses, so take picnic tea over this afternoon. House looks even further from completion than last week, study window is lying on drive and barrow-loads of cement are being wheeled up plank through aperture, drawing-room is piled with plumber's fittings, new bath, kitchen sink, and ankle deep in shavings, and dirt, dust, plaster and broken bricks everywhere. Corral foreman and put inevitable query, as cannot believe they can possibly be clear of house by August 13th. Nor can they, agrees foreman, they haven't nearly done what the estate ordered, and then there's all those built-in cupboards and bookshelves they're doing for me, they all hang out the job. Point out only two cupboards and hardly any shelves, and simultaneously withdraw order, as can always get these put in later. Foreman then says that should make a difference, and he really thinks we shall be able to move in the last week in August. Try not to dwell on abandoned trip to Eire, on which we were to have started to-morrow, and on which we might just as well have gone. Whilst Eve, who was counting on helping with our flitting, speculates, but without much hope, on her chances of obtaining compassionate leave for the actual occasion.

JULY 27   Eve on leave has a most unfortunate effect on my plans for work. Feel that I should be having holiday as well, and have to speak very firmly to myself, though Eve not one to sit pensively sewing fine seam, but is either spring-cleaning the house or stables, arranging the flowers, riding, gardening, swimming, or a dozen other things. (Have always felt that if total human energy in house could be shared out equally, should have twice as much myself, and am more than ever convinced of it at this moment.) Brandy, also with us for duration of leave, but emphatically not on holiday, has had to be ridden over from Silford bareback, as he's grown too fat for girths to meet round his middle. He's also rubbed his mane, which Eve promptly trims off with the surgical scissors from my first-aid box, as I refuse to let her borrow my cutting-out shears. (Have only just rescued these last from the garage, where Adam has been using them on the rubber tubes!)

Eve very salad-conscious at moment, and ready to eat rabbit food at every meal. Lettuce position in most country gardens is usually either none at all, or so many that one can't give them away. Those on our gravelly soil are in former category, having "bolted" the minute they were set out. There is enough at our future home, however, to feed a regiment, but have neither time nor petrol for daily journey now currants finished, so when over to-day to meet electricians, bring back enough lettuces for several days at one swoop. Barbara keeps her lettuces crisp by putting a piece of coal in water with them. Rosemary ties hers in wet butter muslin, and hangs in cool dark place, re-dipping bundle in water night and morning, when she says they'll keep four or five days. Have pulled instead of cutting ours, and put roots only into bowl of water on scullery floor, as have found this way, changing water occasionally, they'll remain in good condition for a week.

JULY 28   Throughout the war years had family tennis lawn just outside my window, but no time to play on it. Since then, have had trifle more time, but no lawn. My racquet now a tangle of broken strings, frocks dyed and worn out aeons ago in attempt to eke out clothing coupons, and shoes completely disappeared. Adam's shoes and racquets have likewise vanished, whilst his "ducks" have provided some first-class banquets for moths and spiders. Do we really want to start again, he asks, and suggests that we plant extra currant bushes on the lawn at Hillingsett instead. Reply firmly that would not know what obtains in towns, in which he unlucky enough to be brought up. But tennis in country is less a game than a social occasion, am looking forward to having own court again, and we're not in bath chairs yet. Had not, however, intended to take active steps until next season. But two invitations to play this coming week-end send me round city shops this morning in search of racquet, if no more, when I acquire appallingly expensive article of which Eve, who is using her grandfather's pre-war one, remarks somewhat thoughtfully that it's "just the job".

Make bread on return home, giving remains of last old loaf to Brandy, who regards it as highly as loaf sugar, and is now so tame that he'll whinny outside the front door, and try to get into the kitchen, if nobody has spoken to him lately. William Cat, who despises bread, but is always on the alert for his rights, promptly appears, and mews for attention and anything else that is going. Whilst bread is baking, at Eve's request concentrate on ice cream. When dressmaking am seldom satisfied to use whole of single pattern, but invariably choose sleeves from one, skirt from another, and so on, with further innovations thought up by myself. And confronted by several elaborate and complicated recipes for ice-cream mixture, find myself following same technique, from which the following emerges. Bring half-pint of milk almost to boil, stir in two well-beaten eggs, put into jug, and cool in frig. Whisk up quarter-pint evaporated milk, 3 oz. sugar, $1\frac{1}{2}$ teaspoons vanilla essence. When first mixture cool, beat all together, freeze in ice tray forty minutes, turn back into bowl and whisk again, then freeze for approximately one hour. Result very good indeed, and neither cooked custard nor scalded evaporated milk.

JULY 30   Telephone rings. Is Eve about, asks Bruce? I know he said she could ride that young horse of his if she could catch it? Well, it's caught and saddled up in his yard now, if she likes to come round. He takes it I don't mind? Have instant's vision of cripple hobbling bravely about on crutches for next fifty years, another of lifeless form brought back to me on hurdle within the hour. I see the piled-up wreaths, the rain-spattered grave, myself at ninety still uncomforted. Did I say anything, enquires Bruce? No, I reply hastily, and add that it's no good tying a string to one's child, if she's going to hurt herself she can do it just as easily by pitching head-first downstairs. Of course she can, why Brian fell off an old horse of his that was as quiet as a sheep, and broke his arm, agrees Bruce heartily. Anyway, he'll have the horse on a leading rein if she likes to be round in half-an-hour, when she can ride round the farm with him.

At 11.45 Eve reappears, unaccompanied, astride large bay horse, and still mercifully in one piece. Brandy, who has already seen her pass and repass on road with Bruce, and hardly been able to believe evidence of his eyes, comes to meadow railing to register more shocked disapproval at this fresh betrayal. "And now she's putting the creature in my stable!" His hairy little face contorts anew as Eve dismounts, and temporarily cages the bay in the loose box. Presently she approaches Brandy with propitiatory offering of oats. Brandy accepts it, though not without a far from playful snap at the seat of her jodhpurs. When he begins to eat, there is a subtle reserve in his munch. The bay is returned to base before lunch, but Brandy sulks for the rest of the day.

AUGUST 2   Weekend downpours make one wonder if the Clerk of the Weather has a definite spite against holiday-makers. Or does his petition department work as slowly as some of our ministries, and is it only now catching up with the country's earlier pleas for rain? Am also wondering how far my last week's purchase of tennis racquet is responsible for local storms, and if I've inherited Mother's fatal attraction for poor tennis weather. Have distinct recollection of girlhood summers when the heavens opened regularly for our Tuesday afternoon tennis parties, and of one occasion when a distraught farm steward begged her to alter her day, as they must get the hay up. She did, a brilliantly sunny Tuesday ensued, and Friday's tennis caught a cloudburst. My appearance on friends' courts over week-end has been signal for showers at least, whilst my inclusion in "wiener roast" party, when we were to toast sausages over bon-fire, resulted in three wet evenings in succession.

Rain, however, does not prevent us sallying forth to view strange animal shot lower down the river at five o'clock yesterday morning. Straw-coloured hairs rise from a pelt of darker-coloured fur. Its solitary hind paw (the other is missing) is webbed, its front paws clawed. Its tiny mouth is shielded by four long, blunt-edged orange fangs. It weighs nineteen pounds. A coypu, I hazard. Adam is certain the operative word copyu. (If it is, I owe him five shillings.) The other onlookers refuse to com-mit themselves, and stick to muskrat. Whilst the man who shot it (and one of his laying hens at the same time), thinking that it was an otter with murderous intentions, is somewhat taken aback to learn that it isn't a flesh-eater, and meant no harm. Am wondering if this is the creature Adam saw sliding out of a tree-stump above the mill-pool a couple of months ago, and if there are any more in the neighbourhood. How I shall miss the river at our door when we move, as, apart from the feeling of peace that running water invariably gives me, its bird and animal life is endlessly fascinating. William finds it equally intriguing, although he has yet to imitate the cat that used to dive for fish in another mill-pool not far from here.

AUGUST 3   Take Eve into Norwich to own dentist for check-up on ministrations of Service ditto, and then pursue quest for new loose-cover material, as our tattered family hand-me-downs practically falling to pieces, and have recklessly decided to have three sofas and five chairs recovered. Am some-what restricted in choice, and dare not get anything outstanding, as (a) it may not "go" with carpet should we ever find one, and (b) shall never be able to afford such an outlay again, so do not want to find we have saddled ourselves with colour and pattern we come to detest within three weeks. Do not see anything we like, however, except one, of which there turns out to be only one-third required yardage left, so repair to car park feeling afternoon thrown away (own dentist has found no fault with Eve's teeth), turn over self-starter, and set off for home.

Have proceeded less than hundred yards when violent commotion behind us, we hastily draw into kerb, and fire-engine screams past. "Quick! After it," cries Eve, with all the appearance of huntsman about to sound his horn. Comment strongly on such reprehensible behaviour, adding fire no joke, etc. But regrettably find myself becoming infected by her excitement and curiosity, and as fire-engine going our way, keep it in sight for length of several streets, and finally see it dash down side-street at bottom of which smoke is coming from chimney in what looks like perfectly normal way. "Somebody came home late and found their dinner burning," a bystander tells us. "They've already put it out. But the woman next door had seen the smoke before they came home and rung up the fire brigade." "Well!!!!" exclaims a disgusted Eve, and we finish our journey without further event.

AUGUST 5 Mystery of "pigeon-hole" ovens at Caister Castle elucidated by correspondent who now lives in Middlesex, but used to inhabit Norfolk, when he was told that brick pigeon boxes had been built into the oven arch, no doubt with bricks from the castle walls, about a hundred years ago. Incidentally, he likes the sound of cucumber with fish. And have I tried eating raw tomato with fried bacon? It's easier on the digestion than when both are fried. Feel he's probably right in this last premise, as recall that the Chinese have a saying that the frying-pan is the undertaker's best friend. But confess that I shall continue to take my life in my hands whenever bacon and tomatoes are paired.

AUGUST 7 How do I accumulate a sugar reserve for all the jam and cakes I make, demands Elspeth. In no honest manner, she is convinced. She can never save a pound. Retort indignantly on the contrary, during war years I once had whole hundredweight of best icing sugar on premises (for rat poison!) and never touched an ounce. And though I did once borrow five pounds earmarked for family's bees, I duly paid it back. My late hoard achieved by always using saccharin tablets in tea, coffee, etc., in milk puddings (at rate of four to pint), custards, and stewed fruit. Sweeten fruit bottled in water by tipping juice into saucepan, bringing it to boil, dissolving saccharin to taste in it, then returning juice to fruit, and leaving it to soak at least one hour. Honey and treacle are used whenever practicable, and sugar rations reserved for fresh fruit, cakes, jam, marmalade, or bottling syrup on gala occasions. Gales of last few days have produced quantities of windfall eating apples. These very good eaten raw either sliced or grated on suet grater, sprinkled with cinnamon, and sweetened with golden syrup or uncoagulated honey.

AUGUST 9   Telephone rings, and Exchange says Birmingham on line, asking for me. Have time to order wreath for Adam's sister (perfectly well so far as I know) and think up half-a-dozen reasons, all equally fantastic, to account for Eve having got there, when male voice comes on line, asks if I remember him, and should I care to give another broadcast talk in near future? Positively purr back, and only when receiver replaced remember what a labour it is to make the script fit exactly into a given number of minutes, and how the inevitable attack of "mike-fright" will shortly have me wondering if I dare send a telegram to say I must cancel the whole thing, as am in bed with broken leg. Then return to attics where am sorting out various treasures as a pre-move measure, being determined this time not to burden myself with too many things that may (or may not!) "come in." Resist temptation to save several piles of old magazines, and ruthlessly stuff small sack full of bits and pieces, and give these to Adam for car-rags, only stipulating that recognisable fragments of underwear shall not be given pride of place in dashboard cubby-holes. Two large bags, each equivalent to three pillow cases, are filled with oddments for patching, frocks whose sleeves and skirts together will make excellent blouses, etc. And reprieve the lives of several outdated garments, odd lengths of ribbon, a broken fan, a child's Indian suit, a Red Cross apron, a large pink cotton mob-cap (cannot for my life imagine where this has come from!) and some distinctly passé hats, by cramming them into the dressing-up box for future Christmas charades. Moths and spiders have made up my mind for me in some cases, and am much incensed to find that they've got into my woollens drawer, too, and had a roaring time amongst my winter jumpers. A pound of wool destined for undies which so far I haven't found time to knit, is perfectly safe in the cellophane bag in which I bought it. Do wish some enterprising manufacturer would bring out a line of similar bags in which to store our winter woollies.

They appear to be perfectly moth-proof, and have the added advantage that one could spot any garment at glance, without turning contents of drawers upside down, as with lesser, non-transparent wrappings.

AUGUST 12   "Hop in, and come up to the harvest field with me," invites Bruce, pulling up beside me on the road. Am really out for exercise, but cannot resist the chance, and presently, watching the combine-harvester snatching up the barley, realise how much I've been missing the harvest fields. A field of ripe corn, the bright colours of farm machinery against a background of golden stubble, a newly thatched stack (and the combines have by no means ousted all these), are among the most satisfying sights I know.

AUGUST 15   Spend greater part of day making new bedroom curtains, and patching old loose covers, having failed to find anything that will do for latter at reasonable price, so ancient wrecks must carry on, and William, who has lately been allowed to do his worst, must once again be firmly discouraged from using chair and sofa arms as claw-strops. In-between whiles I rub out and put into bags the lavender Adam bought from Heacham a few weeks ago, and that cut from our few bushes in the garden, which have been hanging up to dry in the kitchen. These are destined for linen-cupboard, though am keeping a few flower-heads and leaves to use (very sparingly) in soups. And I must try my hand at making lavender toilet vinegar some time. For this, fill a bottle with flowers, cover with white vinegar, and leave in warm spot for two weeks, shaking every day. Then strain, refill bottle with fresh flowers, cover with original liquid, and proceed as before. Repeat the process at end of another two weeks, and a fortnight later the vinegar is ready for use.

AUGUST 16   Builder's foreman these days winces visibly whenever I approach. To-day admits no chance of being out of house by end of month, but thinks I might order furniture van for September 16th. On return home write to furniture removers to say will expect them Friday, September 23rd, and tell Adam that's the day we're moving, and I don't care if they take the roof off.

AUGUST 18   and our wedding anniversary. Since we're having
            to buy so many extras for our prospective abode,
have decided to abandon our custom of giving the house a present
this year, and to exchange small personal tokens instead. Incidentally, how many couples realise that there are other "special"
wedding anniversaries, besides the well-known gold and silver
ones? They are: first, paper wedding; fifth, wooden wedding;
tenth, tin; twelfth, leather; fifteenth, crystal; twentieth, china;
thirtieth, ivory; fortieth, woollen; forty-fifth, silk; and seventy-
fifth (though some say sixtieth), diamond. Am sure there must
be others, and should love to know what they are.

Like all the housebound, my instinct is to celebrate the
occasion by Going Out. This impracticable to-night for several
reasons, so concentrate on festival meal at home instead. Grape
fruit has unexpectedly appeared with the fortnight's groceries,
and have recklessly secured a chicken. The sweet is a pie made
with orange quarters (fresh) and green figs (tinned), an exotic
and attractive combination. The chicken is not such an extravagance as might appear at first sight. The white meat will
provide two meals, as Adam and I are alone. One leg, minced
and reinforced with cooked potato, makes a serviceable pasty (two
eggs broken over the mixture just before the top crust is added
will make it even better); whilst the second leg will end either
as curried chicken, or chicken in aspic with peas, diced carrots,
and slices of cucumber and hard-boiled egg. I prefer to make my
own aspic jelly, using a really good stock made from the chicken
bones and added vegetables, etc., plus powdered gelatine at rate
of 1 oz. gelatine to half-pint stock.

AUGUST 19   Postman delivers registered packet (a pair of
            nylons as anniversary present from Eve) with
greeting "Any message for Gosport?" His wife is just off to visit
her family there, and seeing the postmark on my packet made
him mention it. He was in the Marines for twenty-one years, and
doesn't he wish he were back. Then why not go? I suggest. But
it seems this can't be done, he's finished his time, now he's
pensioned off. He's been in every country in the world except
Russia and Australia. He saw New York during the war, after
being torpedoed at sea. The British were all heroes then, he says
wistfully. You couldn't get out of the pubs, with all the Yanks
wanting to treat you. And the things there were to talk about.

Here, you go into a pub, the men have been hoeing sugar beet all day, and can talk of nothing else but sugar beet all night. Not in harvest time, surely, I murmur tactfully. But can definitely see his point.

AUGUST 21   Can never resist bulb catalogues. And having seen the relevant flowers earlier in the year, know that the brilliant illustrations for once fall short of the real thing. Should like to order the lot, of course. But eventually confined myself to a collection of double-early tulips featuring fifteen varieties, a selection of parrot tulips in fantastic shapes and colours, a bargain offer of mixed crocuses to plant under trees and in patches of rough grass, and a dozen hyacinths for bowls in the house. Order fibre for half these last, but shall use leaf-mould or compost for the rest.

AUGUST 24   How many bottles and/or cans of fruit does the average country housewife preserve per season? My peak three hundred and sixty-five, which I put up in 1945. But have never since approached within hailing distance of this total, and do not really want to, as still have a few of that particular vintage unopened and feel that, unlike wine, too long keeping hardly improves them. This year, faced with move and something like a hundred bottles left over from last season, have done rather less than usual. Peaches, however, are all eaten. So boil up $1\frac{1}{2}$ lb. of this period's sugar bonus with three pints of water, for syrup, and fill up twelve largish bottles, nine with sliced peaches, and three with halves. If one lives in towns, or is in one late on market day, a box of partly "gone" peaches can sometimes be secured at bargain prices, the decayed bits cut out, and fruit then bottled in usual way. Have known more than one housewife who's managed this, though have never been on hand at right moment myself. But wait till price reaches low level, then buy box or two, holding forty to fifty per box, as this way they travel home without bruising, and will usually keep for week or more, allowing me to bottle them at leisure. To-day's batch placed in simmering oven of cooker, after which I set alarum clock for the time they're due out, then temporarily dismiss them from mind. Can recommend this noisy reminder for long-term cakes, etc., too. As it is so easy, when busy, to put something into oven, and forget all about it.

AUGUST 26   Most of us can look back on certain days as landmarks in our lives. One of the more important ones
in mine definitely that one some years ago when, skimming
through some book reviews, I came across one of Doris Grant's
Your Daily Bread. The next step was to buy a copy, the one after
that to get hold of some stone-ground whole-wheat flour, guaran-
teed to be made from wheat grown without the "aid" of
artificial fertilisers, and make up a batch of real bread. Since
when the devitalised stuff that passes for the staff of life in so
many homes has seldom entered ours, Adam takes a loaf with
him whenever he has to spend a night away, and our health has
improved. One thing leads to another, and that on to another
one yet, and so to Haughley Research Farms in Suffolk to-day
to join one of the study week-ends organised by the Soil Association.

Adam and I arrived in time for informal supper at which each
guest has to rise and state his or her name, habitat, and the
reason that has brought him or her there. After which ordeal we
are soon involved in talk and a general discussion. India, Kenya,
Germany, somebody has experienced conditions in each. One
guest is at present condemned to live in a London flat without so
much as a window box, another is about to begin farming in
Scotland, two more are hoping to start with virgin soil in Tas-
mania. But whatever the size of our stake in the soil, we all have
the same absorbing interest in its future, and the discussion is
soon overflowing its allotted time.

AUGUST 27   Morning programme consists of tour of farms,
where various experiments in growing in fields
dressed with compost, fields treated with farmyard muck, and the
orthodox way with "artificials", so that the results can be com-
pared over period of years. More discussion ensues, and we're all
late for lunch. The afternoon finds us listening to Miss Maye
Bruce on the subject of compost heaps and helping her to make
one, after which we're all late for tea. A thunderstorm then keeps
us indoors, so the staff have no cause to grumble about our
punctuality at supper. And the evening ends with a talk on soil
fertility and erosion throughout the world (illustrated with some
quite horrifying lantern slides) given by Lady Eve Balfour and
Miss Bruce, followed by more animated discussion. (Late to bed
once more.)

AUGUST 28 This morning down on agenda as free period, but presently we're all down at New Bells Farm again, this time for conducted tour of that miniature farm within a farm, the acre that Lady Eve has laid out like a full-size holding. Adam much taken by baby tractor, I study hens on deep litter system and secure address of member mentioned last night as having successfully combated big-bud and reversion in black-currants by natural methods, and at one point everybody samples tomatoes. Reach home in time for late tea with minds buzzing, having spent most stimulating weekend in years. In universe where man's misuse and abuse of the soil has led to conditions that make a world famine within the next fifty years a frightening possibility, it is comforting to know that in one small corner at least something constructive is being done to prevent it. Only wish that every housewife . . . and all politicians . . . could spend a similarly educative two days.

AUGUST 31 Look out of bedroom window at 6.30 a.m. to see a covey of partridges on lawn. Am fascinated by sight of so much potential food so near . . . and yet so far. So is William, who has come upstairs to watch us drink our early tea, and is, as usual, stretched out in his favourite "British Lion" attitude along one window-sill. A town-bred cat (and one who has never ceased to believe that we keep a cooked chicken per-petually in the larder, and that it's only our human selfishness that fobs him off with fish), he is new to live partridges. But instinct tells him what they are. And the expression on his furry face as he watches them, now picking at the grass, now immobile and practically invisible against a flower bed, is highly entertain-ing. Then one looks skywards, and sees both of us. On previous visits they have imagined themselves unobserved, and have left at their leisure, squeezing between the wooden palings one by one. This time there is a warning screech, a whirr of wings, and fourteen feathered bullets hurtle over the palings and take cover in the adjacent hayfield. Shall be surprised if they come again, for game birds seem to have developed an uncanny faculty for knowing the date. And although they would be safe enough in our garden, they are not to know that, and from to-morrow think of man as their chief enemy.

4

SEPTEMBER 1   Eve writes that she's been taking part in a recruiting film, her act consisting chiefly, so far as I can gather, in standing on the mainplane of a Firefly aircraft "looking as if we're working", and indulging in (unauthorised) behaviour of the kind that invariably led a late great-aunt to enquire tartly if one had found a "giggles nest". The relief that plain, unadulterated noise is to the very young, laughter undoubtedly brings to the adolescent. And not only to that age. Am not yet immune from attacks of unseemly mirth myself, and am assured by one who knows her that no less a personage than Dame Laura Knight is "a grand giggler" on occasion. Sheer silliness, if not over-indulged in, is a tonic in itself. Should dearly love to see the film when released, but parents being decidedly unrecruitable material, do not suppose the opportunity will come my way.

SEPTEMBER 3   Have I made his tomato sauce yet, asks Adam. Am doing it this morning, using 8 lb. ripe tomatoes, $\frac{1}{2}$ lb. onions, 2 oz. brown sugar, 2 oz. salt, $\frac{1}{4}$ oz. mixed spice, pinch cayenne pepper, $\frac{1}{2}$ pint vinegar. Peel tomatoes (after first dipping in boiling water to make this part easy), cut up, and simmer with chopped onions until reduced to pulp. Rub through sieve, return to pan, add other ingredients, bring to boil, simmer till thick (about twenty minutes). Bottle at once in sauce bottles or jars. Some people simply store theirs at this point. I prefer to play safe, so put jars, etc., into steriliser with nearly boiling water up to their necks, and simmer for half-an-hour. Then attend to tomato chutney begun last night by slicing 4 lb. green tomatoes, and sprinkling them with 2 oz. salt. Put these into pan, and add 1 lb. chopped onion, 1 lb. apples (cored, peeled

52

and sliced), ¾ lb. raisins, 1 lb. brown sugar, teaspoon ground ginger, ½ teaspoon cayenne, ½ oz. crushed mustard seed. Bring pan to boil, and simmer slowly until thick.

SEPTEMBER 4   Last year, when made first appearance "on the air", longed for Adam to come too, but business took him in different direction. This time he is on holiday, we get rail tickets in advance, book hotel room, get addresses where carpets at reasonable prices likely to be found, and plan to have day or so out. Have also, in view of "go slow" rumours, taken precaution of ringing up railway company yesterday afternoon to make sure no hitch likely, and have been told everything is normal, and trains will be departing and arriving on time. Drive up to Norwich, park car in garage, arrive on station, and prepare to relax, as all we now have to do is get on train. Terrific holiday crowd is thronging premises, but do not worry about this as our seats booked. Then suddenly queue shifts, and through gap Adam glimpses notice-board on which is chalked legend announcing that trains are now arriving London end ninety minutes late. Rush to Enquiries, who confirm this, then do some addition sums. Nothing adds up to arrival at B.B.C. at 6.30 p.m., however, and radio waits for no one. "Come on!" exclaims Adam, and grabs my arm, and we bolt back to garage. Luckily we have some petrol coupons, but no maps, no time to play with, and, as we proceed, to Adam's rage, no tea, as I refuse to stop for anything until we're there, and spend entire journey sitting ready to leap out and thumb a lift if car, only just back from overhaul, shows slightest sign of going wrong. In the event Adam actually gets us in with time to check in at hotel and get car garaged before we reach Portland Place dead on schedule. New hitch now occurs. Midland Region has returned my script as just the thing, they don't want a word altered. London producer's greeting is she supposes I know that script of mine is two pages too long? Have been told earlier that about two thousand one hundred words or thereabouts required for fifteen minutes' talk, actual time thirteen-and-a-half minutes, allowing for announcer's little piece at beginning and end. Have also read and re-read my script with watch in front of me. Now learn for first time that news is read at rate of a hundred and fifty words per minute, but talks should proceed at one hundred and thirty, to give the listener time to take it in. Spend next half-hour or so cutting out pet bits that

I've spent hours and hours putting in, producer says she'll stay in with me if I like (which I most emphatically do) and will move her hands quickly up and down if I'm getting behind, and wave them slowly sideways if I'm scampering over the ground, Adam retreats to engineer's den, the red light goes on, and half-an-hour later we're walking down Regent Street, whilst I register vow to come up week in advance next time.

SEPTEMBER 6   Wasn't it the Duke of Wellington who said that to be five minutes early for an appointment was as bad as being five minutes too late? Feel sure he would have disapproved strongly of the miscalculation that lands me on my literary agent's doorstep half-an-hour too soon. But Covent Garden market is barely a dozen yards away, so Adam and I spend an entrancing thirty minutes wandering around it. Lemons, peaches, super grapes swathed in pink tissue, garlic bulbs in transparent bags, sage and parsley au naturel, apples and plums, pears and lettuces, carrots washed and dirty, celery, cabbages, cauliflowers . . . one could go on for ever. Sweet peppers, chillies, and aubergines are my particular fancy this morning. The first two I find entrancing just to look at, and sweet peppers very good eaten sliced with salads, or, like the aubergines, steamed for about half-an-hour, then split, stuffed, and baked in hot oven until filling is golden brown. Almost anything does for stuffing. Grated cheese and well-seasoned breadcrumbs plus a nut of margarine: tomato pulp and onions: minced meat scraps with potatoes or breadcrumbs, and so on.

The "Garden" is a wholesaler's mart, of course. But we manage to flush a retailer, and emerge triumphant with the scarlet and purple treasures that I never seem able to buy at home. Adam can hardly bear to contemplate the inevitable waste. If only he had a lorry, and could cart it back to our compost heaps, he cries. In one corner an ancient pair in rusty-black rags, looking like characters out of Dickens, are poking about in a heap of discarded tomatoes and refuse, stuffing things into sacks. But their object, I suspect, is more probably a barrow in some forgotten back street. Later we lunch at the Chinese restaurant in Glasshouse Street. It was Tom, on leave from Hong Kong, years ago, who first introduced me to chop-suey (a word coined for foreigners, and meaning "little dirty pieces", so I was told), to lichees and cumquats, and Green Dragon tea sipped from tiny handleless cups. Tom used chop-sticks for his chop-suey. Neither then nor since have I risen above a spoon or fork. But I have never lost my then-acquired taste for Chinese food. Are bean-sprouts back again, I ask now. Yes, but there are none for sale, so I shan't be able to take some home to bottle as I did before the war. A big store which once sold tinned bean-sprouts, bamboo shoots, and water chestnuts stocks none of these delicacies at present. So shall have to continue to make my English version of chop-suey as follows. One cabbage (medium size), sliced thinly and then steamed. Two large onions sliced thinly and fried in pan with little dripping, and lid on (this partly steams them). Sliced tomatoes, diced cucumber, mushrooms (if any) cooked in same way. Add cooked diced pork, bacon or chicken remnants and good gravy, and serve in individual bowls each topped with small omelette, and separate dishes of boiled rice and fried noodles. The simplest version of latter is a salted flour and water pastry, rolled thin, cut in strips, then fried. But potato crisps make a good substitute.

SEPTEMBER 7   "I've come for Thirkettle's dilly," announces the gentleman on the doorstep, when I open the kitchen door. Try not to look as blank as I feel. Thirkettle helps us in the garden some evenings, but always uses our tools. We haven't needed a dibbler yet, and there isn't a didle on the place that I can recall, as we're not responsible for cleaning out our small stretch of river. Does he know whereabouts it is, I enquire diplomatically.

"That's up the garden, alongside your wheelbarrow."

It seems my caller has been given some kindling and the odd log or two, and wants to transport them home. Thirkettle's dilly is just the thing for the job. Whereupon light dawns. Thirkettle has lent us a marvellous home-made box-on-wheels-cum-trailer, one-man power. So escort would-be borrower to its lair the while we discourse on probable fuel situation this winter, and agree that every little helps. Yes, that's its proper name, Thirkettle confirms when he calls round to-night to help Adam sort out accumulation in loft. Any little home-made cart that a man can pull or push, that's a dilly. No, he can't tell me if the word is used in other parts of the country, or only locally, or where it comes from. So I put this aside for future investigation. Should also like to know the origin and exact meaning of CIBBER, pronounced "sibby". Miss Barley tells me that when her father was parish clerk at Bawdeswell, this word invariably used when objections were raised to banns, the objector saying "I forbid the cibber".

SEPTEMBER 10   Dinner with the Rivers, where discussion turns on dogs. Major R. has earlier been assisting vet. to remove tails of new litter. I express preference for leaving animals the appendages Nature bestows on them, and recall monstrous beast seen two years ago on Svendborg ferry steamer, who might have sat for portrait of Hound of Baskervilles, but whose fine head marred by ears, or rather lack of them, as these cropped so only trace of original left. Conversation presently reaches retrievers, of which we all have tales to tell. But no one has heard of way to discover best puppy in litter that old gamekeeper gave my parent years ago, which is when puppies a week or two old, but before they begin to crawl about, wait until mother is out of the way, then carry them off to a new "nest". The moment she rediscovers them, she will move them all back, one by one. The first she takes will be the pick of the bunch. This tested out on more than one occasion by family, and incidentally produced Thomas, who in due course was to become something like a legend among our friends, a legend to which his notorious fowl-killing propensities undoubtedly contributed, but which was mainly the result of his prowess when out with the guns.

SEPTEMBER 14   Parents arrive with large baskets of outdoor tomatoes, so decide to bottle some. Dip the fruit in boiling water for easy peeling, then cut in halves, pack in jars, and sprinkle with salt. Elspeth then fills jars with cold water, but I prefer to bottle mine in their own juice: they keep equally well, and have a better flavour. Did not attempt outdoor tomatoes ourselves this year, for moving reasons, but are planting more next season when we propose to grow sweet corn in same plot, and use the corn stalks for tomato stakes. Apparently certain plants have an affinity for others, and experiments in growing tomatoes alone, sweet corn alone, and the two together, have revealed that better crops of both obtained in the third case. Compost produced good crops both indoors and out, of course, without the "aid" of soil sterilisation. But compost containing tomato plants waste yielded better results than compost in which this ingredient was lacking, so must also remember in future to compost the old tomato plants in small distinct heaps.

SEPTEMBER 15   Journeying through the Midlands during the war, our train was invaded at one station by a swarm of children returning from school. It took them some time to settle, and as they raced from compartment to compartment, invariably they left each door wide open to admit Arctic draughts. "Don't ANY of them have doors in their homes?" demanded one exasperated fellow-passenger at length. At Hillingsett to-day am tempted to enquire equally tartly, "Are plumbers, builders, and such never gardeners in their off time?" The former have laid their drainpipes with a fine disregard for climbing roses, shrubs, and flower-beds, throughout and now find that pale pink blossomed japonica has suddenly been reduced from large thriving bush to tiny rootless dying branch crucified against house wall. A small grassy lawn behind the house is now a well-trodden patch of bare earth. And once again I find a couple of wooden trestles sprawling in a bed of gladioli, though there is ample room for them beside their fellows in the gravel square alongside. The nasturtiums have escaped so far, and the seeds, which make an excellent substitute for capers, are just right for pickling. These should be washed, well dried (in sun, if possible), then packed in jars and covered with cold spiced vinegar. Good malt vinegar usually gives pickles a better flavour. But I prefer white vinegar for nasturtiums, boiling half a teaspoon salt and four peppercorns in half-a pint.

SEPTEMBER 17   Our move, like a thunder cloud, overhangs all our present activities, successfully blotting out projected visit to the ballet and similar excursions. Have serious thoughts of retiring to a nursing home and emerging when all is safely over. Since this is impossible, add to already innumerable lists of jobs to be done, and try to curb unfortunate habit of waking in the small hours to demand of a sleep-bound Adam where shall we put that big wardrobe, what day can we get into Fakenham to have the address on our identity cards and ration books changed, did he post that letter to electricity people, etc. Recall with awe and admiration Mrs. Edingthorpe, who moved sixteen times in twenty years, and hope we shall be able to stay put for quarter of a century at least. Life rendered even more complicated by the fact that the Aga cooker leaves for Hillingsett before we do, and will be out of action for several days, beginning to-morrow, so am indulging in positive orgy of baking to-day. Can see us subsisting chiefly on diet of bread and butter as week wears on, so when making second batch of bread, work $\frac{1}{2}$ lb. margarine, 1 lb. chopped dates, 6 oz. sugar, some crushed nuts, $\frac{1}{2}$ teaspoon cinnamon, and some grated nutmeg into dough for the last three loaves, for variety.

SEPTEMBER 18   What is the ideal size for a house? It depends largely on the idealist, of course. Though moving day still ahead, have already settled into Hillingsett Lodge in spirit, and find its length and roominess just the thing. Elspeth would prefer something smaller. Can I imagine what an American housewife would say to that long passage, the warren of store-rooms, butler's pantry, brewhouse, and what not, four attics, and no central heating, she demands rhetorically? But then tastes differ, I tell her, and relate the story of John's bullock-feeder. When the County Council put up some new houses in his district, a sanitary inspector called round to look at one or two of the older and smaller cottages with a view to selecting priority tenants. John having told him that Noah had eleven children, and only a two-bedroomed house, the inspector didn't bother to go inside. "We're building you a Council house with three bedrooms," he told Mrs. Noah, and went his way. "That's what he say," Noah reported later to John. "T'ree bedrumes. That sound all right, I dessay. But fare to me, do they was only to buy us some furniture in the place on it, we could use that other bedrume what we ha' got now."

SEPTEMBER 20   "No one ought never to have more furniture than'll go in a horse an' tumbril," said Ben to me, apropos of his own change of residence some time back. How right he is. Recall my own hasty transference the September war broke out when perforce I had to take to farming, and took with me the minimum of possessions, determined to travel light henceforth, and marvel at the amount of goods and chattels I have since acquired. Furniture removers are booked to deal with these. But lives there the housewife who can contemplate alien hands on every treasure? Daily the list of what I feel I must move myself grows. Manuscripts and notebooks, of course, clothes, bottled fruit; the more precious glass and china. Adam, arriving home, and contemplating the ever-growing array of boxes, baskets, travelling trunks and cartons, wants to know if he shall ring up and cancel the official packers, as soon there won't be a thing left for them to move.

SEPTEMBER 21   Letter from perfect stranger who has heard I want to know the wheres and whyfors of CIBBER, and very kindly proceeds to give them to me, backed with quotations from Hallwell, Forby, Nall, and others. Spelt variously SIBBERIDGE, SIBREDE, SYBBRIT, SIBBETS, CYBREDE, etc., it may be derived from Anglo-Saxon SIB (relative kin) and means "the banns of marriage". He also refers to an interesting entry in the old assembly books of Yarmouth Corporation dated December 25th, 1628. It seems that a number of marriages amongst the poor at that period had resulted in such an increase of persons chargeable on the town that it was decided to "intreat Mr. Brinsley, our minister, to forbear to take any banns, ask any cybbreds, or marry any poor persons" unless they first obtained, in writing, from the aldermen or chief constable of the ward in which they lived, consent to the projected nuptials.

Must confess that words have always fascinated me. And if I had to choose a dozen books with which to be cast away on a desert island, a dictionary would certainly be one of them.

SEPTEMBER 22   and our last night here. To-morrow, if all goes according to plan, we shall be sleeping (or more probably lying awake brooding on all the chores yet to do) in our new home. There is always something rather saddening about "last times", and we have been very happy here. To-night even the low doorway leading from the scullery, on which I have so often bumped my head, has a certain wistful charm. And once again I think how much I shall miss the river, though I've had so little time to "stop and stare" at it, and it's nice to know that our new garden is unlikely to disappear beneath a flood, and water come half-way across the kitchen floor.

Meals have been at sixes and sevens for days, and will undoubtedly continue so for days to come, for though the heating engineer has promised me that the Aga cooker will be working to-morrow night, cannot imagine when I shall find time to cook anything on it. Decide to make a minor flourish for our last evening meal on these premises, so stop stuffing books into sugar-beet-pulp sacks, and prepare two grapefruit halves by working dessertspoonful of honey into each, turn out bottled black-currants for a sweet, and make up a somewhat limited version of Danish smorrbrod for main course. The Danes, of course, use any number of different kinds of bread (English bakers, please copy, one of these days!) for their famous "open sandwiches". Then each slice is garnished in one of a thousand-odd differing ways. Poached egg on a paper-thin slice of ham or meat: one or another of their innumerable sorts of cheese: spiced butter with radishes, cucumber, or other salad vegetables: shrimps: fillets of pickled herring: crab or roe pastes, to name only a few. My effort includes wholemeal bread buttered and decked with anchovy slices: more covered with well-salted butter and slices of hard-boiled eggs: and wheat biscuits spread (*a*) with a mixture of equal quantities of margarine and cheese beaten together with a little sherry, and chopped sweet peppers, and (*b*) sliced tomatoes dressed with lemon juice and a little mayonnaise.

SEPTEMBER 23   As asked, have previously advised furniture removers of number of rooms in house we're leaving, and of existence of such items as piano, refrigerator, etc. Have also called on them to expatiate on amount of furniture acquired via legacies from various relations, now stored in attics, and accumulation of outdoor effects, at the same time extending a cordial invitation to send over member of their staff on reconnoitring expedition, as we're anxious to get everything over in one day. Solitary van now arrives with only two men, who take one horrified look, and immediately exclaim that there should have been four of them at least, and they'll want all to-morrow as well. No good wasting more valuable time in recriminations, so when Mrs. Yarrow and I have stuffed car to roof and trailer to cracking-point, we join in as well, to such effect that men remark admiringly any time we want a job, they're sure their employer will be only too glad to set us on.

At the other end, not only are builder's men still in house, but they're spread over half-a-dozen rooms, a good third of our chattels have to be dumped in temporary quarters instead of going straight to permanent ones, and the bottled fruit ends up in the coal-cellar. To add to the confusion, the stairs, landings, and bathroom floor received their final coat of stain yesterday, it isn't yet dry, and the plumbers have reappeared to panel in the bath. (But that's nothing in these days, the removal men assure me. In nine out of ten jobs they undertake these days, it's just the same, and last week they found the painters still in the house, and all they could do was to heap up the furniture in the middle of each room.) Adam appears at tea-time, and is promptly set to struggling with Aga cooker, which has already gone out twice, and is now threatening to go out a third time. Then we all have cups of tea, what time I wonder audibly what makes people choose furniture moving for a job. "You get around," offers the taller of the two, who in the late "incident" got around to Tobruk, Alamein, and Cassino. "I like to work in the fresh air," says the other, oblivious of the dust he's raised to-day, a goodish bit of which adheres to his person. "And weight-lifting's chiefly a knack." After which they depart promising to return with reinforcements to-morrow, while we take Mrs. Yarrow home, then go on to collect an anxious William Cat and the part of our bed-frame which has been left behind. And so to bed, trying not to wail with Mrs. Tittlemouse, "Will it ever be tidy again?"

SEPTEMBER 25   Try to concentrate on food, taking dozens of unnecessary steps, as cannot recall where half the things have been put, whilst salt has disappeared entirely. Fortunately remembered earlier to put some large cooking apples in simmering oven. Have found if these cooked very slowly (taking anything up to four or five hours) they remain whole, and their skins can be pulled off as easily as of those of potatoes boiled in their skins. I then de-core and stuff them, in this instance with fresh blackberries from the garden fence. But cooked fruit, or jam, particularly apricot, makes excellent fillings.

SEPTEMBER 26   Salt still missing, so make bread without it before cooker, which is still behaving like the leading light of a resistance group, goes out again. William Cat, on the other hand, has transplanted without a qualm. Have never subscribed to popular theory that cats prefer places to people. My own experience has been exactly the reverse. When a place has the greater hold on their affections, I always suspect that the human beings concerned have failed to measure up to cat-standards, by treating their pets with the respect and understanding affection these independent creatures require. Since William was once a lost cat, coming to us via the R.S.P.C.A., and, except in the early morning, is inclined to be somewhat undemonstrative, it did occur to me that he might hanker for known pastures rather than fresh hunting-grounds. But not a bit of it. Never has he been so openly affectionate as on our first day or two here, and now he seems more at home than we are.

SEPTEMBER 29   Took part in Brains Trust at Spixworth last night, when one of the questions asked was "Are modern children pampered too much?" The dictionary defines "pamper" as "to feed luxuriously . . . to gratify (tastes, etc.) to excess". And the natural tendency of most parents is to lavish gifts upon their children, to over-indulge, pet, and protect them, forgetting that in doing so they are stifling their children's initiative, sapping their rightful independence and teaching them, not to take care of themselves, but to be helpless in a world that is merciless to the weak. Rejoicing as I do in the greater freedom accorded to to-day's children, their emancipation from the bad old days when they might be seen but not heard, and when too often arguments were closed with the strap or slipper, I yet wonder sometimes if the pendulum hasn't swung too far in the other direction. And if too many grown-ups, as well as children, are not beginning to sit down, expecting somebody else to get on with the job, instead of taking off their own coats, and setting to work.

Salt found at last . . . in bottom of large box in fourth attic!

SEPTEMBER 30   Telephone call from Eve fetched me from bath last night, to say she has got another airlift, and can I pick her up at four-thirty this afternoon. To-day's weather foggy, ceiling what Adam calls ten-tenths cloud, so spend morning watching sky and trying to control imagination, though latter has sent me racing alternately by air, car, and train to scene of half-a-dozen crashes and hospital bedsides before I eventually collect Eve as scheduled, dead on time. It's most unfair she couldn't get moving leave, she reiterates on way home. But tell her she needn't worry, house still a complete shambles, builders with us (and likely to be) for next six weeks at least, and cannot see us getting straight until well after her Christmas leave.

OCTOBER 1   Have animals and birds a sense of humour? Not once, but many times in my salad days, I watched a pair of wagtails on the tennis lawn tormenting Omar, our Persian cat, into a complete frenzy. Whilst he snaked his way over the grass, flat on his stomach, they would dance nearer and nearer, then dart away just as he pounced. Omar would make one abortive spring after another. Sometimes they would continue to bait him for as long as twenty minutes. Then off they would fly, leaving him with fur on end, tail threshing, almost spitting with temper. Now hear story of rat and Guy's dogs. The other day he heard them barking frantically, so went out to investigate. He found them hurling themselves at the wire front of their kennel run. Outside the wire, just out of reach, sat a large rat, so engrossed in teasing them (for what else could have made him linger just there?) that he never even heard Guy come up.

To-night finished re-heeling and soling the family socks. Necessity drove me to evolve this particular technique in my teens when appointed darner-in-chief to brothers who, in an hour or so, would cheerfully destroy the patient work of evenings. Now when knitting socks and such, I make the leg in the ordinary way, and the foot as follows. Suppose seventy-two stitches on needles, divide for heel as usual, knit heel, and cast off. Using two needles only, and the remaining thirty-six stitches, cast on fifteen at either end, and decrease these newcomers at each end of the original thirty-six in the way I should do if they had been picked up at the side of the heel in the ordinary way, until once again there are thirty-six stitches left. Then knit on for necessary length, shape top of toe, and cast off. Next cast on thirty-six for sole, knot to match upper portion of foot, shape toe, and cast off. The foot is then sewn together, the great advantage being that these stitches can be slit, and new heels, soles, or toes, can be knitted in at any time without disturbing main portion. I also use two strands of wool at once for heels and toes.

OCTOBER 3   Normally Norfolk produces something like one-quarter of the nation's sugar ration. But owing to the long spell of drought, this year's crop will be a comparatively light one. Beekeepers, on the other hand, have had a wonderful season, and wherever I go I pass garden gates displaying "Honey for Sale" signs. Next year we are hoping to have our own bees. But meanwhile am stocking up with honey, for there is no telling what sort of a season next year's will be, or how much our bees will resent my well-meant but amateurish intentions. Stewed pears much improved by being sweetened with honey. For my last batch of spiced date-and-raisin bread, used honey instead of sugar, with excellent results. Have already used it successfully for syrup when bottling fruit. And next year shall experiment with honey for jam-making.

Hedgerows full of elderberries, which can be used in other ways besides wine-making. Am using them to-day, stewed, with stewed apples. And am sure that dried they'd make a useful substitute for currants in cakes.

OCTOBER 4   Is there a noun of assembly for babies? Was sorely tempted to invent one when glancing in at the Baby Show at the Home-Lover's Exhibition in St. Andrew's Hall this afternoon. A wondering. (How solemn some of those infants looked!) A squealing . . . a wailing . . . a bouncing . . . a hubbub . . . All these suggested themselves, as their hopeful mothers brushed and straightened, soothed and encouraged. A sprinkling of grandmothers had come to see the fuss, but only a pair of fathers was visible when I was there. Dare not look in on the fashion parade, having found by (expensive) experience that to attend one is immediately to become thoroughly dissatisfied with own quite adequate garments . . . the parade's main object, of course. Then round the exhibition proper, where I see several articles should like to offer good home, but none of the plastic coverings for kitchen tables I've recently read about and was hoping to meet; and wish I were sure enough of my plans to pause at the stall selling tickets for Bertram Mills's winter circus, and buy some.

OCTOBER 6   Spend morning and early afternoon sorting out books and moving furniture, getting progressively dustier. Then remember hyacinth bulbs still unpotted, so dump these and bowls on front doorstep with bag of fibre, and go in search of compost with pail and trowel. Am in midst of transferring bulbs to bowls, and, as usual, have reverted to using fingers in preference to other tools, when see my first caller approaching rapidly down drive. Toy wildly with idea of pulling face like non-existent parlourmaid, showing her respectfully into drawing-room (which, thanks to Eve, is not only in order, but full of flowers), then hastily removing dirt and disgraceful overall, and strolling in again as though we haven't already met. But no time to put this into execution, as caller, who announces herself as Mrs. Winterton, of Hillingsett House, greets me by name, says I look exactly as she imagined I would (!!) and that she'd recognise me by my voice, anyway, as she listened-in to broadcast last month, with view to finding out what I was like. By time she leaves ice completely broken, and have thankfully discovered that her family (two) about Eve's age, as those in our previous neighbourhood either well under ten, or belong to young married set.

5

OctoBER 7　Plough before Christmas, and the frost will do half your cultivation for you, is one of my parent's well-tried maxims. It breaks up clods bigger than a man's head, fining them down like the soil in a garden. And tractors are at work in his fields hardly before the corn is off, riffling up the stubbles ready for the plough. To-day, Heyhoe on the Case tractor was tearing up the reluctant soil of the field called Swains as I passed on the main road. Under the pale sunlit sky, ridge after ridge of soil curved over and fell against the one before, forming a sea of unmoving dark chocolate waves. Birds chirruped in the hedges. Now and then a jay flashed over the field. A pheasant called from the water-filled pithole once haunted by gypsies, and still known as "Gypsies Pit". But no gulls followed the plough. They wait for bad weather.

Nearer home, I stopped to pass the time of day with Ben, who was ploughing with a team of horses. He owns that tractors are quicker to cover the ground. But in his view you can make too much haste. "You want to give the birds a chance to get at the grubs. Engines, they go so fast, the birds don't get a look in." He also contends that no tractor-driver ever becomes a first-class ploughman unless he starts with horses. "Look at 'em on this yere place. Half the time I hatta set out for 'em. Do they don't make a proper job on it."

A few years back I picked up an old bullock-shoe hereabouts. Ben can recollect, when he was a boy, seeing bullocks yoked to the plough here. Several people I know can remember bullocks being used in other parts of the county as recently as the beginning of this century. In Denmark they are still used occasionally, and also the cows used chiefly for breeding beef-stock, either as a team, or side by side with a horse. But the most unusual team I've heard of to date was that seen by a friend visiting Czechoslovakia in 1934. Behind the plough plodded the peasant proprietor. In front toiled his cow, his sow, and his wife.

OCTOBER 8 At beginning of the week drew attention of builder's men to new water-taps in butler's pantry, which have been enthroned on small piece of wood (exact measurements six inches by three inches by two), in centre of window-sill, thus frustrating any attempt to open window at any time, and incidentally inviting trouble from frost-bite, as window faces due north, and suggest these should be moved back three feet to right, where they will be well out of the way and fully protected by wall . . . a small operation, to my simple mind, and one which, given the tools, could do myself in less than half-an-hour. To date the job has spread over three days, since to move the taps is a plumber's job, to plaster the wall where he's made a new hole, a plasterer's, and nobody but a painter must slap on the brushful of paint needed behind the plasterer. None of the three will touch the piece of wood on the window-sill, as this is a carpenter's job. But cannot face another minute of this, so knock it off with hammer in two seconds, the while I wonder what would happen to the world's work if the housewife began to entertain similar ideas.

OCTOBER 10 Gardens are indeed lovesome things, but as the poet pertinently pointed out, they don't get made by sitting down, admiring the view. And the pace at which weeds multiply the minute nature is left unattended is a lesson in high-speed production. Spend the afternoon removing some of the ground elder and "twitch" grass that is rioting the length of the rockery, and the long flower-bed above. As usual, have forgotten to run my finger-nails across a cake of soap first, a technique equally effective in spring-cleaning if only one can remember it in time. And I have all the average burglar's prejudice against working in gloves . . . it may be the better way, but my hands immediately feel like a claustrophobia sufferer trapped in a lift, so I prefer to get them earthy. Weeding has to be done with care. So has the planting out of our own treasures. For not until the year has gone round shall we discover the full extent of our predecessor's enterprise. Meanwhile more than half our tulips are temporarily homeless, as the beds for which they were destined have turned out to be fully occupied.

OCTOBER 11   Out to lunch to eat Michaelmas goose, coming home in a downpour which continues for the rest of the afternoon. A much-needed rain, but I feel that in a well-regulated universe, showers would fall during the dark hours, and not spoil a good working day. William Cat, who has an infallible instinct for the approach of bad weather, was indoors at sparrow-cheep, and has spent the day in his favourite resting-place of the moment, an empty peach tray he appropriated when I was fruit-bottling. Several people were interested in the tale of William's move. Was told of two cats that returned to their former haunts, but one had been given away to a stranger, whilst the other's new home contained a puppy, a kitten, and a new baby, for whom she was neglected . . . which bears out my original contention. Friends of Miss Tivetshall's take their cat on camping trips, the animal having a wonderful time in the woods beside which they pitch their tent. The Morleys' cats always accompanied the family on holidays, and when Mrs. Morley began packing, all she had to do was to put out the hampers in the kitchen, when the cats promptly jumped in, to be sure they weren't left behind. And I shall never forget Dusty, who came all the way from Yorkshire in an open car when his owners visited us, and returned at the end of a week in the same way. The cat-lover who wonders if she will lose her pet when she moves need have no fear, I am sure, if she remembers to reassure and make an extra fuss of him for the first few days on strange ground.

OCTOBER 15   Do I want a "million"? asks Ben. I have a mar-row but no pumpkin, so gladly accept one of the golden-fleshed vegetables, and introduce Adam to a real old Norfolk dish, pork and million pie, for which I fill a pie-dish with slices of peeled million and diced pork, add seasoning and a little water, pop a pastry crust on top, and bake in the usual way. The million makes an equally appetising sweet pie when apples, raisins, and sugar are substituted for pork and seasoning.

OCTOBER 16   According to Guy, trees are the landlord's so long as they stand, but belong to tenants when they fall. Take good look round our premises this morning, but only one dilapidated beech appears likely to qualify in next decade, and hope it won't, since when it comes down it will inevitably bring both our electricity and telephone wires with it. So order in winter log supply from usual timber feller, wondering what sort we shall get this time, as the various kinds have very different burning qualities. Beech is good, so is walnut. Oak is a slow burner, better used when the fire is well-established. Alder logs will produce an excellent fire, without "incidents". But willow should never be left unattended, as it has a dangerous habit of sending sparks flying out into the room. So has the resinous fir. Chestnut is poor, and the sweet variety, like the willow and fir, has a tendency to sparks. Thorn, if one can get hold of any when hedges are being trimmed, is a wonderful fuel, and burns like coal. But elm, as Ben rightly says, isn't "a mucher", as it tends to smoulder rather than burn. Whilst wood from a tree struck by lightning, whatever its species, will hardly burn at all. Ash, green or dry, is one of the better woods. Apple, of course, is best of all, and in the words of the old rhyme "Apple wood, wet or green, makes a fire fit for a queen." But apple wood is scarce. And what there is of it should never be wasted on fires, as it's invaluable for chisel handles and such. Must confess I hate to see apple logs burning, however bright their glow. Nothing is immortal, and there are many worse endings than to be reduced to ashes which can mingle again with the soil, and so help to produce new life. But memories of boughs foaming with pink-mantled blossom, and branches heavy with ripening fruit, make me feel a caitiff rather than a queen in the presence of burning apple boughs.

OCTOBER 17 Letter received this morning contains details of writer's experience in making crab-apple jelly with honey, using one pint juice to one pint honey, which set in twenty minutes. And how much honey do I use for bottling fruit, she asks? So far, have used half-pound honey to one pint water. But there are various schools of thought on the sugar versus honey question. One favours using half the sugar given in any recipe, and making up the quantity required with honey. Another simply substitutes honey for sugar wherever the latter mentioned. Whilst a third advocates substituting honey, but using twenty to thirty per cent less in weight, on the grounds that it's at least that much sweeter than the sugar we get these days. It certainly is. So, to my palate, anyway, was the sugar I was sent some time ago from Jamaica. The state of my store-cupboard usually rules my procedure. And, as my correspondent says, honey is expensive . . . though not unduly so, considering the amount of work that devolves on the beekeeper, to say nothing of the bees, whilst for sheer good value, honey wins every time.

OCTOBER 18   Adam decidedly off-colour last night, and this morning a candidate for bed. Has obviously picked up one of the germs now "going about", and needs nothing more than rest, warmth, and a light diet for next few days. Prepare to give him these with minimum of fuss, but have reckoned without Our Planners. Apparently one cannot now take to one's bed for more than twenty-four hours without a form, so spend morning finding new doctor (our previous one now outside our area) and dragging him out eight miles (sixteen the double journey) on otherwise totally unnecessary visit, simply to sign a piece of paper.

OCTOBER 19   A telephone call to ironmonger seven miles away and two stations down the line, suggesting he should rail us the articles I have now no time to collect elicits the information that this simple transaction no longer possible. Nowadays a railway lorry must collect the goods, take them to a depot fifteen miles away in the opposite direction, whence they will in due course be railed to us . . . a twenty-mile journey with a change of train en route. Whilst goods formerly consigned to a station two miles away, and picked up on arrival by the consignee must now go on to station eight miles away, from which they're delivered once a week. The trouble with the official mind is that it likes everything to look well on paper, and to take a large view. It makes no allowance for special cases, and life, particularly in the country, is full of these. Since man has only survived the ages because of his adaptability, cannot help feeling that the country that allows itself to become too rule-ridden risks the fate of the dinosaur and other prehistoric creatures. And wonder how I should ever get through my day if I adopted these methods.

OCTOBER 20   Am convinced that only the late W. Heath Robinson was competent to design a ladder suitable for apple-gathering. And before next season I must certainly evolve something in the nature of the blanket held by firemen to catch people jumping from burning buildings, for the benefit of those apples we are reduced to shaking down. After this morning's efforts in this direction, foresee apples in one form and another featuring at practically every meal for the next fortnight. Begin by stewing some, then put them into piedish, and cover with Marjorie's "crumbled crust" instead of pastry. This is made by rubbing 2 oz. margarine (cooking fat or suet will do) into 4 oz. self-raising flour, and 2 oz. sugar. Then bake in pastry-hot oven until crust begins to brown (about twenty minutes).

OCTOBER 22   Much entertained by magazine article entitled "Should your wife be fired?" giving a man's ideas for saving time, and labour, in the home. By his standards I am secure in my job for, being temporarily averse to taking two steps when one will do, and no more fond of backaches than the next woman, have long practised most of the things he preaches. His version of bed-making, whereby one side is completely tucked up and finished before the other's begun, must confess is new to me, now I've tried it out I can't say I care for it, and should like to see his when he's done with it. But all my working tools live in the most get-at-able spot for the jobs they do. My sink and kitchen tables are the right height for me, the first by persistent harrying of builder's foreman, the second by added wood blocks. I have an array of shelves, plate and saucer racks, and a self-designed container for draining knives and silver. And have also thought out countless schemes and devices for saving time, for a minute lost here, two there, have a hideous knack of adding up to an hour or more in the course of a day. And many an overworked housewife has only herself to blame for her plight.

OCTOBER 24   Herring season in full swing, when Guy reiterates his opinion that they'd be more appreciated if the price were higher, as too many people feel that if a thing's cheap it can't be as good as if it costs double as much. Keen members of the Herring Club ourselves. Probably the only way I couldn't eat herring is in the "Stargazing Pie" of the Herring Board's pre-war booklet, for to my squeamish mind those reproachful heads protruding from the piecrust are death to the staunchest appetite. Freshly caught . . . in pre-war days Guy occasionally spent a night aboard a trawler, descending on us next day with a

present of from a hundred to a hundred and fifty fish! . . .
cleaned, split open, fried in butter, and served with mustard
sauce, they are hard to beat. And they are almost as good fried,
austerity fashion, in margarine or cooking fat. Cleaned, put into
a lidded fireproof dish with a finely sliced onion, a bayleaf or two,
peppercorns and salt, and covered with equal quantities of
vinegar and water, then baked in a slow oven for about an hour,
they are good eaten hot or cold. The Danes have a thousand and
one recipes for dealing with herrings, and the good housewife gets
in a store when they are plentiful, preserving them in tubs or
stone jars in layers of salt, or spiced vinegar.

OCTOBER 26   Raining heavily at daybreak, and keeps on rain-
              ing all day. Could have wished for more helpful
weather, as contractor is moving over our compost heaps, I have
to superintend this, and also collect first instalment of two
thousand five hundred young currant bushes from fruit farm
some twenty-five miles away; the painters, who should have
finished off stairs, bathroom floor and remaining kitchen wall
yesterday, ran out of paint and want to work to-day; and there
are at least a dozen more conflicting chores to fit in. Am also
highly dubious of my prowess with car-trailer, as cannot back it
at all, and do not know with how heavy a load decidedly ancient
Austin Seven can cope. Car doesn't, either, and we have several
anxious moments on slippery hillsides coming home, when I can
see myself jettisoning bundles of currant bushes in manner
reminiscent of sleigh party chased by wolves, who buy time by
pushing off weaker numbers one by one. Manage to reach home
without taking this drastic step, and just as lorry drives in with
first load of compost. Currant bushes temporarily earthed up in
slit trench in garden. Must remember, when they're planted out,
to see that they're set "on the slope" and that the "union" is
buried. After which every bush must be cut down to the ground.

OCTOBER 27   Am always fascinated by seed-catalogues. And
              am certain that the average housewife could be
much more adventurous when planning the crops for her kitchen
garden. My list for next Spring's planting includes currant
tomatoes, apple cucumbers, Chinese cabbage (to be eaten both
raw and cooked), celeriac, the old-fashioned Jersey bean, sweet
peppers, Northumberland pot leek, South African marrows (the

fruits, the size of a cricket ball, are cooked whole), and, for next winter's decoration, a packet of ornamental gourds.

Windfall apples still very much with us. Sliced and fried with the breakfast bacon, they make a good substitute for tomatoes. To-day am also making Cornish apple flan. This requires four large apples (rather more when apples are somewhat wind-battered), ¼ cup chopped seeded raisins, ¼ cup sugar, ¼ lb. almonds if available, ¼ teaspoon ground cinnamon, one lemon. Peel, core, and chop apples into saucepan, add blanched chopped almonds, raisins, sugar, cinnamon, and the grated rind and juice of lemon. Cover and stew until apples are cooked . . . about five minutes. When cool, put into previously made pastry case (I use ¼ teaspoon cinnamon in the pastry), dot with fragment of butter (margarine), and make piping hot in oven before serving.

OCTOBER 30   Clocks back to Greenwich Mean Time, followed by usual argument as to whether Summer Time is a good or bad thing. To the mothers of young children that extra hour of daylight is an unmitigated nuisance, leading as it does straight to wakeful nights and fretful mornings. To the farmer it too often means another wasted hour waiting for the dew to go. Factory and office workers probably find it a boon. But since Summer Time means that they get up an hour earlier anyway, this could be achieved without meddling with the clock. Or could it? A visitor from Mars might well gape at our behaviour. But the fact remains that illogical man will happily rise at six if the clock tells him it's seven, but turn over for another nap if the hour hand gives the correct time.

NOVEMBER 1   Overnight that incomparable artist, Jack Frost, has been busy touching up the landscape with his wizard's brush. Exquisite fern fronds cover the window-panes of our bedroom windows this morning. Delicate flowers, miniature trees, and a thousand other fanciful images are sketched on the windows downstairs. Outside each blade of grass is coated with a dazzling layer of crystal. A commonplace wire-netting fence is transformed into a barrier that belongs to a fairy tale. The needles of the firs in the drive and beside the tennis lawn glitter like silver in the sun. The bare branches of the leafless trees are hung with a million diamonds. Even the compost heaps have acquired sparkling mantles. Whilst a thin film of ice covers the puddles in the yard and sits on the top of the water tanks. How thick is it? I poke an experimental finger through. Would a duck skate over it or fall in? The former, I fancy. So now we can make what Ben would call "a nigh guess" at the approaching winter's weather. "Ice in November to bear a duck. There'll be nothing after but slush and muck", runs the old saying. And it's not a bad guide.

NOVEMBER 2   Breakfast early, then set off to collect balance of currant bushes and the three hundred gooseberries we've ordered with them. Admiring countryside scene en route . . . a gorgeously apparelled cock pheasant slinking along beside a fence: a covey of partridges which might be mole hills or grass tussocks until they move: a herd of cows being driven to pasture that actually stays on the grass verge for me to drive past, instead of following the more usual bovine practice of straying all over the road: horses at plough, their breath rising in clouds of steam into the frosty air: a blue plume of smoke waving above a garden-rubbish fire: the russet and gold of hedgerows and woods: . . . I overshoot my proper turning half-way, as I feared my attempts to back the trailer merely results in the latter taking a sharp right-angled turn of its own, and I have to make a five-mile detour to get back to my route, getting rather more scenery than I have time for at the moment. More drama ensues when a large car sweeps round the corner from the opposite direction just as I am about to turn into the fruit-farm gate, a bus roars up behind, and in desperation I abandon car and trailer, and rush post-haste for the fruit-farmer to deal with the situation before I create a traffic block.

Can I save myself another journey? Yes, if I don't mind bushes in the car as well. So presently six hundred Wellingtons are stuffed behind and beside me, filling the car with their pungent, spicy smell, whilst the trailer is piled high with the remainder, the gooseberries on top. He supposes our man knows how to plant gooseberries, remarks Mr. Stratton at this point. I don't, at all events, and feel it would do no harm to learn. So off we go to field, where Mr. S. hauls up a bush, and gives a demonstration. Apparently gooseberries, unlike currants, grow on a "leg." So roots must be trimmed off to give "leg" about eight inches long. When planting, bury roots only. This means bush will be on top-heavy side, so build a small mound half-way up leg, and heel it down. This will hold bush firm and protect it from winter gales, and can then be hoed away in Spring.

Return journey made more or less without incident. Resolve, however, to take trailer to wide-open spaces without delay, and settle once and for all who is to be master.

NOVEMBER 3   Obviously the compleat housewife should take a course in electricity, how, why, and what. Had no idea that washing hands in an ordinary fixed basin, far from switches, could be lethal until Simon, touching tap and water simultaneously in cloakroom last night, receives a violent shock. Current nowadays often earthed alongside water-pipes, he proceeds to explain, when faulty earthing, defective plugs, etc., can render water "live" as in this case. To turn on a tap with one wet hand whilst the other in water (as he's done), is to invite disaster if anything's wrong, enlarges Simon, proceeding to gruesome details. So is to pull out the bath plug whilst still in the bath. This last my invariable habit, and foresee I shall never dare indulge in it again, especially if in hotels or other strange baths. Had also never before realised that the slightest "shock" when dealing with electrical appliances is a very definite danger-signal, to be dealt with by experts immediately, not put off as one usually does with a vague "I must remember to have that kettle (or whatever it is) looked at some time."

NOVEMBER 4   Christmas puddings, cakes, and mincemeat, need time to mature if they are to be at their best for the great day, and early November is none too soon to make them. Whilst Great-great-grandmother believed in making them one year to eat the next. The Minister of Food (am strongly of opinion that this post should be held by a practising housewife) has not yet released our meagre fruit allocation, and I have been thoroughly improvident earlier with my hard-won little hoard. However, can produce enough to make mincemeat according to Great-great-grandmother, who used 1 lb. apples, $\frac{1}{2}$ lb. each currants, raisins, and suet, the juice and grated peel of one lemon, a pinch of salt, mace and nutmeg, with brandy to taste. To this add on my own account 2 oz. peel, 2 oz. crushed walnuts, and $\frac{1}{4}$ lb. sugar as a rule. But this time am substituting honey for sugar.

NOVEMBER 6   Remembrance Sunday. Have not yet summoned enough courage to attend a public service, so keep the Silence at home. Does time heal? Perhaps a new skin grows over the lacerations on heart and mind as the years pass. But some wounds go too deep for healing. And no day is without its pang of remembrance.

NOVEMBER 7   "When are we fetching those three pigs?" demands my parent on telephone. "They should have been collected weeks ago." Only one answer to this, which is when we can dislodge builder's men, etc., from pig-sties. One of latter has been fitted with stove, and is evidently firm's branch office. Two more are paint shops and stores, and the fourth is filled with our stuff, as we can't get possession of work-shop or more than half of garage, and altogether everybody seems settled in for the winter except us. Climax reached when two large wood and corrugated iron shapes like sentry-boxes decorate drive for week-end. Have been convinced for some time that repairs to other premises are being conducted on ours, am now sure of it, and proceed to say so with much ill-feeling, and a certain amount of effect.

NOVEMBER 9   Tin of floor stain I purchased recently appeared to be little more than darkened paraffin. Unable to find anything better, I used it on bookshelves with much grumbling. Continuing my growls to Mrs. Peacock to-day, am given recipe for first-class stain that can be made at home. This consists of equal quantities of boiled linseed oil and terebene, both of which can be bought at ironmongers. For old boards nothing more is necessary. For new wood, or where a darker colour is wanted, add a little Berlin Black. Soak the boards with the mix-ture, and allow to dry thoroughly, which takes about twelve hours. Friend who gave this to her, adds Mrs. P., stained one landing seven years ago, it's the most walked-on place in the house, and it still looks as good as new.

Flowers for house the usual problem at this time of year. Had hoped the small outdoor chrysanthemums in kitchen garden would have been safe for weeks yet. But recent frosts have made it necessary to cut any survivors, and put them into pails in the old brewhouse, hoping this will prolong their lives a little. Late m arigolds, an odd delphinium and lupin, and the last Michaelmas daisies have turned to blackened pulp overnight. Some tiny scarlet ramblers, however, continue to defy the season. So do the chestnut trees, which are sporting numberless sticky buds. And several of the old currant bushes are unfolding new leaves.

NOVEMBER 10   Have found that when one's hands are busy, one's brain will often range far and wide. But time spent stoning raisins to-day results in no great thoughts, merely calculations as to how many ounces the stones account for, and speculations as to who first bred the seedless variety: a married man whose wife had stoned one raisin too many, I make no doubt. Then for the Christmas puddings. Ought I to make the austerity model . . . ½ lb. each flour, suet, breadcrumbs, currants and raisins, ¼ lb. sugar, 2 eggs, boiled 4–6 hours? Or can I reduce and adapt grandmother's more generous recipe? Quality wins the tug-of-war, and presently the mixing bowl holds 6 oz. each breadcrumbs, suet, sultanas, chopped apple, 12 oz. raisins, 4 oz. flour, 3 oz. sugar, and 2 tablespoons of honey, 2 oz. mixed peel, 1 oz. crushed walnuts, the grated rind and juice of one lemon, a glass of sherry, a little milk, a dash of mixed spices, a pinch of salt, three eggs, and a number of sixpences. Should love to have had Eve able to join in the first "stir" in our new home, but as this isn't possible, Adam and I take turns and wish, and then give a stir for her. Then into the basins the mixture goes, to boil for 6–7 hours, in the fruit steriliser.

NOVEMBER 11   Some are born photogenic, some achieve this desirable state, and some are distorted almost beyond recognition by the camera's lens. Belong to the last order myself, so when asked for new photograph for publicity purposes, cannot help viewing the situation with alarm and despondency. Recall visit to eminent photographer who heard my murmured misgivings with the air of a headmaster listening to anxious parents endeavouring to explain that whilst little Tommy's heart is in the right place, he is a little difficult and needs especial care, etc., but when proofs came to hand, had to ring me up and confess himself defeated, his concluding remark being, "This isn't you as your friends know you. But I think it looks literary!" Whilst when one was taken on the farm, everybody who saw it spontaneously admired the look of the tractor in the picture ("That tractor have come out WELL."

"That's a good 'un of the tractor." I can hear them now), but was extraordinarily reticent about the appearance of the woman at the wheel. Altogether it seemed simpler to try one of the multiple unit kind this time, hoping that, like a tommy-gun, with so many shots to fire, one at least should land on the target, if only in the outer ring. At the studio children are evidently the chief sitters, and I am adjured to smile in turn at scrapbook ducks and swans, horses and lambs, kittens and dogs, and so on. "Now smile at the bunny!" By this time the smile so carefully pinned on at first is working loose, and sagging into a grin that would do credit to the Cheshire Cat. And can see myself lacking the courage to open the envelope when the proofs arrive in a fortnight's time.

NOVEMBER 12   Builders successfully ejected from pigsties, arrangements made for owner of stud boar to collect pigs from Silford and keep them for few days, troughs hurriedly fetched from loft, when suddenly realise that we've forgotten to get in clean straw and remains of bales unused in compost heaps far too wet. Ring up contractor and ask if he can deliver one ton at once. Only ONE ton, enquires incredulous voice. Only three pigs, I retort smartly, and we digress to talk about feeding-stuff rations. "You know how to make pigs pay, don't you?" the voice finally addresses me. "Put 'em in the pot." An old man he knows always used to. (That was before the days of only two domestic pigs a year, I interpolate). He daresays it was. But the time he's talking about, there wasn't all this interference, and the old man had just killed a soler, must have weighed all of forty-eight stone. A friend of his happened to drop in just after, and was horrified by its size. It was far too big, he'd never kill one like that, he said reproachfully. "You never want to let your stomach know you've had a bad market," was the reply. Sound advice, the voice concurs. And he'll send that straw along first thing to-morrow.

NOVEMBER 14   Collect James off London train, and am just thawing him out with cup of tea, when front door bell squawks, and discover on doorstep author of beekeeping book I've recently been reading, and from whom I've ordered bees to arrive in May. As he happens to be in Norfolk, Mr. Westgate has nobly called round with view to advising me on one or two points, notably where hives should be sited, and what hives to buy in first place. Since it's already dusk, defer offer of cup of tea to latest arrival until we've made hasty tour of premises (accompanied, inevitably, by William Cat) and choose spot at far end of kitchen garden behind plum and pear trees. If I prune those boughs a bit, and stand a wattle hurdle just in front, the bees can take off from hives and proceed about their business without disturbing anyone gardening near by, says Mr. Westgate. And adds it's a great mistake to imagine that a sting is the first sign of their displeasure. To sting means the bee loses its life, and it's no more anxious to die than I am. The angry bee emits a high-pitched whine, and comes straight for your face, he goes on. When all (!!) you have to do is to fold your arms and walk slowly away. The bee will escort you to a safe distance from the hives, still sirening, but won't attack. And if it does? I murmur dubiously. Mr. Westgate has a fund of sting stories, each, to my mind, more painful than the last. "But what are a few stings?" he concludes. What, indeed?

NOVEMBER 15   Fog early and late, but a gorgeous day in between which James and I spend "guide-booking" about North Norfolk, visiting various coastal resorts, and no less than twelve churches. What a wonderful heritage of these last we have in our county. But what a responsibility and financial burden the upkeep of each entails only the individual parish knows. Could wish, however, that Knapton could spare time and money to remove the disfiguring paint and varnish from its rood screen, and so make it a fitting companion for the nave's magnificent roof. At present the screen looks a good deal more like nineteenth-century deal instead of fifteenth-century oak, and at first the former was what James insisted it must be.

No chance to visit *The Times* book exhibition, so glad to hear account of it from James, who had. How interested is the average man in the mechanics of cooking? Judging from Adam, I should have said not at all. But James disagrees. Cookery books were one of the most popular features at Grosvenor House, and an equal number of both sexes were delving into them.

NOVEMBER 17   Store cupboard now resembles Mother Hub-bard's as far as fruit is concerned, but the Christmas cake is just out of the oven. The recipe has been a family favourite for years, and used at other times of the year as

well, examples travelling overseas to my parent in Egypt in
World War I, and, if allowed, would keep for twelve months in
a tin at home. It takes 12 oz. flour, 8 oz. butter, 8 oz. sugar, 4 oz.
each currants, mixed peel and sultanas, 2 oz. glacé cherries, juice
and grated rind of one lemon, 3 eggs, teaspoon baking powder,
and baked in medium oven two to three hours. Have used margarine instead of butter in mine. But this will not be expected to
keep for any length of time!

6

NOVEMBER 18   To Chrysanthemum Show at Norwich, where, as usual, I am filled with demons of envy, and wonder whether, if I order plants of some of the big, frilly mop-like varieties, for which I have a weakness, they'll grow so well for me. (Decide they won't, so spend my money on joining the local Bee-Keepers Association instead.) Decorative classes, lovely, as always, and long for Eve, who is so good at this sort of thing, to see them. Should love to linger, but Adam is away, and pigs are scheduled to arrive in mid-afternoon. Car and large trailer appear half-an-hour after I get home, and from latter three black and off-beige Wessex Saddleback young ladies are decanted with remarkably little fuss. One has a large "saddle", one a smaller one, the third's saddle begins well but disappears abruptly in mid-pig. We'll be able to tell them apart, anyway, announces their late host, as he pockets the modest inclusive fee for their bridal, honeymoon hotel expenses and taxi fares. And adds cryptically that that little black one's the first, that large one with the big saddle comes next, and the middle-sized one is Number Three. But you never can tell with gilts, so ring him up if we have any trouble.

Have previously decided to christen all members of our pig population with names beginning with H, and the prefix Hilling-sett, so lead off with Hepsibah, Hazel, and Helen.

NOVEMBER 21   The ideal Christmas present contrives to be both a surprise and something we long for. But how seldom we achieve this ideal combination once we have ceased to hang up stockings at the foot of our beds. Lamenting this when having tea at the Vicarage this afternoon, was presented with ideal solution to this problem. As children, my hostess's mother kept a "wish book", in which each child wrote down the presents he or she would like to get. "Father Christmas" was then able to make his selection, confident that the recipients would be pleased with their gifts, yet keeping the element of surprise. The custom has been continued ever since. And henceforward it is sure of at least one new follower!

NOVEMBER 22   How does one discover the correct distance between two points? My way into Norwich, after sundry divagations in a maze of country lanes, now follows the Holt road for a dozen miles or so. Signposts and milestones bestrew my route, but are as about as unanimous as the delegates at a U.N.O. meeting. Whilst my speedometer disagrees with all of them. Have come to the conclusion that time taken, not mileage, is the best way of reckoning. But should like to know who is responsible for the official mileages, and why signposts and milestones standing only a few yards apart differ in their conclusions by three-quarters of a mile.

NOVEMBER 23   Letter from James, now back in the purlieus of W. 12, to say that Angela has another touch of sciatica, and have I any more of those herbs, as they seemed to do the trick last time? So pack up a selection from the young sheaf hanging from the attic rafters, the while I recall the cheerful grin, the bright succory-blue eyes, and the Father Christmas beard of Henry Knights, pottering about in the wooden shed which housed a car nearly as old as himself, and bundles of the herbs he collected at appropriate seasons.

Many were the stories told of invalids who visited him for the first time driven in a dog-cart or pony-trap, so "set fast" with rheumatism or lumbago that they had to be helped down from their conveyances. Sent away with a bunch of dried "harbes", plus instructions on how to use them, their next call would be paid on foot, sometimes from a distance of several miles. His remedy for both complaints was much the same. Agrimony: a tall woody-stalked plant with a spike of small yellow flowers, succory: another woody-stemmed plant with blue flowers, which is also known as chicory, and wormwood, were its chief ingredients. A good-sized bunch of the first two, with a dash of the third . . . or succory or agrimony used alone . . . to be thrust into a saucepan, partially covered with boiling water, then simmered from two to three hours. The resultant brew, in taste and texture not unlike strong, slightly bitter tea, to be taken in quantities roughly approximating two pints per week for three weeks (or longer should, by any chance, the condition persist). Henry Knights could toss off a day or two's ration at one gulp without apparent ill-effects, but the general rule was a wineglassful three times a day, preferably after meals.

Rheumatism and its kindred ills were not the only ones for which he was consulted. As a child, and in early adolescence, I suffered torments from recurrent attacks of eczema. The succession of doctors to whom I was taken advised numberless ointments, sulphur baths, and two bananas a day. The attacks went on. Henry Knights owned a small market garden business, and one day my family called to buy some plants. I didn't know him then, and was none too willing at first to produce my bandaged arm for his inspection. "That's right! Scratch it! Scratch it!" he exclaimed when I told him that the irritation was such I could hardly keep my fingers from it. "Then rub on this here." And he wrenched a handful of elder leaves from a neighbouring bush, and held them out in his grimy paw. Having recently taken a first-aid course, I couldn't bring myself to follow the first part of his advice too literally. Home again I gathered more elder leaves, put them through a mincing machine, applied hot fomentations instead of finger nails to the three-inch-square tormented portion of my arm, then dabbed on the thick green juice with cotton wool. The constant irritation of the past sixteen weeks subsided in two minutes. Within three days the whole thing had healed, and not even a scar remained.

The elder bush provides another lotion, less potent, but more congenial for those who flinch at the thought of bright green stains on their persons. Henry Knights gathered the flowers in season, left them to dry in a paper bag, and then poured a little boiling water on the dried blossoms for use when required. The root of Solomon's Seal, crushed, and applied to spots on the face with one's fingers, was another remedy he advocated. For internal use, as a blood purifier, he used "cleavers" (goosegrass), his recipe being three pints of water to a bunch "the size of a house-sparrow's nest." Simmered in the same way as the agrimony brew, he recommended a wineglassful per day, though when I knew him, old Henry kept a jug of the mixture handy through-out the summer, tossing off a mugful whenever he felt so inclined. "You never see me ailing," he would say, with a twinkle in those succory-blue eyes.

For constipation he prescribed rhubarb root, the thick brown root for adults, the younger and lighter-coloured roots for children. Shredded into a cup in small flakes until the cup was one-third full, the cup was then filled with boiling water and allowed to stand, the dose being one teaspoon after each meal, or a tablespoon before bed, to be taken until the condition disappeared. To stop bleeding he believed in the application of a piece of the large white fungus known locally as a "puff-ball", and, in its absence, the good old Norfolk remedy of a spider's web. For attacks of "vertigo", he recommended three or four drops of oil of fennel, taken before going to bed. For other ailments, other herbs. A few he grew in his garden. But most he collected from hedge and common during the summer months, waiting until each was dead ripe and at its best, always choosing a day just before the moon reached its zenith for the gathering.

Adam swears that I shall end up as a minor "wise woman", and probably be thrown in a pond to see if I sink or swim, if I live long enough. For ever since a sharp attack of sciatica during the war years re-aroused my interest in "harbes", I have kept a supply of agrimony, and as much of the more elusive succory as I can come by. And more than one friend and acquaintance has offered to write me a testimonial as a result. I have also received a letter or two from strangers who want to know where they can find various herbs. One, to whom I sent a small bunch, subsequently wrote to say that whether it was the change in the weather, my witches brew, or the natural course of events, he couldn't be sure. But anyway his lumbago had gone. Why didn't I commercialise the stuff, he suggested. And enclosed a highly entertaining "Spiel" for an advertisement, presented me with a name for the mixture, "Gipsibroo", and assured me that, properly handled, it should make my fortune!

NOVEMBER 24 What exactly are the duties of a housewife? Judging by a one-hundred-and-fifty-year-old cookery book in my possession, they include the management of cows, poultry, rabbits, sheep. Then she should know how to build a haystack, to stucco a house, to cure a pig, make lotion to prevent falling hair, "chopped lips", and similar ills, besides dealing with the more usual chores of cooking and housekeeping. No doubt the old-time housewife would consider her modern counterpart's life a lazy one. But I am certain she would approve my activities this morning, however, which include filling a skep with cabbage leaves, and handing them over to Helen, Hazel, and Hepsibah. As they gobble, I glance anxiously towards Helen's rear. Yesterday I was horrified to notice it hanging down as straight as a rat's, which is universally agreed to be a Bad Sign. To-day am much relieved to see that it looks like a young corkscrew.

NOVEMBER 26   To eat a mince-pie before Christmas means a happy month after, or so they say. (To ensure a carefree year, the necessary number must be eaten in twelve different houses, of course.) Make certain of one month at least by using up the odd amount of mincemeat left after filling the jars three weeks ago. Have recently had a " grazing " craze, so line a shallow round oven-proof dish with the remaining pastry, fill it with raw grated apple (skin included), sprinkling a little sugar between layers of apple, and grating nutmeg on top, then put this into the oven with the mincepies to see what happens. Remove twenty-five minutes later, when am distinctly gratified by the result.

NOVEMBER 28   Much drama and incredible amount of noise over week-end, thanks to Helen Pig, who begins to limp one day, and run at the nose the next. Am sure that she has cut her foot on the broken glass that keeps turning up whilst the yard is dug out, but any efforts on our part to look at the injured member result in complete non-success. (Either she leans heavily on it or us, or skips out of range with surprising agility.) The new symptom appearing, we hastily consult text-books, when we are horrified to learn that the two together may mean foot-and-mouth. We cannot believe that Helen has it. But since this fell disease must start somewhere, and at present we are as imaginative about them as a mother with her first baby, Adam rings up the vet. The vet. arrives, takes a precautionary glance at Hepsibah and Hazel, then opens the door of Helen's stye. An unbelievable uproar immediately commences. Am sure the entire neighbourhood must imagine a particularly brutal murder about to be committed, William Cat mews in sympathy from the ridge of the stye roof, the builders cease work and as one man gather round to offer advice, whilst Helen's screams redouble.

(At all events, this is no mortally sick pig, I screech thankfully to vet. at one point.) All this is caused simply by an attempt to pen the invalid in one corner of the stye, and put a halter on. Once this is accomplished, her shrieks give place to a heartrending whimper, her temperature is taken (she hasn't one), and her feet are examined. (One has a small cut.) Presently vet. departs, leaving us some medicine to be put in her food, night and morning, till bottle done, and says keep her where she is for next five days, letting him know at the end of that time if she hasn't recovered. This morning Helen presents a perfect picture of piggy placidity, with her limp almost gone.

NOVEMBER 29   To see ourselves . . . Admittedly my face not one calculated to launch a thousand ships, or even push a model yacht from bank of duck-pond, but do I really look like that? I appeal to Adam, after one shattered look at my photograph proofs. Not in the least, he assures me stoutly. Wonder if this is the truth, or husbandly tact. But recall the prolonged and suspicious scrutiny given me by the Danish official who once tried to reconcile the portrait on my passport with my actual visage, and take heart. Since this sheet even worse than the last, decide on another attempt in near future. But first should spend an hour or two in front of a looking-glass to discover the best "angle", then have the entire forty-eight taken that way, when one may turn out passable.

DECEMBER 1   Make Hot Mill Cakes for tea. These only need $\frac{1}{4}$ lb. dripping or margarine to three breakfast-cups flour, plus 1 teaspoon cream of tartar, 2 teaspoons carbonate of soda, pinch of sugar, one egg, a little milk. Mix all ingredients together, roll out on pastry board, and cut in rounds $\frac{1}{4}$ inch thick. (I use an eggcup for this last.) Bake for ten minutes in really hot oven, split, dip both inside portions in saucer of melted butter (marg.), clap together again, and serve. (Left-overs can be re-heated another day.)

DECEMBER 5   One of my earliest memories is of a wild-eyed man accosting our old steward in the farmyard with the words "You've got my wife!" It turned out that the latter, sick of being haled from her household chores to open railway gates, and tired of waiting for her husband to fulfil his promise to find another home, had answered Brampton's advertisement for a housekeeper. To-day, as precious minutes slid by as I waited at a level crossing for a train to appear, I wondered how many man and woman hours are wasted daily by these contraptions. They must add up to a terrifying total in the course of a year. Surely a system of traffic lights, operated by the approaching and departing trains, could be installed instead?

DECEMBER 7   Have sought in vain for ground almonds this year, so the almond icing for our Christmas cake will consist of $\frac{1}{2}$ lb. each icing sugar and soya flour, $\frac{1}{4}$ lb. margarine, 4 tablespoons water, $1\frac{1}{2}$ tablespoons almond essence, 1 teaspoon lemon juice. Method is to melt the margarine in the water, then add the remaining ingredients less $1\frac{1}{2}$ oz. of the sugar, which is kneaded in after turning mixture out on a board. Half a pound each of ground almonds, icing sugar, and castor sugar, plus $\frac{1}{2}$ teaspoon each of orange-flower water, sherry, brandy, lemon juice, and almond (or vanilla) essence, and three egg-yolks, make a wonderful almond icing for those lucky enough to command the ingredients.

DECEMBER 8   Ever since our arrival, have been irritated by sight of decaying tree trunk sprawled within a few yards of garage door. The time long past when I could speak to Marsham, and the matter would be promptly dealt with by half a dozen men, a tractor, and a cross-cut saw. Far more urgent jobs are screaming for the attention of Our Man. So this afternoon pounce on axe, and start on it myself. Portions of the centre have rotted so much that I can, and do, scoop out quite a lot with my fingers. The rest is tougher, the minutes fly, my hair becomes progressively more windswept, my face more puce, my hands filthier, and my outlook disheartened. At height of dishevelment, I catch sight of two respectable male figures advancing down drive, and dropping axe, sally forth to intercept them. We met at a Spixworth Brains Trust, he thinks, begins the taller one, eyeing me somewhat doubtfully. We did, I agree, though I'm surprised he recognises me to-day, I add candidly, recalling the navy suit, red hat with eye-veil, etc. with which I graced the latter occasion, and guessing at the figure I look at present in dilapidated slacks, wooden sabots, and rest of working garments. Object of visit then emerges, which is to ask if I'll give a course of lectures (twelve!!) for the W.E.A. They evidently don't know my limitations as a lecturer, I tell them pityingly. Nor am I one of those fortunate individuals who can get up, without preparation, and give a talk to anyone on anything at any time. Twelve lectures, each lasting an hour, by B.B.C. Talks timing alone, would mean something like a hundred thousand words, I go on, warming to my subject. That's longer than a full-length novel, and would take me every bit as much time. I then give them a brief précis of my working day, and enquire interestedly when do they suggest I could fit it in? They agree it doesn't add up, either. After which they depart in search of fresh prospects, and I go back to my axe.

DECEMBER 9   What a fascinating place to wander in is a toy-shop. Could spend hours among the farmyard animals, the clockwork engines, jig-saw puzzles, paint boxes and bricks, balloons and pedal cars, the cuddly bears and such that throng the shelves and stand about the floor. The difficulty is to decide on what will most appeal to a niece rising nine, a two-year-old nephew, and a lady of ten months. To fit the gift to the recipient needs a Solomon, I feel. But at least I can avoid the mistaken kindness that presented a nine-year-old hoydenish me with a large and handsome manicure set!

DECEMBER 10   What, Elspeth wants to know, can she do with her weekly half-pound of so-called sausage meat, for a change? Ours is the same amount, and I can recommend the following. 1. Add salt, lemon juice, a pinch of paprika, 2 sage leaves (chopped or crumbled), a medium-sized onion (grated) and two or three good-sized grated raw potatoes. Mix well together, put into fireproof dish, and bake about twenty minutes in hottish oven. Serve, if available, with bottled tomatoes. 2. Use the same mixture, minus the potatoes. Scoop out the centre of a cabbage, stuff in the prepared sausage meat, put in covered fireproof dish with about $\frac{1}{2}$ pint water, and cook in good oven until done: about an hour.

DECEMBER 13   More than once in recent months I have murmured wistfully "How I should like a day or two in bed!" This wish now granted, and like the family in W. W. Jacobs' gruesome story, *The Monkey's Paw*, I couldn't

care less for the idea as I look at the thermometer, and wonder
if there's a single part of my anatomy that doesn't ache. Unlike
other one-man businesses, the housewife cannot close the
shutters, and retire to bed to be ill in comfort, since sick-nursing
is one of her multitudinous jobs. And whilst no afflicted business
man expects the office to telephone him for instructions every
hour or so, nothing can save the housewife in similar plight from
frequent queries as to how, what, and when, to say nothing of the
visions she has of finding an empty store cupboard when she gets
up again. Luckily Adam has to be away for a few days, so hotel
staffs will look after him, the pigs are provided for, and I have
only meals for myself and an anxious cat to provide. My own
requirements limited at moment to hot-water bottles and hot
lemonade: and as I have had the forethought to have a power-
plug installed in the wall on one side of the bed (and the telephone extension on the other) these are no trouble. Regret to say,
however, that lemonade used is of the bottled variety, since have
neither lemons nor energy to make the correct invalid kind. This
requires 1 lb. loaf sugar and six large lemons, the lemon skins
being grated into a muslin bag, then placed in a bowl with the
juice and sugar until dissolved, water being added to taste just
before drinking.

DECEMBER 14   Cancel appointment with hairdresser, and cry
off a couple of cocktail parties, but suppose I can
be thankful the germ has attacked this week, and not next,
when we shall be decorating the house and the Christmas tree,
dispatching the last of the cards and presents, baking mince pies,
and icing the cake. Am leaving the finishing touches of this last to
Eve, who loves playing with icing syringes. Over my almond
icing I shall use royal icing, made from 1 lb. icing sugar, 2 egg
whites, and a little lemon juice, working in an extra ½ lb. of icing
sugar if I need it with the help of a little extra lemon juice.
Incidentally the icing syringe can be employed with great effect
when preparing party food. A cheese spread, made of equal
quantities margarine and grated cheese, plus a dash of sheery
and pinch of paprika or cayenne, coloured green, red, or similar,
can be used on biscuits and in a dozen different decorative ways.

DECEMBER 15   Don't think I have a temperature this morning, but am in no position to find out, as broke

thermometer yesterday when trying to shake it down. (Trust that mercury and glass chips won't create an incident later on, as William, that indefatigable fur-licker, is asleep on the bed, and I seem to have retrieved remarkably few shards and quicksilver balls.) Am still uninterested in food, so whilst William consumes boiled fish in the kitchen, I sip more lemonade upstairs, and remind myself that at least I'm obeying the old adage to "starve a fever", and that my figure should benefit, if nothing else. In mid-morning the telephone rings, and a voice asks if the spraying outfit has arrived yet to do our currant bushes. Reply, no, and we aren't expecting it, either, as have not had promised confirmation, and so are without the extra help they wanted. Let him know when outfit arrives, and he'll send it on somewhere else, promises a voice. I ring off, there is a clanking sound on the drive, and machine is there. Voice's number is now engaged, so don all dressing-gowns in sight, plus a blanket, and risk pneumonia by conducting long and involved conversation with sprayer-driver from window, the upshot of which is that if he once misses us out, goodness knows when he'll be in our district again, and anyway he can manage with help available. Presently I see clouds of spray drifting across the tennis lawn, and think of the Fenland farmer who, forbidden by his doctor to roam his farm, built an extra storey on his house, and used it for a watchtower. William Cat, who cannot bear to miss a thing, has disappeared in the sprayer's direction, and can only pray he doesn't come in completely covered in tar oil.

DECEMBER 17   Rosemary rings to ask how I'm stuffing my turkey this year. One of the family is killing a pig, so we shall have some real sausage meat for it. The ordinary variety, however, can be greatly improved with a little extra seasoning, lemon juice, and chopped parsley: or better still, used with an equal quantity of boiled chestnuts.

DECEMBER 18   Still in bed. Blame this on Hepsibah Pig, who two days ago took occasion to escape from yard, and patter up the drive below my windows when nobody else was about. So, beset with vision of her gaining the public road, and causing an accident, to say nothing of damaging herself, I had to don mackintoshes over dressing-gowns and descend to deal with the situation. Adam, who is not pleased with either of us, and feels that both should have known better, says he shall ring up the doctor first thing tomorrow, and meanwhile, even if the house catches fire, will I kindly stay in bed, and confine my activities to ringing up the fire brigade.

DECEMBER 19   Doctor arrives just as I am calculating that two days more in bed is the utmost I can afford, as Eve, now stationed in Northern Ireland, is due home on Wednesday. And presently I am being told that I must stay where I am for several more days at least. If I am allowed to get up on Christmas Day, I must certainly not go out. And if he were me he would certainly cancel our house-warming party planned for the twenty-ninth. He suspects jaundice, the doctor adds, and goes on to sketch a pleasing picture of the brilliant orange complexion I can expect next week if he is right.

More disaster, as Hepsibah and Hazel have to depart on second honeymoon, so our hopes of a March piglet family now pinned on Helen.

DECEMBER 20   Whoever speaks of the country as quiet has evidently never spent a day in bed listening to the "noises off". The banshee wail of cocks near and far begins while it is still dark, and continues at intervals throughout the day. Then a car starts into life, a dog barks. Presently there is a chorus of quacks from ducks on a distant meadow. Nearer at hand a blackbird calls a tentative good-morning, a thrush utters a slightly scolding reply. Sounds thicken and swell as the day proceeds. More birds sing. A distant train can be heard, an aircraft passes overhead. Geese gabble, cows low, a calf cries for its mother, and one hen after another announces with a sublime lack of modesty to the neighbourhood that she has laid an egg. We are well off the main road, but cars and lorries add their quota. Sometimes a tractor roars down a side road, with trailer bumping behind. Oftener one can be heard chugging away in the fields. Now and again comes the screech of an indignant pig, a distant shot. The most prevalent of all are the joyous screams of children at play. (Surely one of the cruellest commands a grown-up can give a child is to "Play quietly", which for the young must almost always be a contradiction in terms.) During the afternoon comes the brisk clip-clop of a pony pulling a trap, and later the slower clop-clump of cart-horses going home from work. The hoarse cackle of the geese is heard again. Dusk falls, and with it comes the unmistakable goodnight call of the blackbird. The rising wind sets leaves dancing down the drive. Sparrows scuffle in the jasmine over the porch. A pair of cats are brawling in the currant bushes. When all else is quiet, the rats begin to scamper up and down the attics above my head.

DECEMBER 22 Jaundice it is, and I can resign myself to spending bulk of next fortnight in bed, though I can get up for an hour in the evenings, starting with Christmas Day. Telephone calls of sympathy have revealed that almost every caller has had jaundice, is having jaundice, or knows someone who's got ‑it. (Had no idea there was so much of it about.) Also hear of (*a*) a victim who ate a whole tin of sardines in one go and promptly recovered. (*b*) another who went for a hundred-mile car trip, which cured him. If this is so, why am I having best part of month in bed? I want to know. To which doctor replies some people don't even know they've got it, some are dead in a week.

CHRISTMAS DAY "O Dirty December, for Christmas remember" wrote Thomas Tusser nearly four hundred years ago, bidding husband and housewife make ready "to welcome good neighbour, good cheer to have some". He continues with a list of some of the things he considers necessary to achieve this desirable object.

> Good bread and good drink, a good fire in the hall,
> Brawn, pudding, and souse, and good mustard withall.
> Beef, mutton, and pork, shred pies of the best,
> Pig, veal, goose, and capon, and turkey well drest.
> Cheese, apples, and nuts, joly carols to hear,
> As then in the country, is counted good cheer.

And there is nothing there, he observes, that should cost the good husbandman a penny: it is only "good household provision", and he has left out "a many" other things that the normal household should provide in the ordinary way of living. How he would open his eyes if entertained in the austerity style that prevails to-day. Though I think he would have approved of some of the innovations that have cropped up since his time. Christmas cards, for instance, which only celebrated their centenary seven

Christmases ago. And the Christmas tree, a lovely custom that one is apt to think he ought to have known, but which only came from Germany to England about the time our Queen Victoria married Prince Albert.

Since I cannot eat it anyway, Adam and Eve presently depart for the family's luncheon party, to return home again in time for tea upstairs with me. Then I descend for my allotted hour. Not exactly the day I had planned for the first Christmas in our new home. But Christmas remains Christmas whether we spend it bed-bound or in radiant health, one day in the year when peace and goodwill capture the upper hand. It is for all of us to see that the spirit remains when the holly and decorations are taken down.

DECEMBER 27   Have often heard the phrase "a jaundiced outlook", but never until now has its full meaning struck home. My complexion, though still suggestive of a bronzing seaside holiday, is no longer a sunny yellow ochre picked out with lemon. But fond as I am of reading, this amusement palls a little as for the third time in as many days Adam and Eve set off for a party, whilst I settle back on my pillows with a nice book, an over-age Cinderella for whom no fairy godmother will call. There is also the question of food. Eve has brought back masses of confectionery and butter from Ireland. A delightful chocolate cake from Warsaw is among my presents. There is the usual Christmas fare. But fats and such are not for me. I am even denied the pleasure to be got from staying in bed in miserable weather, for the day has been amazingly mild, with long sunny spells. Jaundiced outlook is the word.

DECEMBER 28   One trial of the bed-bound housewife is cooking at long range, since it is one thing to look at a dish and pronounce it cooked, and quite another to explain exactly what it should look like at the crucial moment. Whilst when she does crawl into her kitchen for a moment or two, nothing seems to be in the place in which she is accustomed to find it. Am now allowed up for an hour or two each day, and spent part of this morning's quota making bread, retiring to bed between whiles. Content myself on this occasion with making six straight wholemeal loaves and two spiced, plus (Irish) fruit. Next week, for a change, shall make some oat bread . . . 1 breakfast cup oats, 2 lb. ordinary flour, 1 teaspoon each baking powder and bicarbonate of soda, mixed to a dough with warm milk (water will do) and baked as bread . . . and some wholemeal biscuits, for which I dissolve 2 oz. margarine and a pinch of salt in half-pint boiling water, stir in 1 lb. wholemeal flour, roll out thin, cut in squares and rounds, and bake in hot oven.

DECEMBER 30   Christmas to us is so inseparable from winter that it is sometimes difficult to remember how different the weather may be elsewhere. Miss Smith, writing from the Queensland border, talks of feeling quite exhausted by the heat. They have also suffered much from flooded roads during the past three or four months, and only now are these being repaired so that they can reach the neighbouring towns. The big ranch Christmas tree had to be abandoned. But a case of toys for the ranch children was eventually delivered by horse-drawn lorry.

7

JANUARY 1   "How thankful I am to have done with the forties", writes Freda, when wishing me a Happy New Year. Certainly the nineteen-forties, as seen by the historian, have little to commend them. Yet, for the individual, ten years is a long time. And even ten such years as now lie behind us have produced roses as well as thorns. If they are responsible for one of the deepest sorrows of my life, they have also given me one of its greatest joys. There has been much work, a little play, but many friends. Inevitably the new and untried seems to promise fewer pangs than the familiar, the known. A new year, a new decade, appear big with hope, happiness and opportunity. And so they are. Simply to be alive is a wonderful, a marvellous thing. And our personal share of grief and adversity is a small price to pay for it.

JANUARY 2   Thanks to books, I have made countless excursions these last three weeks, exploring the Gobi Desert, the land of the *Saturday Evening Post*, the differing Englands of Jane Austen, Thackeray, Dickens, and many more. But much as I enjoyed them, at the moment I would cheerfully trade the lot for a potter round the garden I can see out of my window. Have also been re-reading Parson Woodforde's *Diary*, which has added interest for me as I was born within a few miles of Weston, and just before the war lived for some years at a neighbouring village in the old mill house at which he called in 1778 to buy a "Ream of writing Paper". How different is his England, too, when the prudent guest went home early unless there was a moon, for fear of highwaymen. But perhaps the greatest change is in our food habits. When niece Nancy kept house for the diarist, and three guests came to dinner in 1781, the first course consisted of a pair of boiled fowls, a tongue and a boiled leg of mutton with capers and batter pudding. The second was two roast ducks, peas, artichokes, blancmanges and tarts, followed by almonds, raisins, strawberries and oranges. Cannot imagine what he would say to our present-day rations. But which of us could do justice to his gargantuan meals?

JANUARY 4   The doctor calls, says that I can get up for longer and sees no objection to my putting my nose out of doors for a moment, either. Which is just as well, as Eve was rushed off to nursing home last night with view to having two obstreperous wisdom teeth removed this morning, she'll be home again tomorrow, and I feel that two invalids in the house is definitely one too many. Get up in mid-afternoon, and although the weather is dull and cloudy, take a hurried walk round, escorted by William Cat, who greets the painters (busy on pig-stye doors) with such enthusiasm that he gets a large dab of green paint on the top of his head and one paw. Take apples and carrots to Brandy, who so far this leave has only been hoofs on the drive to me, and who is now hanging a disconsolate head over the meadow railings. There are five pale blossoms on a primrose plant in the kitchen garden. The jasmine that frames the front door is starred with yellow blossoms. And the birds are certain that spring is here.

JANUARY 5   Eve home, full of penicillin, and a somewhat pre-judiced view of life in general and wisdom teeth in particular. Have already acquired some bones from the butcher and simmered them for hours with two of Brandy's carrots, one shredded potato, one onion, half a small cabbage, two table-spoons rice, two chillies, salt, a stick of celery (outside bits only), the last of some vegetable extract, enough water to cover, and a bacon and cheese rind or so. (The French put almost everything into their stock-pots. And how right they are.) White soup will be the next, made by peeling and slicing 1 lb. potatoes, and one onion, cooking these for five minutes in 1 oz. of margarine melted in a saucepan, then adding two pints of boiling water and sim-mering until soft. Rub through sieve, return to saucepan, add half-pint milk, bring to boil, stir in salt, pepper, one tablespoon crushed tapioca (or similar) and cook until tapioca is clear.

JANUARY 6 Twelfth Night, and time to take down all the Christmas decorations. The witchballs Eve bought in Buncrana are packed away until next December. Holly, ivy, fir boughs and tree will finish in the grate or on the garden bonfire. The mistletoe is not yet joining the funeral pyre, however. Superstitiously speaking, a berry should have been removed for each kiss taken under the bough. But we have kept ours intact, as I intend to have yet another shot at growing our own. An established tree is necessary for host, or the guest may kill the tree it grows on, as it did the sapling apple at Silford. The ancients preferred an oak, since they believed that it increased the medicinal qualities for which they valued the plant. (They used it for ulcers, apoplexy, palsy, and "the falling sickness" amongst others.) I am trying a number of berries on apple and pear trees, in some cases making a tiny slit and squashing the berry into it, in others simply smearing it on a branch, as the birds do.

JANUARY 8 What a minor history of England could be compiled from a study of the names of the fields and pastures on her farms. In one village I know one at least has a pre-Conquest date, whilst a couple more commemorate a long obsolete fair, originally held yearly under the auspices of the local nunnery. The prefix "Black" usually denotes previous human occupation, sometimes of Roman date. The Pound Field is a reminder that the lord of the manor had the right to impound straying livestock, charging the owner (when found) so much a hoof for the release. "Friars", "Monks", "The Nun's Meadow", were pious gifts to one or other of the religious houses that once flourished up and down the land. "Mautby's Hall", "Stewkes Hall", and such, mark the site of long-vanished manors. "Coney Hill" was part of the lord's warren, to whom John Paston wrote in the fifteenth century asking for "six couple black conies or running rabbits, or some black and white to the same number". "Bloodfields", "The Hangman's Piece" and others enshrine some sinister memories. "Sidegate Breck" and "Three Gates" remain, though the toll-house on the turnpike went years ago. At the bottom of "Limekill Breck" are traces of the old lime kilns. And though nobody at Silford can remember any bridge there at all in recent years the dredger has fetched up several lumps of ancient masonry beside the meadow and field known as

"Three Bridges". At Binham, "Saffron Breck" recalls a crop no longer grown. At a farm four miles on, "Dutchman's" acquired its present name when early in the present century a party from Holland camped in one corner to show my uncle how to grow some sugar beet. "Mavis Piece", and "Dicky's Piece" speak for themselves (only "foreigners" need to be told that the first refers to the song-thrush, the second to the humble donkey). "Mill Hill" is a reminder that windmills were once a common feature of the landscapes. "Doles", the old East Anglian word for boundary, still shows traces of a banished coach road. In a corner of "Leasepit Breck" a boggy morass marks the site of the old leech pit, from which local apothecaries caught their store. But what is the origin of "Hellman Hatchett"? Of "Guiltcross" and "Gunspear"? Who lived in "Crabbs Castle"? And who were the prisoners of "Prisoner's Close"?

JANUARY 10   In mice it takes ten generations for a habit, originally acquired, to become inborn, or so I am told. Since this house was built nearly two hundred and fifty years ago, the mind blenches at thought of the numberless generations of rats that have haunted its attics, slid down inside its walls, and bitten bottom corners off doors. Their present descendants possess all their ancestors' evil habits, plus an allergy to traps and similar deterrents. This morning (my first breakfast downstairs, as Eve has to be taken into Norwich to see dentist), I find a rat disporting himself in the kitchen. My female forebears for the last half-score generations undoubtedly greeted every such manifestation with a piercing shriek, for my reaction is instinctive and immediate. And within two seconds I am outside on the back lawn invoking help. Help arrives and chases the rat round and round the kitchen, behind the cooker, below tables, and in and out of the refrigerator engine chamber, whilst I direct operations through one kitchen window, and a completely disinterested William Cat looks on. After some twenty minutes, when rat is back in engine again (the latter refusing to start up and frighten the rat out, though in the ordinary way it seems to be for ever running) I suggest the machine be pushed against the open door, as I can bear no more. It is, and rat promptly escapes to the kitchen garden. By this time have lost all interest in breakfast. And arrange to spend afternoon heightening door sills.

JANUARY 12 A perfect spring day, so Eve and I leave the clamorous household tasks, and spend an hour or so replanning the garden. As usual, wish it were possible to alter its layout. But trees cannot be moved with impunity or without expense, though a Norfolk landowner once successfully uprooted and replanted enough to make an entire avenue to greet his visiting Sovereign. And the treasure of flowers and shrubs left behind by a previous tenant is enough constantly to make me think of Dr. Rigby's epitaph at Framlingham Earl, which reminds the reader that the doctor's true memorial is to be found, not in the church, but in the many trees he planted in the neighbourhood. This morning we are chiefly concerned with the patch of rough grass in front of the narrow belt of trees above the tennis lawn. Can excessive rolling and lawn-mowering reduce its tangled surface to some semblance of smoothness in time? Should we tear it up and re-seed? Or shall we construct large flower beds, interspersed by wide grass walks? We decide on this last, and the eye of faith is soon envisaging a lavender hedge, a riot of lupins, delphiniums, in every shade of blue and purple and a rainbow of other blossoms. Some at least we hope to see in bloom this summer. If not, I can see Eve's coming-of-age party preceded by an orgy of the pot-plant style of gardening that graces agricultural shows.

JANUARY 14 Letter from Norah, asking for a recipe for bottling odd pieces of pork, and wanting to know if bottled meat keeps, is it safe, eh? Have been meaning to try out just such a recipe for ages, but so far have got no farther than buying some special wide-mouthed jars for sausages, when unexpected visitors descended on us, and we ate the sausages instead. The method given me, for poultry, meat, game, etc., is to cook the meat, pack at once into warm sterilised jars, cover with stock (or leave "dry", if preferred) put on rubber rings, tops, and clips, then place the jars in a lidded steriliser with warm water reaching three-quarters of the way up them. Allow the water gradually to reach 200°–210° Fahrenheit, maintaining this temperature for two hours. Remove jars, and leave for forty-eight hours. Then re-sterilise as before, keeping temperature at 190°–200° for two hours. The official view is that only pressure cookers can deal adequately with meat and vegetables. But have encountered so many instances of satisfactory meat-bottling before these were heard of that, when I make the attempt, shall certainly use my steriliser.

JANUARY 16   The city housewife can, and often does, do part of her shopping each day. Her country counterpart necessarily takes a slightly longer view, and a good deal of mine is done by fortnightly telephone calls. But which of us, I wonder, has the least idea of how much food our family consumes in six months, or would care to order our groceries at such intervals? It was ninety years ago that Great-uncle George, crossed in love, left his Norfolk home without a word to his family and took ship for Australia. Followed ten grim months in that country which, however, resulted in a fortunate friendship that led him to New Zealand and put him in charge of a large sheep farm, helped by six assistants, and with equipment that included a brace of revolvers in his belt, since the Maori wars were in progress. Presently he replied to a sister who asked for details of his housekeeping. Beef and mutton could be bought for twopence and threepence a pound, though actually they slaughtered their own each week. Fruit and vegetables were also grown on the premises, peaches being so plentiful that the surplus was fed to pigs, and Great-uncle George thought nothing of eating five pounds of grapes a day. But groceries and such had to be ordered for the half-year, and included half a ton of flour, half a ton of sugar, a hundred pounds of plums and currants, fifty-six pounds of tea, and fifty-four pounds of coffee, besides "various other little delicacies".

JANUARY 18   Eve certified "fit to travel" tomorrow, so to-day full of the usual preliminaries of departure. Fortunately the sun has elected to shine, since these include a fourteen-mile ride, as Brandy has to be returned to base, and have his shoes removed at the blacksmith's en route. Then saddles and bridles and such must be cleaned and put away, and unwanted civilian clothes put to bed with mothballs, the while I remark at intervals that anything which can't be squeezed into her suitcase and hold-all for the journey is to be made into ready-to-post parcels by its owner NOW: and if the boot-trees over which everybody has been tripping for the last two weeks are not soon returned to their hunting boots, there will be grave trouble, and lots of it. In between whiles I make up batch of cakes, etc., for the traveller. When last in Norwich, she begged for a coconut, and the grated remnants of this now end up in buns made from my coconut cake recipe, by creaming $\frac{1}{4}$ lb. each sugar and margarine, adding 1 teaspoon lemon juice, $\frac{1}{2}$ teacup milk, two well-beaten eggs, 1 teacup coconut, then stirring in $\frac{1}{2}$ teaspoon carbonate of soda and $\frac{1}{2}$ lb. flour, and baking in quick oven.

JANUARY 20   Having seen Eve into London train, returned home yesterday and to help ward off threatened attack of what is known in our family as "we mothers", started on first stage of marmalade needing twelve Seville oranges (approx. 3 lb.), two lemons, $6\frac{1}{2}$ lb. sugar, and five pints water. Not owning the correct machine, and having no time to slice by hand, as usual have washed fruit, cut into quarters, worried out the pips, then run fruit through ordinary mincer. After which pips, in muslin bag, have been set to soak overnight in half-pint water, while the fruit soaks in the rest. In the past, Stage Two has seen me spending long evenings sitting by the fire, a book in one hand, a wooden spoon in the other, and the preserving pan on a primus stove on a tray on the hearth-rug. (The alternative was standing for hours beside the kitchen stove.) Since owning a heat-storage cooker, the necessary two to three hours preliminary simmering is replaced by allowing the fruit to spend the night in the cooker's simmering oven. So this morning I have only to bring it to the boil, add the sugar (warmed) and muslin bag of pips, and boil to setting point, contrasting as I stir the warmth of the kitchen with the biting cast wind whining outside, and wonder if Eve has had a good crossing.

JANUARY 21   Hepsibah, Hazel and Helen allowed into our one-acre piece of meadow for first time, and within half an hour they've had hurriedly to be driven out again. Though all three have rings in their noses, within ten minutes they have ripped up a patch of turf as big as the floor of their styes. There are several be-nettled plots we want cleared of rubbish, so as soon as these can be wired in, shall employ them in there.

JANUARY 23   A minor difference between the town and country home is that the latter almost never owns a number. Except, perhaps, in the case of the new council houses, there is seldom any need for one, for everybody in the neigh-hood knows the abode (not to mention the business!) of everyone else, and the name of the village is usually a sufficient postal address. Progress, however, has now caught up with us, and a letter from our Rural District Council informs Adam that we have been allotted a number, which we are requested to affix in some prominent position within seven days. Presumably we are not alone so favoured. And since we are a law-abiding race in the main, no doubt the gates and doors of the countryside will shortly be a-shine with these adornments. But will anyone pay the slightest scrap of attention to them? I doubt it. Our own number, according to the soothsaying fraternity, is a fortunate one for me. But this does not tempt me to order forthwith a new die-stamp and a fresh supply of writing paper. And since the house has borne a name for well over two hundred years, I cannot suppose that in future it will be referred to by the figure on one drive gate. Cherry Tree Farm will remain Cherry Tree Farm, I am convinced. Horses will still be shod at the blacksmith's, not No. 10, The Street. The postman will continue to deliver letters at Mrs. X's, Jack Y's, and old Miss Z's. And can anyone imagine that men will arrange to spend an evening at No. 81 or No. 56, instead of meeting at the "Pig and Whistle", or the "White Hart"?

JANUARY 25   "Who do you think will get in this time?" asks the lorry-driver, as he unloads the last straw-bale. I have no more idea than he has. And no party has yet come out with the programme I should like to see for agriculture. Since healthy citizens are the result of good sound food, and healthy food is the product only of healthy soil, there should be an acreage bonus for all fields properly composted and mucked. As a corol-lary, if rationing of feeding-stuffs could not be done away with altogether, a more elastic system of allocating them should be introduced. Why, for instance, may the newcomer keep pigs, or poultry, but not both? And where a farmer does not use his basic ration, why shouldn't this be transferred to someone who will? The county committees, who know the local conditions and people, should be empowered to deal with these and similar problems on the spot, instead of being forced to refer them to a distant Ministry whose officials are more concerned with adhering to the Rules as Laid Down than treating cases on their merits.

Imports need some drastic revisions. Granted that at the moment we must import some of our food. But the housewife who bought apples when her larder was stacked with trays full of those from her orchard, would rightly be considered extravagant and improvident, if no worse. And no more than a family can a nation afford to import other countries' surplus, and let its home-produced food rot in hales and stores.

JANUARY 27   How much does a level tablespoon hold? Or a breakfast cup? And as my teaspoons vary considerably in size, how can I be sure that my heaped teaspoon is measuring the amount the recipe intended, and neither more nor less? The average teaspoon, when used for flour, sugar, salt, or fats, holds $\frac{1}{4}$ oz. when level, $\frac{1}{2}$ oz. when heaped: whilst the contents of a level tablespoon weigh $\frac{1}{2}$ oz. and heaped the full ounce. A tablespoon of jam or treacle equals 2 oz., of rice amounts to 1 oz. A breakfast cup holds 8 oz. of flour, the average egg cup equals 2 oz. of butter or suet. And if you have mislaid your smaller weights, three pennies weigh 1 oz., a dozen of them $\frac{1}{4}$ lb. Incidentally the edge of a penny is an excellent thing for removing spots of paint from window-panes.

JANUARY 28   "Now all things rear . . . For all the year," is Thomas Tusser's advice at this season. But what can we do with the ground like iron, as it's been for the past fortnight, demands Adam. Richard, a keen rose-grower, has found something. Already he has a man out, searching the hedges for likely briars to remove to his flower-beds, where in due course they will be budded with first-class roses. Dan was another collector of briars. His own garden, on the edge of the village heath, where he lived in a tiny one-up, one-down cottage, was a jewel. But it was far too small to contain his love of roses. During autumn and winter he would roam the neighbourhood. Whenever he found a suitable briar in a fence, he would importune the farmer for it, and mark it for his own. Later in the year he would bud the briar where it grew, stipulating that the roses should be his. Somehow he made time to attend countless rose shows. Perhaps it was at one of them he first met Queen Mary. If not there, then somewhere else, and at one time he grafted roses for her at Sandringham. He was over seventy when Amy first knew him. Re-visiting the village a year or two ago, she found that his cottage had grown new rooms, and was occupied by strangers. But the fences still speak of Dan.

JANUARY 30   Were the good old days so very good? Re-reading the Paston Letters, those fascinating records of life in the fifteenth and early sixteenth centuries, one wonders. Wars abroad, our French possessions lost, the enemies a-prowl around our coasts grown so bold that they kidnapped the unwary, holding them to ransom, and played on Caister Sands and elsewhere "as homely as they were Englysche men". At home there were civil wars and insurrections, and "riotous felaschepes" attacking and murdering men even in church. Nor were they safer in their homes. Whether or no John Paston gained possession of Sir John Fastolf's lands by a forged will, he had little good of them. Caister, "the fairest flower in our garland" Drayton, Hellesdon, were all the scenes of riots and pitched battles. And though his title to Gresham, bought by his father, was clear enough, his family were twice forcibly driven out of it. Before the second ejection, Margaret Paston wrote urgently for cross-bows, wyndaes, and quarrels, longbows being useless as Gresham stood so low. But she was helpless against the thousand-odd "riotous people" sent by Lord Moleyns, who carried her out, cut asunder the posts of the house and let them fall, and carried off goods and chattels to the value of £200 (at least £3,000 to-day). Police, as such, did not exist. Justice was often bought by the highest bidder. Posts, newspapers, telephones, radio, are commonplaces to-day. Then, John Paston the younger could offer as a valid excuse for not having written to his father, the fact that he knew no one bound for London.

But if manners and customs have changed much, human nature has altered little. Families still fall out and in again. Extravagant sons are told how much better their fathers managed, but continue to pawn their goods or run up bills in the manner of Sir John who, when asking his mother to collect his new hose from the hosier at Ludgate, added that if she pays for one pair, the other can go "unpayd for". Daughters fall inconveniently in love. Margaret Paston speaks for all mothers when she bids her eldest son look to his brothers in France, "for some of them be but young soldiers, and know little of what it means to be a soldier, nor to endure what a soldier must do". And now, as then, we suffer from "cyetica", and our clothes from the ravages of "mowghtes".

JANUARY 31   The air is raw, damp and cold. Fog envelops woodlands and fields in a clinging grey-white cloud. Every "grup" and "holl", rut and hollow, is full of water. Drops hang from every twig, branch and bough. Patches of spilt oil on the road surface look like fragments of fallen rainbow. Sodden heaps of gorse and "browings" disfigure the banks of fences. The wind wails through the telephone wires until it is difficult to imagine anything but messages of disaster flying along them. Cows huddle in small groups on the meadows, whilst perfectly healthy horses stand about looking broken-kneed and broken-winded. A large flock of rooks is ripping the thatch from a wheat stack; they rise in a black cloud when I appear, but are back at their work of destruction hardly before I am around the next corner. The deserted fields are discoloured and lifeless. The woods, so inviting in summer, that border the road for part of the way, have a bleak and desolate look, especially the small forest of giant Christmas trees whose tops bar off the sky, leaving their trunks imprisoned in a black and lightless cavern. (Can they be destined for pit props? If so, they are certainly being conditioned for it, growing up in that murderous gloom.) In the distance the cry of a jay sounds like a prophecy of doom. A distant explosion sets the pheasants alarmedly calling. Not an ideal day for a walk, perhaps. Yet there is something exhilarating about it, neverthe-less. The gorse stubs are putting out new shoots, a last year's branch has a cheerful cluster of yellow bloom. There are fresh green leaves on the twining honeysuckle tendrils. Tight little hazel catkins are beginning to think of bursting open. Spring is not yet here, but her harbingers have arrived.

FEBRUARY 2   "Candlemas Day, the good housewife's goose lay. Valentine's Day, yours and mine may", remarks Miss Barley. We own no geese at present, but are already enquiring about the possibilities of some month-old goslings in May, since from that age they can live entirely on grass.

"So far as the sun shines in on Candlemas Day, so far will the snow blow in before Old May" continues Miss Barley, as a shaft strikes through the window on to her lap. Ben always says "If Candlemas Day be fine and clear, the shepherd had rather see his wife on a bier". Another local rhyme has it that "half the winter's to come and mair". But the sun has vanished well before noon, and clouds have taken possession of the sky. By six it's raining heavily again, and the wind is raging at gale force. So perhaps we've had the worst after all. Or have we? For most of the ancient weather sayings were old long before 1752, when we adopted the Gregorian Calendar, and men rioted, crying "Give us back our eleven days". Almost two centuries have passed since then, and with each another day has been added to the lost eleven. So to be accurate, no doubt, we should search the skies thirteen days from now if we wish to learn what weather lies ahead.

FEBRUARY 4 The last egg in the house used, and immediately Adam wants one of his pet steamed puddings, which needs two. So make one of my childhood favourites instead. This takes $\frac{1}{2}$ lb. flour, $\frac{1}{4}$ lb. marg. (dripping, or butter), $\frac{1}{4}$ lb. sugar, small teaspoon carbonate of soda, two tablespoons jam (or. marmalade). Mix all together. Steam 3–4 hours. Serve with jam (or marmalade) sauce made by stirring a little cornflour into another two tablespoons jam, add boiling water, and cook till thick. Used wholemeal flour instead of the ordinary variety on this occasion, with first-class results.

FEBRUARY 5 Pursue theme of geese on our meadow at dinner to-night. She shouldn't have geese if she were me, says Jessica at once. They had four one year, and it didn't matter where they were put . . . once it was on a far-away meadow with lashings of grass, another time in the orchard with eight-foot wire netting . . . nothing ever kept them in. Sooner or later (mostly sooner) there they were at the back door of the house. They nearly chewed the bottom of it öff in the end. The only reason she can give for it is that they must have been brought up to be fed at the back door, as she bought hers at a month or so old, too. Then they invariably attacked anyone who looked the least bit afraid of them. Her maids were terrified. The two elder boys were inclined to look sideways at them, whereupon the geese would simply fly at them. Michael, the youngest, merely said "Out of my way, goose", and they went. But they were a menace to everyone else. So will that grass be if something doesn't eat it off, we can't trust the H's., and Brandy's only there on Eve's leaves. Perhaps our geese, when we find them, will have better manners.

FEBRUARY 8   For the last two years February Fill-dyke has scarcely contrived to fill a tea-cup. But this year it looks as if she has decided to make up for lost time. Already we have had nearly as much rain as in the previous two Februaries put together; and the alleged ha-ha that links the two arms of the drive, and which I always suspected of being a "holl" in disguise, has come out in its true colours, and is two feet deep in water. The soil is unworkable so, penknife in hand, I launch an attack on the daisies, plantain, and . . . can it be succory? . . . that disfigure the tennis lawn. Cannot say that this is a job I particularly care for. And, anti-chemicals as I am, can see myself in near future setting off on witch-hunt for a selective weed-killer that will deal with it instead.

FEBRUARY 11   Melt a jelly in one tablespoon of hot water, whip up the contents of a tin of evaporated milk that has been in the refrigerator for forty-eight hours, combine the two, cool for half an hour, and you have a delightful quickly made "Fluff" for a party sweet. But it must be jelly jelly, not crystals, Barbara impressed on me when she gave me the recipe some eighteen months ago. Unfortunately this isn't always available. Couldn't gelatine be made to do instead? I wondered to-day. And having discovered pots of stem ginger selling at half their Christmas price, couldn't I use some of the syrup and chopped-up ginger as well, and make a ginger cream? So I put 1 oz. powdered gelatine into saucepan, add two tablespoons ginger syrup, four of hot water, stir over boiling plate until dissolved, then beat in the whipped milk, plus one tablespoon sugar. Result most satisfactory. But as it set almost before beating was finished, I feel $\frac{1}{2}$ oz. or $\frac{3}{4}$ oz. gelatine should be enough. For those who have no refrigerator, if a tin of evaporated milk is placed in a saucepan of boiling water, boiled five minutes, then left overnight to cool, this then whips equally well.

FEBRUARY 14   "Good Morrow, Valentine. Draw up your window-blind. I've got a little pocket to put a penny in. If you haven't got a penny, a ha'penny will do. If you haven't a ha'penny, then God bless you." Amy would never produce her coppers until the verse was sung right through. But in my home village, though it was only about eight miles from Amy's, I doubt if the children knew it all. At any rate, they never got farther than the first three words, which were repeated *ad lib*, in a rising crescendo. They called at midday as a rule, when they scrambled for pennies, apples, and oranges. Then, at dusk, would come a thunderous knock at the front door. As one child we rushed to open it, and there on the step would be a large parcel, which immediately set off down the drive, apparently of its own accord, the moment we bent to pick it up. When finally captured and torn open, it might contain anything, from a bar of chocolate to a piece of coal. Not for years did we realise that Thurston, the groom, and a piece of string, were the secret of its mobility. And even after she had discovered the truth about Father Christmas, Eve remained convinced for years that "Mr. Valentine" was genuine.

This morning, having previously ransacked the shops for the most sentimental "Valentine" cards we can find, Adam and I exchange these tokens of esteem. I was under the impression that the Saint's day commemorated the date of his martyrdom. And that the ancient belief that "On Saint Valentine, all the birds in couples do jine", had led in time to the custom of exchanging lovers' greetings on this day. An East Suffolk correspondent, who remembers children coming round with garlands of snowdrops and ivy, gives a different version. "The custom of observing February 14th was, of course, much older than St. Valentine", he writes. "But it came to bear his name because people in his day had what the Church described as 'an ancient and evil custom' of drawing the names of their lovers in a sort of lottery or sweepstake, held in honour of the goddess Februata. St. Valentine caused the billets to be inscribed with saints' names instead."

FEBRUARY 16   Several friends have assured me that the after-math of jaundice is a tendency to brood on suicide. Seem to have escaped this, but suffer from more than usual amount of witlessness, which reaches a peak to-day when I am confronted by newly arrived pair of beehives, which Mr. Westgate has nobly made up for me. Long before this, I had intended to study my bee books until I could pass with credit any examination on bee lore. But this, like several other good resolutions, has so far gone unfulfilled. And am appalled when I contemplate the pit of my ignorance, and the one-thousand-and-one things I have to do between now and mid-May, when the colonies are due.

"I suppose you wouldn't care to take them on?" I suggest hopefully to Adam. "They're an absorbing hobby, I'm told. Look how Guy dotes on his."

"You know what I said at the start. I'm not touching them", says Adam firmly.

"A great big man like you afraid of a tiny bee!" I scoff. "Who eats most of the honey in this house, anyway?"

But Adam is not to be caught. And can see myself, damp towel round head, hot-water bottle at feet, working frantically at the books, and later on, pestering all my bee-keeping acquaintances to be allowed to watch them handling their charges. Like so many people, before I began to consider bee-keeping, I imagined that the owner did little more than remove the honey at the end of the summer. Instead it looks as if I shall have to work as hard for my honey as the bees.

8

FEBRUARY 17   At East Bilney to-day we found the little flint
church locked, alone, and aloof, on its hillside.
The green frost-touched slopes of the meadow to westward were
empty and silent. No birds sang. Not a human creature other
than ourselves was to be seen in the pale late afternoon sunshine.
We gained an impression of ineradicable, abiding peace. Yet both
church and meadow have known turbulent times, for it was on
these same slopes that Kett's men once gathered, pulling down the
church tower's upper storey before they left. And a century or so
later a battle of the Civil War was fought on "Bloodfields", so
they say. At all events, old weapons, sword-hilts and spurs, and
other fragments of martial paraphernalia have been found
roundabout from time to time since. It was in this village, too,
that Thomas Bilney, the martyr, was born. He was burnt at the
stake in Norwich for his beliefs more than four hundred years ago.
But the little half-timbered cottage he once called home still
dreams on the rise across the valley.

Suddenly the peace was shattered. A tree inside the church-
yard, bare-branched and lifeless a second ago, was blossoming
with starlings. Aptly is their flock known as a "murmuration".
There must have been well over a hundred of them, all murmuring indignantly in unison. The noise redoubled as we came
down the path, and a few broke away to murmur aloft in the
boughs of an oak in the lane. They were murmuring with ever-
increasing vigour as we escaped to the car, and drove off.

FEBRUARY 18   Reach home in the small hours (William, as
usual, is sitting disapprovingly on the hall mat!)
after a thoroughly enjoyable time at the Press Ball. I suppose the
day will come when we don't want to go to dances any more. But

I hope that it will be a long time coming. What a lot the non-dancing housewife misses. Apart from all that goes with "Soft lights and sweet music", we spend so much time in sober, workaday clothes that it is a tonic in itself to put on the other kind, forget all about the pots and pans, and saunter through an evening looking (one hopes) elegantly useless down to the last varnished finger-nail. "We ought to do this oftener", I sigh, as I reach for my cooking-apron.

FEBRUARY 21   Shrove Tuesday and Pancake Day. For the pan-cakes there are batters, and batters, of course. Great-grandmother substituted small beer, or clean snow and a very little milk, for eggs in hers, if eggs were scarce. And at the other extreme used seven yolks and four whites, one pint of cream, and two to three ounces of flour. My standard batter is 4 oz. flour, one egg, half-pint milk (or milk and water), and a pinch of salt. Two eggs are better. A little sugar is an improve-ment. Nutmeg and ginger make a good addition for a change. And if I'm feeling extravagant I cream 2 oz. margarine with 2 oz. sugar, add two well-beaten eggs, and 2 oz. flour, then stir in half-pint of warm milk. (This, like all batters, should be allowed to stand for an hour or so before using.) Sometimes I bake my pan-cakes in the oven, using separate oven-glass plates for each (they take 20–30 minutes). Usually I fry them in the ordinary way, but as I'm anything but a skilful tosser, on these occasions I mostly play for safety and turn them over with a fork, then serve them with lemon juice and sugar (my favourite), or treacle, or jam. Pancakes came to be associated with Shrove Tuesday to symbolise the using of the last of the rich fats before the Lenten fast began. In some churches (East Dereham for one) a bell known as the "pancake bell" was rung at midday. Certain Midland churches still ring a "pudding bell". And Dereham's present vicar tells me that he is reviving the ringing of the "pancake bell" there. It would be interesting to know how many more Norfolk churches once followed this custom.

FEBRUARY 22   Rout out every old box, carton, tray, kitchen-drawer, etc., and use all available table and bench tops for "chitting" potatoes, but still have nine hundred-weight unspread. So ring up the family with an S.O. Potatoes, and rush off with the trailer to borrow forty trays. Depart in such haste that not until I get there do I remember custard (with my currant ration in it), baking in oven at home, now ten miles away. Attempts to hurry are frustrated in turn by (*a*) the car sticking in mud and having to be pushed out of it; (*b*) by herd of Red Polls wanting to pass just as car and trailer are in position, so both have to be moved again. Home again, I dash to oven, where, as I feared, pudding now only fit for pig-bucket. So solace myself by making flapjacks for tea. These take eight tablespoons coarse oatmeal (if of the "pinhead" variety, I use two table-spoons flour to six of oatmeal), three tablespoons brown sugar (two tablespoons white sugar plus one dessert spoon treacle make an effective substitute), two tablespoons butter (margarine). Rub in together, press down hard in flat tin, smooth off with knife, and bake very slowly until just brown; if really brown, they taste burnt. Finally cut into squares when cool. Make a double quantity to-day, adding some grated nutmeg and powdered ginger to one half of mixture for variety.

FEBRUARY 23   Back to our old neighbourhood to vote. On our way encounter few who appear to be on same errand, though at Ashwell we pass an elderly dame proceeding towards the school at the rate of half a yard a minute, leaning heavily on a possible great-grandchild the while, who can be abroad for no other reason, and who looks as if she hasn't been out since the last election. At Roxstead there are only ourselves and elderly couple, the female of whom immediately sets the returning officer a poser, as it appears that her name is Lottie Maud X, but she's featured on the voters' list as both Lottie X and Maud X. The female returning officer suggests the obvious solution that one of these be crossed off. Her male opposite number protests at once that this will make his list All Wrong. Lottie Maud obligingly offers to vote twice. Question still un-solved when we depart, running into Ben as we reach the car. "Who do you think will get in?" asks Ben. "The party that wins the biggest number of seats", I answer brightly. Whichever that may be, I hope it promptly tackles the problems of peace and the H bomb abroad, and the housing situation at home. How I wish that the Minister responsible for the latter (and his family) could be made to share a house and kitchen with another family until the number of those without houses of their own was reduced to less than three figures. Only those who have to endure it appreciate the ceaseless strain that sharing living quarters entails, the daily irritations, the lack of essential privacies. Young married couples who start out on their great adventure in such circumstances do so with their little boat loaded well above the Plimsoll line, and many overturn for no other reason. Personally I would rather live in a derelict railway coach on an abandoned searchlight site, than share a palace with a family of angels.

FEBRUARY 24 Eve's mid-week letter two days late, the result of a long week-end's leave in Dublin. The theatre full, the museum locked, but she visited the National Art Gallery, managed to ascend Nelson's Column, after an enormous meal, ate several more enormous meals, walked leagues, and indulged in an orgy of shopping which left her with the handsome sum of one shilling and twopence to last until next pay-day. Much entertained to hear that purchases include yards of tulle and taffeta (at one-third of the purchase-taxed price we pay over here) since only three years ago it was a major operation to get her out of jodhpurs and into a skirt, whilst the mere mention of dance frocks was received with contumely and scorn. But don't we all? To paraphrase Shakespeare, "First the dribbling infant, bonneted, embroidered, shawled. Next the hoyden, torn of garment, rough-haired, dirty-nailed. After her, the niceish miss, curled, frilled, and furbelowed. Follows the bride, white-veiled, mystic, wondering. Then the mother, pelican-wise plucking her feathers for her nestlings, but keeping back a few for pride's sake. Next, the grandmother, ewe with a touch of lamb. (Why not? Life's dull enough without!) Last stage of all. 'I care not for the colour of that shroud. It ill becomes me. And wants a gusset in't'."

FEBRUARY 25 Last harvest's stubble in several unploughed cornfields gave the landscape an oddly autumnal look. Pussy-willows with silver-grey paws peeping from chestnut sheaths swayed the balance towards spring. Round a corner the sight of early lambs frisking just over the fence stamped the season with a certainty. We wished, of course, for they were the first lambs we'd seen this year. Quite possibly they're the only ones we'll see, for ewe flocks are few and far between in Norfolk now, though not so long ago few large farms were without one. And where there was a flock, there was a shepherd.

Shepherds are not born fully blown. They must begin young.

But one seldom sees an immature member of the species. Like tramps, they always seem to be the same age. And when, as a small child, I first set eyes on Old Kirk, already he seemed ancient (fifteen years later, he looked exactly the same, and, to our astonishment, suddenly owned to an antique parent still living, tucked away in a distant corner of the county, and still hale and active). Shortish, blue-eyed, with hair of an indeterminate dusty, sandy colour, and a long patriarchal beard of similar hue, his working dress was invariable. (One could have sworn, too, that the identical garments were worn year after year, for we never caught him in anything new.) Dust-coloured corduroy trousers, tied below the knees with string, a dust-coloured, dust-covered smock: an incredibly shapeless, weather-stained old felt hat on his head, and his crook in his hand. In wet weather an old cornsack over his shoulders would be added to this outfit. On highdays and holidays his nether garments remained unchanged, but above them were superimposed an ancient frock-coat and bowler hat, both acquired at a rummage sale he had once visited.

For much of the year the sheep he tended were penned on various parts of the farm, feeding off this and that. But round about Christmas a miniature town of little straw houses would be built in a sheltered corner of some convenient field. Presently each ewe occupied her own little home with her babies: mostly twins, but sometimes three, four, or even quins. The air would be filled with the shrill clamorous "maa-a-a-a" of the lambs, and the deep-throated reassuring "murr-murr-r-r-r" of their mothers. For weeks Old Kirk seldom took his clothes off. And if he slept in his "shepherd's hut", a large wooden box on wheels drawn up beside the "town's" outer wall of gorse and straw, it must have been with one eye open and both ears pricked. Lambing is the shepherd's harvest, and a weary anxious time as long as it lasts. And Old Kirk took the loss of a lamb as a personal affront. He could sense the onset of a ewe's labour pains almost before she was aware of them herself, and many a frightened animal was soon soothed by his voice, or the touch of those roughened, short, square, and incredibly gentle hands.

He knew every member of his four-hundred-odd flock, but woe betide anyone who enquired its total. Though he can tell in a moment if one is missing, no true shepherd ever courts ill-luck by admitting to an exact number. One day brother Noel, fresh from school, determined to count the newly severed lambs' tails to discover the total of lambs. When Old Kirk defied him, he went in search of the "Guv'nor" to back him up. The moment he vanished through the field-gate Old Kirk picked up two double handfuls of uncounted tails, and stuffed them down inside his trousers. "Now he may count 'em all he like. That 'ont make no odds", he remarked placidly to his astounded assistant, who many years later told the tale to me.

Each year the sheep had to be dipped. And to make this tiresome but necessary task as easy as possible, Father had a sunken concrete bath built, six feet deep at one end, and steps for the victims to flounder out at the other, the whole surrounded by hurdle pens to control the incoming and outgoing sheep. Half the village turned out to watch the dipping, and the day that Old Kirk tripped, overbalanced, and followed one of his sheep into the dip, is still remembered with joy in the neighbourhood. So, but with awe, is his language, his opinion of the incident taking fully thirty minutes to deliver, during which period he was not once heard to repeat himself. He had other opportunities to display his vocabulary (unequalled in the county, according to his contemporaries) as the popularity of motor vehicles increased. Some farms have little or no traffic on their premises, other than their own. Several stretches of minor road ran through our domain, not to mention a mile of so of the Norwich turnpike, and moving the sheep nearly always meant negotiating a stretch of them. As his charges bolted through gaps, broke back the way they had come, or wedged themselves around and under the offending vehicles, despite the frantic efforts of himself and his dog to control them, Old Kirk would keep up a running commentary of abuse at "them —— moty-cars". But he was reconciled to them in the end. As he grew older, though his outer man appeared unchanged, he was no longer as spry as before. So Father bought him a donkey to ride. Old Kirk, with his beard, his smock, and his crook, astride the back of his old "dicky" and surrounded by his flock, was a sight indeed. And his enemies, the motorists, forced to keep still whilst the sheep swarmed past them, were overcome by the picture he offered. First one, then another, then a continuous stream of "them mucky varmints" begged him to pose for a photograph. And never was his complaisance rewarded with less than half a crown.

Old Kirk had left to herd celestial sheep before the family eweflock was dispersed some years after the 1914–18 War. At one period his son followed the same career in another county. Recently I stopped my "mucky moty-car" to offer a lift to a young man in R.A.F. blue. We got to "mardling", when I discovered that he was Old Kirk's grandson. He talked of staying in the Air Force, and I wondered what Old Kirk would have had to say about aircraft. I think I can make a "nigh guess", as Ben would say. And there are times when I wonder if he would have been so far wrong.

FEBRUARY 27   Three cups of tea on the tray, one for Adam, one for me, and one, with no milk or sugar in it, for "cup of cold tea" cake, the recipe for which has just been given me by our vicar's wife. Put the cup of tea into a saucepan with $\frac{1}{4}$ lb. lard, $\frac{1}{4}$ lb. sugar, $\frac{1}{2}$ lb. fruit, and 1 teaspoon mixed spice. Boil three minutes. When cool, add $\frac{1}{2}$ lb. flour, one teaspoon bicarbonate of soda. Mix well, and bake $1\frac{1}{4}$ hours: in a medium oven for one hour, low for the last quarter. Cyclamen in pots thrive on cold tea, so my parent tells me. She waters hers with nothing else. I have employed it as a carpet brightener, and as an emergency dressing for minor burns. I wonder what other uses can be made of it.

MARCH 1   "For every frost in March, there'll be a frost in May", or so Sam says. If he is right, one at least can be expected in the latter month, since this morning the ground is like cement, and covered with white crystals. The too-optimistic bloom on the winter jasmine has shrivelled overnight. Buds on the flowering shrubs have a pinched and starved look. I haven't the courage to inspect the currant bushes. But the sun is shining, and continues to shine. The orange and purple crocuses shake off their icy wrappings, the grass is green again. Birds are singing. There is a subtle exhilaration in the air. I suppose one can have too much of a good thing. Those who live in sun-drenched lands say that they long for the sight of a grey sky, or even a good thick fog. Personally have never had the opportunity to tire of the sun. I find a dull day as depressing as bad news. But sunshine seems to lighten the heart as well as the day.

MARCH 3   There was another car approaching, and a sharp bend in the road just ahead, so I was forced to slow down on my way back from Norwich this afternoon, and thus obtained a good view of one contribution of private enterprise to the solution of the housing problem. The cart, drawn by a thick-barrelled, rough-coated chestnut pony, was on the small side, the sort in which one used to see a small higgler driving round, a crate of chickens under the seat. From its axle dangled two tin pails. A couple of bicycles were slung behind. A stack cover of sorts roofed it in, the short length of piping protruding drunkenly from the top evidently doing duty as a chimney. I longed to stop and ask if I might look inside, for where in the world could the barest necessities be tucked away? (Perhaps the driver had once lived in a submarine.) The last of the diddy-kais, or the van of an army determined on homes of their own, I wondered, as I shot past, silently wishing them good parking and good pasturage.

MARCH 5   Every housewife knows those days when meals, however artfully contrived, seem to develop a horrid sameness. One wants something different, yet hardly knows what, except that nothing in the larder seems to fill the bill. To deal with these crises I keep a small "extravagance" shelf, replenishing it with stuffed olives, outsize prawns, tins and bottles of peculiar fruits and vegetables, on birthdays and similar occasions as a present to myself. Tinned sweet peppers, with or without home-bottled tomatoes, go equally well with fried fish or scrambled eggs. A bottle of assorted Chinese fruits in syrup makes all the difference to bottled strawberries. Add a little grated onion, chopped parsley, mint, lemon juice, pepper, and salt to a tin of tomato juice, chill and serve as tomato cocktail on a warm day, or cook your fish or chops in it on a cold one. Cape gooseberries vanished from my shelf early in the war years, but I hope to see them back one day. With patience and a small pair of scissors the berries can be removed (without damaging the "chinese lantern" portion) from the home-grown variety. But, unless the summer has been really hot, the berries are so sour that they're not worth the trouble involved.

MARCH 6   A perfect spring day, sunny and warm. Yellow blossom decks the forsythia branches, japonica buds open into scarlet cups, green daffodil sheaths thrust from clumps of leaves, and the willow boughs look as if William has been scrambling among them, shedding tuft after tuft of grey fur. It is far too good a morning to spend indoors, so desert my pen for a small fork and hoe. Our ignorance of what may be in the various beds has inclined us to leave them undisturbed until the flowers give some indication of their whereabouts, which has given the weeds a flying start. Grass flourishes everywhere except where it's wanted. However, it's all grist for the compost heap. And, incidentally, refreshment to the jaded mind. For each of us is another Antaeus in a small way, needing contact with the earth to renew our strength.

MARCH 8   Make determined effort to study bee book, but find almost nothing "clicks", as I can't even tell one part of a hive from another. And hurried visit to workshop, with illustrated catalogue in hand, to look at own hives, leaves me almost exactly where I started. It also dawns that I have been gaily referring to my future bees as "colonies" when the correct term is obviously "six-frame nuclei", which is something else again. These latter, says book, should be manipulated as little as possible in early stages. So hastily write off to secretary of local Bee-keepers Association, who has enquired earlier whether I am willing to allow a demonstration in "your apiary" in early June, and recall my previous consent. Then re-read list of minimum equipment suggested by Mr. Westgate. Veils come high on the agenda, and veils presuppose headgear of some kind to hang them on. As price of absolute bare essentials adds up to startling total, look round for something already on premises, and wonder if wartime tin hats will now "come in". My star turn, decorated with wheat sheaves and flowers, with crossed carrots on a soil-coloured square as my "divisional sign", disappeared from my coat-hook at a wartime dance, and was never seen, by me, any-way, again. But have two less interesting versions of the species packed away in the attics, and shall give these a trial anyway.

MARCH 9   On alternate Thursdays, minions of the local R.D.C. descend upon our village and, provided we have left the objects in "appropriate containers", bear away our empty tins and bottles. Fortnightly I bless those responsible for this service. But how I wish the various councils would make it retrospective. Rusting milk churns, superannuated saucepans, vintage bicycle wheels, decayed sieves and disenamelled basins, leaking cans and kettles, protruding from the surface of a willow-fringed pool, or spilt across a tree-studded hollow, hardly add to the beauties of our rural landscape. Nor are our main roads immune. Recently men have been at work "browing" the fences along stretches of the Norwich–Holt road, and what a harvest of household debris has come to light. The browings have been neatly heaped and burned. The fences, pruned of too-high tops, too-spreading branches, and encroaching undergrowth, are now trim and orderly. The unlovely rubbish remains, a monument to our national vice of untidiness. Good luck to the St. Faiths and Aylsham Rural District Council, who, at their meeting this week, decided to tackle this evil.

MARCH 10   Our first essay in the mathematics of the gestation period for pigs suggested that Helen's family was due about March 5th, our second that it may arrive any time between March 8th and 12th. For the past few days we have been hovering around like anxious would-be grandmothers awaiting the birth of an heir to an ancient title. Meanwhile Helen continues merrily to root up nettles and docks as if nothing was farther from her thoughts than maternity. Adam says she is waiting for my birthday tomorrow, as a graceful gesture!

MARCH 13   My birthday parcel from Eve on Saturday having included a pound of desiccated coconut, I use $\frac{1}{4}$ lb. of it to-day for coconut loaves, with two whites of eggs whipped stiff, and 3 oz. sugar, dropping the mixture in lumps on to a piece of greased paper spread on a flat tin, moulding them into cone shapes, and baking in moderate oven. Use more for coconut ice, made by adding coconut to taste to American fondant mixture . . . $\frac{1}{2}$ lb. icing sugar, half teaspoon cream of tartar, and one tablespoon cream (top of milk, in my case). Save the remainder for sprinkling on cakes whose surfaces have first been lightly brushed over with jam.

MARCH 15   "With husbands away, wives can dine from a tray", I say to myself, as Adam departs for Birmingham. So spend the day preparing seed-beds for flowers to be grown especially for my prospective bees (and the rest in the neighbourhood, no doubt!), and carting compost about the "estate" with car and trailer, since this is infinitely quicker than letting Our Man work unaided with the wheelbarrow, and also eliminates the risk of wheel-ruts in the drive. At 4.5 p.m. we set off for a local saw-mill, to return in triumph with a trailerful of bags of sawdust. (Have become so compost and mulch-minded that I can hardly pass a dead leaf on the ground without coveting it.) Day closes with my being asked if I will make one of village team to embark on quiz combats with other Village Produce Association groups. Feel my inclusion is tantamount to knocking out the home side in first round, since my memory invariably has to be supported by platoons of notebooks, with urgent matters on a sheet of notepaper fastened to my person, and shall never be able to grapple with questions that must be answered within sixty seconds. But since the selectors are willing to risk this, I accept, and trust that inspiration will intervene at the critical moment.

MARCH 16   To Oulton to meeting held for purpose of forming a local association in support of the Girl Guides. It is impossible to over-estimate the importance of the work done by Guiders and guided, especially in these days when the State undertakes so many of the duties and responsibilities that belong to the individual, thus stunting initiative and ingenuity. Camping, particularly, is both an active joy and a training in resourcefulness, so much better for any child than simply listening to the wireless, or sitting at the cinema.

Much entertained, once the business of the meeting is over, to be asked by new acquaintance, "Has Helen had her pigs yet?" Am sorry to say no, she hasn't, unless they've arrived at dead of night, and she's promptly eaten them.

MARCH 17   7 a.m. Take a look at Helen, who for once does not "woof" good morning, but stays in stye, looking distinctly pensive.

7.45 a.m. Our Man reports that he thinks Helen will farrow some time this morning. As he will be hoeing on field across the road, perhaps I'll keep an eye on her, and fetch him if he's wanted. Murmur that my parent says the great thing is to LEAVE them ALONE, and wish fervently that Adam, who wanted to keep pigs, wasn't still in Birmingham.

8.10 a.m. Take peep at Helen, who grunts, but doesn't move. Decide I'd better read relevant chapter of pig book instead of bee-keeping tome when breakfasting.

At 10.15, she answers my greeting with a non-committal

"Hrrumph". At 11.0 she's finishing up her breakfast potatoes, and Our Man's reconsidered opinion is that he shouldn't be surprised if those pigs don't arrive until night-time. Only hope they will, as Adam due home about 7.0. So get hurricane lamp filled and trimmed in readiness.

Afternoon's post brings letter from Eve to say she has been chosen for the Royal Tournament P.T. display, and is so excited she can hardly think! Of course, she isn't sure of a place yet, as altogether three hundred Wrens have been selected from the different stations, and only forty-five are needed in the actual display, so will we keep our fingers crossed. The special uniform consists of round-necked sleeveless dress with skating skirt ending six inches above the knees, white undershorts and shoes, which can be bought afterwards, so if the worst comes to the worst she can always give us a private display on the lawn.

Reply at length to this, but mind still very much on Helen. Latter proceeds to eat a good tea, and by time Adam reaches home, is peacefully sleeping.

MARCH 18   Wake at intervals throughout the night, and suggest to Adam that really keen pig-keeper would hop out and have a look at Helen. Adam replies with "hrrumph" this time, and declines to do anything of the kind. Half-past six is quite time enough, he mutters, at the nth prod. And events prove him only too right. At this hour no sign whatever of Helen's family, and by feeding time she's as lively as a young kitten, and clamouring to be let out. In mid-afternoon Adam says she's spent ten minutes tearing up her new bedding, and making a nest with it. Also he's looked in our copy of *Home Doctoring of Animals*, and this, whilst admitting that 115 days is the average period of gestation, says that 126 is possible, and 143 has been known. But personally am beginning to feel that Helen is no more likely to produce a family than William Cat!

MARCH 20   Week-end full of alarums and excursions, but no piglets. Premises now re-infested with swarms of carpenters, painters, etc., and preparations for re-painting the outside of the house and buildings in full swing, the welkin resounds with rasp of saws on wood, knives scraping against glass and boards, and the roar of blow-lamps, whilst William Cat insists on scaling ladders to within an inch or so of the roof, then can't get down, and mews for rescue. (Understand this incursion will probably last six weeks, and wonder how many "incidents" will result, as men cuprinoling beams in farthest attic contrive to dislocate cut-out and overflow water tank within an hour.) One of carpenters also a pig-keeper, so ask him to look at Helen, when he remarks that it's a funny thing to him if she's in pig. He was sucked in just the same over one of his, he enlarges. She did have a litter later on, but never more than the one. Just wouldn't breed. You get them like that sometimes. Now his sow, he adds happily, has just had half a score beauties.

Return to house, to find painter busy scraping frame of study window below which my writing table lives. Does every bit of old paint have to be removed, I enquire, with teeth on edge. No, but there must be a flat surface, or the new paint will flake off. How much paint is wanted on a house this size, I pursue, remembering that next time it's done it will be our worry. The amateur covers about sixty square yards with a gallon of paint, the expert seventy, and spraying will do eighty, is the reply. Have been told by another painter that September is the best month in which to apply it, not spring, as then the paint hasn't to face too strong sunshine too early in its career. My new mentor confirms this, but is somewhat taken aback to learn that I am seeking this information to use six years hence. I may not be here, none of us may be here, he observes. This is very possible, but since I come of farming stock, to think ahead is as natural as breathing. Like every trait, however, this has its darker side. How many of us are apt to put off for a problematical to-morrow the fun and happiness that can be ours here and now, to-day.

MARCH 21   and the first day of spring. According to Ben, this day sets the weather for the next three months, and should an east wind be blowing, it will keep it up until mid-June. What wind there is, is westerly. But evidently we can expect our usual variable weather, as the day produces frost, fog, sea-mist and sunshine, and though no rain falls at Hillingsett, I manage to be mackintoshless in Norwich when a smart shower descends. Home again see no painters about, but traces of them all over the place. Shavings have blown across the rose beds and lawn in front of the house. There are used-up bits of sandpaper on the beds below the windows. From various parts of the drive I retrieve three cake papers, four paper bags, six empty cigarette packets, some chocolate biscuit wrappers, a matchbox or two, and a number of similar treasures. Put all these into large cardboard carton, and a couple of painters presently reappearing, announce to them that for the future carton, to be kept in stables, is official litter bin, and that if I find any more lying about, I shall take their names and addresses, and descend upon their homes and gardens, one by one, with contents of my outsize wastepaper-basket.

MARCH 23   For months I have been searching for kitchen roller towels, the rough, fluffy kind, not the smooth linen variety which never dry one's hands. Lamenting at length on this at our W.I. meeting last week, was told by fellow member that old "honeycomb" bedspreads make very good substitutes, and that they used to use these in hospital. Two of these articles came to me with furniture left me by Aunt Sarah. So this morning retrieve one from the farthest corner of the linen cupboard, and my roller towel problem is now solved.

MARCH 24   Now definitely established that Helen is NOT in pig. And feel more like cuffing than scratching the head she thrusts hopefully up at me this morning, when I think of the trouble she's been, and all the extra food she's eaten. Pigs have been sent to the bacon factory for less, I remark tartly. To which Helen merely replies "Hrrumph" and looks round to see if I've brought her a cabbage.

9

MARCH 25   Heard at the North Harriers Point-to-Point at Sparham to-day. "Aren't they lucky in their weather? A really fine spring day" . . . "Well, whatever you think about blood-sports, you can't help enjoying this!" "I was glad when clothes coupons stopped. They grow up so fast, don't they? And schools are so tiresome about uniforms". "Six runners and not one horse finished! I've been to dozens of point-to-points, and never seen that happen before". "Funny being at one race-meeting, and listening to another. I wish Monaveen could have won, though I didn't back him". "One of the things I like about these local meetings is that the whole family can go, though I shouldn't care to bring a three-month-old baby myself". "I wanted to put some money on her. But she'd won her last two Ladies' Races. I didn't think she could possibly do it again, and she only eighteen, anyway". "If anyone else says they haven't seen me since I was so-high, I'll . . . I'll spit at them!" "See you next Saturday at Litcham. I never miss a point-to-point if I can help it".

MARCH 26   So many of the ancient songs and rhymes, many of which have been handed down through the centuries from generation to generation, are being lost in this one, since modern youth is much more interested in "swing". Amy has a fund of them, acquired as a child from an elderly village woman who could neither read nor write, but possessed a marvellous memory, Amy's is none too bad, for after forty years she can still recite her favourite.

I had a little hobby horse,
His name was Dapple Grey.

124

> His head was made of peastraw,
> His tail was made of hay.
> He could nimble, he could trot,
> He could carry the mustard pot,
> Three times round the chimney pot
> Heigh—gee—whoa, the ploughman go.
> What shall we have for supper, O?
> Barley cakes as black as the hakes,
> Without a bit of butter, O.
> Where's the butter? The cat ate it.
> Where's the cat? On the church hill,
> Cracking nuts with a five-farthing beadle,
> I'll have the nut. You have the shell.

Have often heard the expression "Black as the hakes", but never grasped its exact meaning. Apparently old-fashioned kitchen chimneys had a bar above the fire from which hung by a hook a short chain ending in a second hook, used to suspend the cooking pot over the flames. This tackle was known as the hakes, Amy now tells me, and that they had one at home. The five-farthing beadle, however, was a mystery to her until a few years ago, when she discovered that it was a small flat-iron that used to be sold for that sum.

MARCH 28   How I abominate firms who accept an order, promise delivery within ten days, then apparently hibernate for the rest of the season. Our prospective "walking-tractor", promised for the first week in February, has still not appeared, whilst two enquiries as to exactly when we may expect it, have merely winged into the void. So ring up local agent of another concern over the week-end, and ask have they machines in stock, how soon can they demonstrate, etc. Result: motor hoe tried out on premises yesterday afternoon, bought then and there, and an hour's work put in at once. To-day Our Man hoes one acre of currant bushes, and does a considerable amount of ploughing ready for potato planting with it, whilst I take over during his lunch hour and tackle the future chrysanthemum plot. Foresee country walks are off for the next few months, and instead my walking exercise will be taken behind our new acquisition.

MARCH 29   Open day at the local county primary school, with specimen work of every description on view, and the building crammed with prideful parents. What a frightening load of responsibilities the teacher carries. But what a worthwhile job it is. I wonder how many parents realise the extent of the debt they owe to those who instruct their young, and if they co-operate with them as much as they might. Eve's earliest school held "parents' week-ends" at intervals, when parents and teaching staff were able to air their views and problems together, an idea which could usefully be extended, I feel.

MARCH 31   Our greenhouse having advanced no further than wishful thoughts, and the cold frame being stuffed with seed-boxes, we have been using the kitchen window-sills as auxiliaries. Started off the currant-tomatoes in a shallow wooden box on one, and to-day am cutting cress set eight days ago in a one-time peach box, on another. Outside, the kitchen garden is full of promise, but performance at the moment is limited to bolting cabbages, burst-out sprouts, and a small parsnip hale. The parsnip is not one of my favourite vegetables. But it can be greatly improved by (*a*) mashing when cooked, with a little pepper, salt, and margarine; (*b*) parboiling, then roasting underneath the weekly meat ration; (*c*) parboiling, then frying. Rice, boiled with a few chillies, salt, and a sliced onion, and served with chopped parsley on top, helps to fill the vegetable gap, and is also good eaten cold with salads.

APRIL 1   But nobody tries to fool me before noon, and I forget to lay an appropriate trap for Adam. Weather at to-day's point-to-point is showery, with a blustering wind, but a good day in spite of this and our getting trapped in one line of the leaving queue which apparently was invisible to the traffic police, so that we were forced to watch hundreds of cars that left their places on the course well after us, get away well ahead. The usual number of small boys busily taking car numbers both coming and going. Should love to know the rules of this apparently absorbing game. And do the participants, I wonder, live in hopes of the day when Inspector Sherlock pulls up with squealing brakes to pant: "That green coupé that just went by! What was its number?"

APRIL 3   To-day hopeless for potato planting, or any other land work, as week-end weather has done its worst with thunderstorms and the best part of half an inch of rain. So take another look at contents of parcel arrived by post this morning. Have earlier ordered five dozen frames for beehives, expecting them to appear ready made up. Instead of which I am confronted by what looks like a bundle of kindling, and might just as well be as far as I'm concerned. Our Man equally clueless. So ring up Mr. Partridge, a beekeeping acquaintance, to ask if I bring them over, can he show me how to put them together? With pleasure, says he. But then goes on most unnecessarily, I feel, to enlarge on number of stings I shall soon be getting. Do not care at all for this line of talk, and have no hesitation in saying so. Ah, well, replies Mr. Partridge cheerfully, we all end up at the doctor's with tremendous swellings sooner or later. He remembers one time . . . "I'll be over on Thursday morning", I interrupt, and ring off hastily, as much more of this, and can see myself advertising equipment already bought, for sale at bargain price, and writing to Mr. Westgate to cancel bees!

APRIL 5   Eve has to be collected from Norwich to-night, I have a thousand-and-one things to do, so of course "incidents" develop in all directions. First, Our Man reports that the motor hoe won't start. Adam does various things to its engine, and dries the plug in the cooker's simmering oven . . . (if his breakfast tastes of petrol, I remark, he has only himself to blame), but there's nothing for it but to ring up the service depot, who say they will send a man the moment there's a van available, he should reach us before lunch. Painters then want every window open (the day is fine, but cold, and an arctic wind is blowing); the R.D.C. vehicle arrives to pump out our septic tank (the soakaway in the new drainage system is refusing to soak away, owing to our high water table and recent rains), a small boy appears with a wheelbarrow containing some special early seed potatoes that were due six weeks ago, and no sooner have I dealt with these, and got back to my writing-table, than a carpenter appears to say can they borrow Our Man, as they want to take down those old garden railings by the pigstyes and put up new ones? (Am rendered almost speechless by this, as two packets of hollyhock seed planted beside these railings only last week on the understanding that nothing more than a single new post was involved. And my new mint bed has already been trampled to death a fortnight ago when they suddenly decided to replace the window just above it.)

At twelve o'clock Hazel Pig, confronted by newly erected wire gate, takes one look, then flips it open with her nose, and all three race out. At two I ring up the service depot, to ask what has happened to their engineer. At four the engineer arrives, partially dismantles hoe, and discovers scrap of paint on second jet. That's the trouble, he says, as he begins to put it together again. They've had one or two like this. He pulls the starting cord confidently. After several more pulls, all equally unproductive, he takes the whole thing to pieces, watched by Our Man (who will have to deal with future trouble), whilst I feed the pigs. Presently the hoe is reassembled, with the same result, or lack of it. Adam appears to have a go, I produce cups of tea, the clock-hands race on. The engineer says despairingly that there are two hundred of the same model in the county, and this is the only one that's given any trouble. Finally he loads it on to his truck, and departs with it, telling us he hopes to bring it back tomorrow.

After all this, am quite prepared to find Eve has missed her connection, and is not on train. But happily we are spared this.

APRIL 6   Morning spent on sundry errands, which include taking Eve and miscellaneous collection of saddlery, etc., to fetch Brandy: visiting Mr. Partridge to learn how to put frames together, when I also take quick look at his bees (which seem remarkably active to me, though he says not, and he won't be opening them up for another month), and calling on ironmonger for extra strong bolts and hinges for wooden gates capable of circumventing the enquiring nose of Hazel. Home again, open series of doors and windows for painters, hurriedly consume two mouthfuls of food, and begin on delayed cooking programme. At once Our Man appears. Can he have a brace and bit? Painters want the kitchen windows open as well, callers arrive, Eve reappears with Brandy, and clamours for something to eat. Am just starting on second mix of pastry, destined for tart-let and flan cases, when the front door bell rings. Haul Eve back from the kitchen garden, where she is gathering daffodils, and say will she fend off whoever it is, as my hands are covered with flour, and if the roof falls, this lot is going in the oven. This time it is the county bee-keeping instructor, who happens to be our way, and has called in to answer my earlier pleas for information. Spend next hour or so assembling more frames, playing with hives, and smoking out the premises, emerging a decidedly wiser woman, and the unwilling possessor of yet more "sting" stories. (Query: Do all beekeepers develop a tendency to sadism? As have yet to meet one who doesn't torture the novice with terrifying tales.) After listening to these last am returning the comparatively flimsy veils recommended by Mr. Westgate, and bought earlier for Our Man and self, in favour of much more elaborate protection. Am also now on the look-out for two ex-R.A.F. white boiler suits, and preparing to fashion all sorts of bee-gloves, cuffs, and mittens, in readiness for mid-May.

APRIL 7   Piece of salmon gaffed by Hugh in Scotland last Wednesday week has been a block of ice in refrigerator drip tray since its arrival here, as we wanted Eve to share it. (Have already kept sausages here and in ice trays for six weeks, without disaster.) To-day thaw it out and simmer (approximately ten minutes to the pound) in water to which have added two bay leaves, some fragments of dried tarragon and thyme, and fresh sprigs of mint and parsley. Serve with mayonnaise, and slices of cucumber purchased at great price for the occasion. Mayonnaise made by beating $1\frac{1}{4}$ cups olive oil into 2 egg yolks to which pepper, salt, and half-teaspoon made mustard have been added, then lastly beating in three tablespoons vinegar. Use up left-over egg whites, whipped stiff, for angel buns, using half quantities required for angel cake. Latter takes 4 egg whites, $\frac{1}{4}$ lb. each flour, margarine, castor sugar, 3 oz. cornflour, half teaspoon almond essence, one teaspoon baking powder.

APRIL 8   Much ado about Helen Pig, but no piglets. A certain amount of fuss over Hazel, believed, erroneously as it turns out, to be the next expectant mother. No commotion at all over Hepsibah, who yesterday afternoon was suddenly seen pulling straw from the straw bale wall of the pen, carting it into her stye, and bed-making like mad, and this morning is discovered beaming at twelve little pigs. Feel there is a moral in this somewhere, though I have not yet decided what it is. One pigling, a weakling at birth, has vanished in rather a sinister fashion during the day. Otherwise all are doing well, and Hepsibah is proving an excellent parent.

EASTER SUNDAY   Easter cards on the chimney-piece, Easter eggs again, and outside, daffodils everywhere.

(Recall Richard's remark to me three years ago, when I was hesitating over the purchase of flowering shrubs, as we were hoping to move at any moment: "I never let that worry me. If I'm planting flowers here for somebody else, I like to think that in another garden someone is planting things for me." But never thought we should have the luck to follow somebody so flower-conscious as the previous tenant of Hillingsett Lodge.) The church also full of spring blossoms, most of them from the congregation's gardens. But not the lilies on the altar. These last, according to ancient practice, have been subscribed for by those who wish to remember their dead to-day. It is a comforting custom. For if the fact of death remains unalterable, the little things that may still be shared with our lost ones seem to lessen, if only for a moment, the distance that separates us.

April 10   How seldom we're blessed with really good weather for a public holiday. Yesterday's gales were at least unaccompanied by rain. To-day at Fakenham Steeplechases the first three races were run in pouring rain. And though the sun condescends to peep out after that, it's not until the bulk of the spectators are pretty well wet through. It also minimises one of the great attractions of these affairs, which is the opportunity they usually give to have a word with the many friends that one seldom has time to see anywhere else in these days of shortages, frustrations, and queues. For Eve the weather has its brighter side, however, as Virginia, over from Kenya, takes refuge in our car, and before she leaves it, there is talk of a possible trip out for Eve when her time is up in the W.R.N.S. (and when we can raise the fare!). By the time we arrive at the Race Ball in the evening, she has lost what little interest she had previously in that function (she doesn't share Adam's and my love of dancing at present, and half-way through is declaring audibly, "I can't think *what* you see in it!") and is planning to help Virginia start a racing stud within sight of Kilimanjaro. Dawn is breaking as we start on our forty-mile drive home . . . quite thirty too far in Adam's opinion, on top of a day at the races as well. "If it was a mid-season Hunt Ball, the idea is for everybody to turn up at the Meet in the morning as well," I murmur sleepily. But Eve is with us in being thankful that there's no such possibility this morning.

APRIL 12   An American reviewer, writing in 1942 of my book "Farmer's Girl," voiced a personal regret that so much of my work was administrative, as she would have liked me to have more dirt on my hands. Feel that she would have rejoiced to see me dropping potatoes into furrows this morning, and at sundry moments last week. And am wondering if said hands, which have acquired additional decorations from a glancing knife, the ripping claw of a too-playful William Cat, and a neat line in oven burns, will ever be the same again. Eve advises colourless nail varnish on one's nails when doing dirty work, and says this is a great protection when dealing with aircraft. Must remember this for future operations. At the moment am thankful to say that all but a few pounds of our three-quarters of a ton of seed potatoes are in. Motor hoe not home again until yesterday. Helen Pig returned from stay with gentleman friend at neighbouring farm this morning. "A nice sow, that. A very nice sow," remarks the farmer, as we chivvy her from his yard on to the road. "Handsome is as handsome does", I retort, and hustle Helen off in the direction of home.

APRIL 13   Have been on look-out for birds' nests for some time, but not until this morning, when a blackbird starts out of a holly bush as I pass, have I found one. The sensible thing, of course, would be to pull it out at once, since to leave the greenish, brown-speckled eggs unscathed will only mean more thieves amongst the black currants in due course. But cannot bring myself to do anything of the kind, so shall have to think up an efficient bird-scarer instead. Weather still cold and wet, so abandon salads, and curry the wreck of the meat ration. Slice an onion, fry lightly in a saucepan in a little dripping, then stir in a small grated apple, desert spoon curry powder, teaspoon flour, pinch of salt, dessertspoon mango chutney, half-pint gravy, and simmer 10–15 minutes. This sauce equally good with cooked white fish, or hard-boiled eggs cut in halves. Served boiled, but not overboiled, rice with it . . . every grain should be separate.

APRIL 14   Eve and self to Spring Flower Show, which has the usual effect of making us thoroughly dissatisfied with all the flowers at home. Envisage row of double cherries (James Veitch, for preference) just inside the kitchen garden, and some double peaches and Pyrus Lemoini, in front of the house.

(No seedsmen will ever take orders for these at this time of year, however, and am sure I shall forget to order them in September, as I did last year.) Take firm line with Eve, who, if she had her way, would bespeak a fellow to everything in sight. And remind her that at moment she's committed to saving for boat-tickets, not bulbs.

APRIL 15   To Drawing Match at Bawdeswell. Not having attended one before, I was under the impression that competitors brought their own horse, ploughs, etc. But all tackle provided, and anyone may attempt to draw a furrow on payment of two shillings towards the church funds. Urge Adam, Eve, and Monica to "have a go" but not they! What about me, suggests one of the organisers? I back hastily away, protesting my utter ignorance, and positive conviction that the horses will bolt the minute I touch the reins, but am finally brought to the starting line. "Keep the stick at the end between the horses", I am adjured as I set off. This is easier said than managed: first one solid dappled rump and then the other swings inwards, and my furrow quickly acquires some distinctly inelegant curves. "Carry away the stick at the end", warns the man who is walking beside me, just as, in my ignorance, I'm doing my best to leave it standing. The general opinion is that it might have been worse (though not much, I suspect). Ploughing, like so many simple-seeming farming operations, is an art, of course. Incidentally, how festive horses look when plaited, brassed and be-ribboned, and how dull and utilitarian in contrast are the tractors.

APRIL 17   Spend morning using up most of accumulated sugar and fat, etc., for cakes, buns, and biscuits for Eve to take with her. Make lemon pie for immediate consumption. Since I am in the habit of making up half a dozen pastry cases at a time, and storing them in a tin until wanted, have now only to make the filling. Mix one tablespoon cornflour, two egg yolks, grated rind of one lemon, then pour on one cup of water, and three-quarters cup sugar, which have previously been brought to boil, stir until thick, and put into case. Then add the egg whites, beaten stiff (with a little sugar) and brown lightly in oven. (One egg will do if these are scarce.) Another good filling is to mix the egg yolks with bread or cake crumbs and a little milk, adding juice and grated rind of one lemon, sugar to taste, and cook lightly in oven before adding whipped whites as in the first method.

APRIL 18   How I wish that "occasions" would space themselves more conveniently. For years I have longed to see a ship launched. For months a possible launching has been dangling, dateless, in front of me. Now letter this morning announces it's fixed for May 3rd, in middle of week already crammed to bursting. Spend day cancelling appointments right and left; writing to Mr. Westgate to beg him on no account to send bees that week, and to chrysanthemum grower to say I can't collect cuttings as arranged; and back out of Quiz Team. And in evening have sorrowfully to refuse invitation to dinner (complete with Woodforde menu) to be given in honour of the one-hundred-and-fiftieth anniversary of the poet Cowper.

APRIL 19   Journey into Norwich punctuated with Eve's affronted laments of "I knew it! The good weather's starting now my leave's up". And the station as usual seems to me to be saturated with leave-takings, though common sense tells me that it must witness quite as many home-comings as departures. See Eve into her seat, when we resolutely cut short those lacerating and useless moments when one hangs about reiterating last-minute messages and farewells, blocking the carriage doorways: and depart to shop in city, calling in at Cook's to enquire about seats for the Royal Tournament, and discover the heights of Kenya fares. Am staggered to learn that if she contemplates a voyage in October next year, Eve should register now, as in matters of this kind feel that eighteen months is much too far to look ahead. But put her name down to be on the safe side. "Your daughter will see the countries that you've always longed to visit", a fortune-teller told me years ago. She may be right.

APRIL 21   "Annual income £20, annual expenditure, £19 19s. 6d., result, happiness. Annual income £20, annual expenditure £20 0s. 6d., result, misery", was Mr. Micawber's verdict. Feel that "Weight according to health charts, etc., X stone, actual weight the same, or minus Y lb., result happiness. Correct weight X stone, actual weight X stone plus Y lb., result unbecoming to say the least of it. But like Mr.

M., I find precept one thing, and practice another, and my waist-line suffers accordingly. Have at least three diet charts, one of which has worked wonders in the past. But at the moment strength of mind is in as short supply as some of the necessary ingredients. Am assured by one who has tried it that to limit one's daily intake of liquid to one and a half pints has a most gratifying effect. Started (and abandoned!) this on what subsequently proved to be the hottest day of last summer. Now that the weather is cooler, and the slimming effects of jaundice are wearing off, am giving this another trial.

APRIL 24   "Oh, to be in England, now that April's there . . ."
with sleet, frost, snow, gales, flying tiles and falling boughs, and all the impedimenta of a ruthless January. Hepsibah's piglets put pink noses out of their stye, and hurriedly retreat again. Their mother has shut the day out of sight by balancing a straw bandage across her eyes. Dare not think of what is happening to the black-currants. And the plum and pear blossom that I fondly hoped would be there to welcome the bees when they arrive, has all been smashed from its branches. The night is as wild and as cold as the day. I wonder if any Norfolk people are sitting up to watch the church porch, to see who goes in and out. Not so long ago it was staunchly believed that on St. Mark's Eve, those who were to marry during the coming year could be seen entering the church together, and presently coming out again, whilst those who were to die went in one by one and remained inside: and more than one Norfolk porch was carefully observed.

APRIL 25   Finish making up our year's accounts for our modest venture on the soil, and am immediately reminded of the old saying that there are three infallible ways of losing money: horses, women, and farming your own land, the first being the quickest, the second the pleasantest, but the third the most certain. Couldn't agree more with this last, except to add that it isn't necessary to own the land, a tenancy can do just as well. Those who like to imagine that the farmer's life is one long riot of prosperity, home-produced eggs, bacon and cream (to say nothing of feather-beds!) should take a look at the reverse side of the medal . . . the heavy capital outlay involved, the endless restrictions, the spiralling costs, and the unending battle with the weather. Crops can be ruined by frosts, flood, or drought, or rendered worthless by an influx of imports. And it is only in the minds of townsmen and in the imaginations of ship's captains who plan to farm when they retire, that every cow gives at least a thousand gallons of milk a year, and each hen lays two hundred and fifty eggs.

APRIL 26   Much entertained by newspaper account of Lord Sempill's present of a loaf to Lord Alexander in the bread debate in the House of Lords, and disagree strongly with the latter's contention that to reduce the extraction rate would be enormously to increase the amount of wheat used, since all our own experience goes to prove that one is satisfied with much less when eating real bread. Wholemeal flour also makes excellent cakes and puddings, and if I want a less coarse flour, a gravy strainer makes a handy home extractor, the extracted bran being useful for coating fish, etc., or for any hungry horses or birds one may have about the place. Apropos the latter, feel more like putting poison on the bird board at present. "As gay as a chaffinch" says a French proverb. They build exquisite nests. They eat an incalculable number of weed-seeds, insects, and caterpillars. Some claim them to be among the gardener's best friend. They are certainly a boon to seed merchants, destructive little wretches. But the primrose heads now strewing the garden paths make me feel far from friendly when I hear their perky cry of "Spink! Spink! Spink!"

APRIL 28   Have not yet perused book entitled *The Individuality of the Pig*, but can heartily endorse its title, for individuals they certainly are. Hazel no bustling housewife like her sister, Hepsibah, but altogether more lethargic, and yesterday afternoon was quite content to retire to a ready-made straw bed in her stye, without adding so much as a solitary straw. By eight o'clock she was the mother of six. At nine-thirty the score was thirteen, but nett this was no more than ten, as three were born dead. This morning Adam decides that one looks a weakling, and nine enough for a gilt to bring up anyway. So nine it is. Trust that it stays at this figure, as cannot forget fellow-guest at recent dinner party on subject of his Large Black sow's latest litter . . . a tale hideously reminiscent of the Ten Little Nigger Boys.

APRIL 29   Decide on cheese soufflé for change. Melt 1 oz. margarine in saucepan, add 1 oz. flour, stir in 1 gill of milk. Mix thoroughly with 3 oz. grated cheese, remove from stove, and add three egg yolks. Just before cooking, lightly stir in three well-beaten egg whites, pour mixture into well-greased soufflé dish, and cook 20–25 minutes in moderate oven. (Watch it, but don't leave the oven door open too long when you look).

MAY 1   If a housewife has to leave her household for three days, it seems to require as much advance preparation as an army commander needs to start off a major attack. (Query: Has anyone ever considered mobilising housewives for service in this latter capacity? As am sure they'd prove invaluable.) Spend day helping Miss Barley fashion sting-proof suits against imminent arrival of bees (have been totally defeated in attempt to track down ex-R.A.F. boiler-suits), making ever-growing list of jobs that must be attended to the minute I get back, packing frantically, and cooking enough to last the household whilst I'm away. Small quantity of minced beef having appeared with meat, stew this gently for fifteen minutes with seasoning and gravy, put in piedish with two sliced hard-boiled eggs, implement with layer of grated raw potato, cover with pastry crust, and bake till crust cooked. Then stow this away in larder for future warming up, so that one course can be produced with minimum of trouble.

MAY 2   Up with dawn . . . which at this stage may be rosy-fingered, but if so the condition is caused by a sharpish frost and generally unpromising weather . . . and soon after seven, having reduced luggage to minimum, praying the while that hold-all won't burst on journey, am on my way to rendez-vous with Marigold and Simon. Taxi queue at Liverpool Street so long that by the time our turn comes, it's far too late to catch our scheduled train at Euston, so Marigold suggests we proceed via Oxford Street. "I hear it's full of barrow-boys selling nylons. And I'm down to my last pair." The taxi-driver enters into the spirit of the hunt, and off we go. The first three barrows we locate, however, are only selling peanuts. Then Simon catches sight of the right cargo on the far side of the road, leaps from the taxi, and vanishes in its direction.

"Can't stop here", the taxi-driver tells us, so he cuts across the traffic and comes round on the other side, hoping to collect

Simon as he cruises by. Unluckily at this moment an earnest policeman looms upon the pavement, Simon and the barrow-boys disappear as though Messrs. Maskelyne and Devant have taken charge of the proceedings, and the taxi-driver hastily moves on again. It isn't until we're coming round for the third time, and have practically given him up as sunk, that the taxi-driver sees Simon, and hauls him aboard, complete with nylons. After which we make for Euston, where, following lunch and fresh adventures, we board special train, by which Her Majesty the Queen (who is launching the ship) is travelling, two minutes before it pulls out of station. At Crewe the Royal coach is taken off, with more packs of top-hatted officials grouped on platforms and scrambling over railway lines, whilst passengers as one man and woman disobey printed injunctions to refrain from putting their heads out of carriage windows. And so to Liverpool.

MAY 3   Simon has inadvertently left home hatless. (He's always doing that, remarks Marigold. He must have quite thirty there now.) Marigold has left her new headgear behind deliberately, having taken a last-minute dislike to it. So directly after breakfast we dash in different directions to remedy this, then back to hotel to pick up remaining member of our party at ten. Proceed via Mersey Tunnel, as Simon thinks I ought to see it. (Am glad to have done so, though can never control my imagination on these occasions, and spend most of time in it full of direst visions of chaos and catastrophe should roof fall in.) And presently have navigated shipyard and are in our places quite half an hour before the time requested on our tickets, and two hours before the actual launching due.

Already the shipyard is thronged. Spectators are ranged on other platforms, on adjacent ships on their stocks, on scaffolding, on roofs, and in the yard. Above us towers the vast hull, pale blue above, chocolate below. The sky is dull and overcast. But it won't rain, my neighbour assures me. It never does when a Cammell Laird ship is launched. At intervals bands play, choirs burst into song. Simon and a shipping friend begin to talk of other launches. The most anxious men in the yard to-day, says Mr. Horsfall, are the shipwright (carpenter to me) and the draughtsman, for the one is responsible for the work, the other for the incline. I'd be surprised at the things that can go wrong at a launch, he enlarges. One ship he launched at Londonderry during the war, "crept".

When she'd gone about fifty feet, she stopped, and nothing would budge her. A few days later they had another go, first fastening her with a rope to a tug, so that if she "crept" again, she could be towed off. Instead she set off at such a pace that she hit the tug, and cut it in two, and men were jumping into the water all over the place. Another time, when he was in France . . . whereupon, a perfect stranger standing by introduces himself as French shipping man, and I attend by proxy launches in Italy, France, Flushing (where ships are launched into water aswim with boughs) and elsewhere. Presently the guns of the *Illustrious* begin to boom, and we speculate as to how many are fired at one time, since the salute is said to be twenty-one, but there are only ten bangs. The members of the Girls Nautical Training Corps lining the rails below us with arms behind their backs spring smartly to attention. The crowd cheers Her Majesty all the way to the launching platform. The service starts. We sing "Oh God of Jacob", and "Eternal Father", and join in the printed prayers, that in all our hearts being "May she never need to fight in war". The great moment arrives. The bottle, wreathed in red, white and blue ribbons, is swung back, poised, then released to shatter against the hull. (For her ill-fated predecessor the launching bottle was crashed four times against the hull before it broke, but there is no hitch this time.) There follows a momentous pause. Has she moved? Is she moving? Then, almost imperceptibly, the new *Ark Royal* glides gently forward. The next moment foam is creaming her stern and she is waterborne, her cradle floating away, the sound of her anchor rattling down, with that of the splash with which she enters the river, lost in the deafening roar of ships' sirens, cheers, and the engines of Seafires and Sea Hornets overhead. Everyone agrees that it has been the perfect launch, and the omens couldn't have been fairer. Though am staggered to learn that there's probably another three years' work on her still to do.

MAY 4   Catch the 8.15 a.m. from Liverpool, diverting ourselves on journey by identifying one another in newspaper photographs. (Marigold certain she can see her hat, I'm equally sure of mine. If we're wrong, no one can prove it!) and wondering in a housewifely way how it is that British Railways have so much sugar that we can have two lumps in any cup of tea and coffee, when rations won't extend to half a grain at home.

MAY 5 Only been away three days, but trees seem to have got in a fortnight's growth, and the pig families developed enormously. Hazel litter still numbers nine, and Hepsibah's eleven grow more adventurous and comically lovable every day. Quiz Team, as I foresaw, has profited immensely in my absence, and come out top in its first round.

10

MAY 8   Last year, when Horticultural Officer suggested that we should grow early chrysanthemums this, he has said he'll be calling back again long before planting time, when he will give me all necessary instructions. Accidents, however, can happen to any of us, as he has been painfully learning, his promised visit has never taken place, and all I have to go upon is a book purchased with a gift token last Christmas. This says decisively that cuttings should on no account be planted out in wet weather, it has been raining heavily off and on for the past week, it has poured during the night, and it is still raining, not to mention foggy, this morning, when I am due to collect cuttings. Cannot ring up nurseryman asking him to hold these for a further week, as he's not on telephone. But have various chores to be worked off in Norwich, so deal with these, calling on nurseryman on way back to say will he keep them for some days longer, only to find cuttings already lifted and boxed, and a letter of instructions from Horticultural Officer waiting for me with them. Have come without the car trailer, of course. But boxes finally wedged in on back seat and beside me, leaving just (but only just) enough room for me to cope with gears, and return home through thickening fog to round up Our Man, tell him to stop what he's doing, and start planting cuttings out at once. Letter mentions fillis string and two-foot canes. (First I have heard of either of these, so none in readiness, of course!) Posts and wires are also required, but not for a month or two. Spend rest of afternoon with secateurs cutting out substitute canes from nut bushes, willows and lime trees, producing just over three hundred in two hours, and wonder when I shall find the time to cut the rest, as there are a thousand cuttings altogether.

Nobody comments on date, which passes almost unnoticed.

Cannot believe as I switch on the lights at evening without first closing shutters and curtains, that five years ago we were doing this for the first time in nearly six years.

MAY 9   Look into grocery cupboard and count, all too quickly, miserable store of sugar. Calculate demands likely on this during next few weeks. Recalculate, but no amount of mathematical jiggery-pokery makes it add up to my lemon curd, which takes 1 lb. sugar, 4 eggs, $\frac{1}{4}$ lb. margarine, and two large lemons. So decide to try honey. Stand 1 lb. jar of this on side of cooker until melted, melt margarine in saucepan, add juice and grated rind of lemons, stir in honey and well-beaten eggs, and thicken carefully on simmering plate, stirring constantly (approximately 5 minutes). Admittedly the colour is creamy yellow instead of the bright buttercup of the original recipe. And the pure lemon flavour is slightly obscured by that of the honey. But the result is a most edible mixture. And I shall certainly make it again.

MAY 10   To Women's Institute Exhibition at St. Andrew's Hall. Mere man has staked out one small corner, and a few (very few) of the species are to be seen here and there in the crowd, but it is really Woman's own exhibition, and she has made the most of it. Could linger all day in the produce section, and long to be asked to tea by several makers of biscuits and cakes. Lose my heart to several knitted garments, and various entries in the embroidery and basket sections, and decide not to mention the horse in "toys" to Eve, who would immediately want me to track it down for her collection. Altogether a great exhibition, and worthy of the great movement it represents.

MAY 11   Theoretically the author-housewife-smallholder should be able to write and cook on wet days, and garden on fine ones. In practice, pen, kitchen, and soil all demand attention simultaneously and continuously, and it needs a Solomon to sort out their claims. My writing table is overflowing with un-answered letters, and virgin pages of foolscap screaming to be written upon. Except for the bread tin, the larder is virtually empty. But the sun is shining, Adam is away, and the weeds out-side have evidently learnt their lesson of growth in the same school as Jack's beanstalk. Bee Day is almost on me, so stay indoors long enough to make 2 lb. of my precious sugar into feeding syrup (bees' sugar ration is not, alas! issued until bees are *in situ*) and ransack the premises for something to hold their water supply . . . not so easy a task as it might be, Adam having purloined all spare shallow baking tins for piglets. Then take hoe into garden. Am told that shepherd's purse grows to seeding capacity within six weeks of itself being a seed. Can well believe it, and feel other weeds must be worse. If only vegetables were as hardy and as rapid, what terrific crops we should have.

MAY 12   Am cutting chrysanthemum stakes from lime tree on drive when hear telephone bell shrilling through open front door, and dash in to seize receiver. The bees will be put on rail at Hatfield, passenger train, this afternoon, announces Mr. Westgate at the other end. And they should get to King's Lynn at seven-fourteen. Since King's Lynn is thirty miles from Hillingsett, no doubt I sound as unenthusiastic about this as I feel. They could go on to Littlethorpe North, reaching there at eleven-five, Mr. Westgate suggests as an alternative, though I have obviously gone down in his estimation. No bee is going to drag me out at that time of night, I retort firmly, and add no doubt the station will ring me up first thing in the morning. No need to be nervous, says Mr. W. soothingly. My womanly touch is all they'll want. Personally, feel that one ounce of experience worth any amount of womanly touches and say so. Then pick up my secateurs again, wondering for perhaps the two-thousandth time why I ever thought of keeping bees.

MAY 13   Sure enough, British Railways on telephone at 7.15 a.m. to say they have two boxes of bees addressed to me, and how soon can I fetch them? Feel like answering in well-known words of a certain radio comedian, but compromise with "Not until after breakfast", and presently Adam and I set off for Littlethorpe. Visions of escaped bees loose in car has decided us on taking trailer. But though boxes are making sounds unpleasantly reminiscent of bombs about to explode, the return journey passes without incident. Home again I follow instructions to "allow to cool for one hour, under the scullery sink is a good place". Then, feeling that whilst curiosity may not kill the cat in this case, it is more than likely to lead to some severe stinging, I shut up a too-interested William, cart the boxes

down to the stand at the bottom of the kitchen garden, remove
the gauze from the entrances, and depart with more speed than
grace. Weather permitting, the bees should be transferred from
travelling boxes to hives at five o'clock. Since it is dull, cold, and
windy, finally decide to leave them until to-morrow, whereat the
sun immediately comes out. So dash indoors, don bee-suit, and
new veil (which looks like fencing mask) and Father's discarded
hunting bowler (this, he has suggested, is better than proposed
tin hat), and armed with smoker and hive tool, go into action,
what time Adam (at a safe distance) remarks that it's as good as a
music hall turn. Have one horrid moment before picking up first
frame bristling with bees, when I wonder if after all, gloves
wouldn't have been superior to mittens. But all twelve frames
are transferred without incident. And half an hour later, more
conventionally attired, am on my way to dinner with parents,
the bee sugar form (which must be signed by a "responsible
person"), in my bag. Evening closes with torch-lit procession to
hives to give the bees some syrup, when William, hitherto
invisible, appears purring on hive stand just as I remove the first
roof. Luckily they're all inside, so no untoward results this time.

MAY 17   No sign of bee-sugar permit to date, and sunless
          weather has kept bees in eating all our personal
rations. So have none to spare to-day for custard tarts, so use four
saccharin tablets for these in one pint milk and four well-beaten
eggs, melting the saccharin in a little warm milk before adding
to the rest. Line flan and bun tins with pastry; fill cases three-
quarters full of custard, grate over a little nutmeg, and bake in
moderate oven until custard is set: about half an hour. Take care
not to get pastry too thin, soft, or rich, lest custard end up
underneath pastry instead of inside. And make sure the oven is
not too hot, for if the custard is allowed to boil, it will be "holey"
or watery.

MAY 19   Bottle some rhubarb in syrup by using honey at rate
          of ½ lb. to one pint water. Next go through existing
stores, make rough plan of season's preserving, and order all
necessary rubber rings, new tops, jam covers, etc., right away,
instead of waiting until I actually need them, only to find shops
have sold out. Then ring Mr. Partridge to ask how long I must
go on feeding bees, as at rate they're guzzling syrup, they'll soon

have finished all their sugar, and be borrowing from me again. Have I noticed the direction of their flight? he enquires. As they ought to have found a field of kale-seed or something by now, when feeding can stop. How to dress for a demonstration? A veil and a light raincoat should do. If I wear anything more I shall probably be laughed at. But keep my hands in my pockets as spectators are often stung on these occasions. Still, what are a few stings on hands and ankles? Much too much, as far as I am concerned, I tell him. And though I may attend my first demonstration with no more protection than he suggests, if a bee comes near me, the next one will see me armoured from top to bottom. After which I depart for bottom of garden, to study bee flight. A constant going and coming in progress, but not, as I expected, into the garden. Instead they rise to the top of the thorn and holly fence behind the hives, circle in a manner reminiscent of carrier pigeons, then dart off and away. While the return home is a lightning downward zooming like that of a jet-propelled aircraft, and conducted at such speed that I feel they must all be equipped with super-efficient brakes, since all make perfect landings.

MAY 23   A really fine sunny day at last, so open hives to see how the bees are getting on. Not very rapidly, so far as drawing out the new frames is concerned, though there is more than enough activity for my liking, and am not sorry that juggling with occupied frames is unnecessary. On return to house have time only to remove veil and hunting hat, before a caller appears waving Ordnance Survey map, which he is checking over. Having ticked off name of house, he inquires if I have any views on the retention or otherwise of the final "e" that has recently appeared in the village's name. Reply that I have made sundry inquiries, and cannot find the least historical justification for said "e", do not use it myself, and have no intention of doing so, whether the Ordnance Survey finally decides to adopt it or no. Then remove remainder of bee-costume, and book up state of hives.

MAY 24   Yesterday's sunshine only a flash in the pan, and to-day is dull, cold, and windy again. Am not in the least tempted to cast any clouts ere this May be out, nor to call down on my head the old warning "Bathe in May, you'll be buried in clay, before the end of the month", which in our child-hood was quoted at us by a mournful nursemaid every time a warm spell in May sent us flying riverwards. Thomas Tusser takes a slightly more cheerful view of miserable May weather. "Cold May, and windy. Barn filleth up finely", says he. At the moment am following his advice to "slack never thy weeding". The cold has killed off dozens of seedlings, stunted some plants, and set back others. But nothing deters the weeds, it seems.

MAY 25   Order some rice, and at the same time tentatively inquire if there's any ground rice about, when I am astonished to hear that there is, and that I can have as much as I like. Feel that it has probably been obtainable for quite a time, but nowadays, one gets so used to being told that nothing one wants is in stock, that by the time it is, one has quite forgotten to ask for it. Celebrate with "maids of honour", made by lining tartlet tins with pastry, putting dab of raspberry jam into each, then covering with filling mixture, and baking in sharp oven 15–20 minutes. Filling: 4 oz. margarine, 4 oz. castor sugar, 2 oz. ground rice, 2 oz. currants, one egg, few drops almond essence. Lemon essence or juice is equally good. And the mixture will go further if 1 oz. sugar, 2 oz. ground rice and another egg are added. At same time make up flan and tartlet cases for future use, and suddenly think why not use tins upside down for these, moulding the pastry round the outside. This works beautifully, and gives better shaped cases.

MAY 29   Asked in advance what he would like to do for Whit-sun and his birthday, Adam's choice is a quiet time at home. Accordingly plan for this. But, as usual, "incidents" abound, keeping us on the run the whole week-end. Eve's unexpected forty-eight-hour leave well worth it, in spite of the fetching and carrying involved. But my breaking the front spring of my car, Adam having to have a tooth out, and the escape of Helen just as we are about to set off to a christening, all high unnecessary complications. (Christening goes off peaceably, baby receiving names of various relatives in ordinary way. But cannot help thinking of old Suffolk custom mentioned earlier by Guy, whereby child receives first name that comes to father's mind immediately after the birth. The instance Guy quotes took place some thirty-five years ago, at the critical moment the father was reading a newspaper account of the sinking of a German ship, and the unfortunate infant was presently baptised Fraulein Deutschlandia.)

Most of to-day spent peacefully gardening, taking time off to make a treacle tart. Freda makes hers by lining a sponge sandwich tin with short-crust pastry, adding the filling, then cooking both together. I prefer to cook my pastry case in advance, so now have only to decide on the filling mixture. Elspeth mixes her treacle with cake crumbs or coarse oatmeal. Freda beats in an egg. Kate puts currants and chopped peel in hers. I generally use breadcrumbs with mine, and on this occasion try melting the treacle in a saucepan first, adding the crumbs, and partly cooking the mixture (about 3–4 minutes. But not too fast, lest it should turn into toffee!) before tipping it into the pastry, then baking it in the oven for about twenty minutes. This a distinct success.

MAY 31   Sun out at last, so feel bees should now be able to support themselves. Am most affronted with them at moment, as last night I compassionately gave them an extra feed of syrup (made from my sugar ration), and got stung in the process. Obeyed the ancient adage to "tell the bees" by airing my frank opinion of such ingratitude before departing for the house for antiseptics, the sting sticking in my chin like a miniature dart the while. But so far am bound to confess that nettle stings acquired earlier in the day were much more painful. And I did NOT swell, as so confidently predicted by my beekeeping friends.

JUNE 1   As always, the Archaeological Society excursion is amazingly lucky in its weather. This afternoon's outing is to the Barninghams and Holt. The former, one parish at Domesday, but now three—Little (alias Parva), Winter (or Town), and Norwood (North)—lie in one of Norfolk's lovelier corners, to-day at its best, and needing a brush; not a pen, to record its beauty, since there are not nearly words enough for the myriad shades of green, with their shades within shades, that illumine the countryside, although the narrowness of its roads makes one hope that few unarchaeological travellers are about to-day to encounter our procession. Our meeting place is the house built by Sir Edward Paston in 1612 (and extended to the design of Humphrey Repton in 1805) and by permission of its present owner we are allowed to explore it inside and out. (During this perambulation, constantly encounter married couple who greet me cheerfully each time, but whose name I cannot recall, though I recognise their faces. Am still wondering who they are at end of day. Have a perfectly appalling memory for names, and shall never forget the occasion when, under the impression that this was someone else whose name had slipped my mind, I accosted perfect stranger, asked after the children, etc., and not until ten minutes after we had parted, realised that although her face was reminiscent of a distant acquaintance, we'd never met before.) We next walk down through the buttercup starred park to the ruined church, of which only the chancel is now in use, to look at the Wynter brass and other monuments. Then we go on to Norwood church, whose south wall contains part of an earlier eleventh-century structure. Here we listen to a talk on Norwood's history, and also of the Palgrave family, several of whose monuments are in the church, including one to that Sir Austin, whose behaviour (when High Sheriff) in 1617 to Thomas Mingay, then Mayor of Norwich, resulted in the Lord Chief Justice ordering him to stand with head uncovered while the Mayor sat in state in the disputed chair. Tea at Holt (with most unarchaeological discussion with fellow member on bees!). After which duty sent me flying home, so I missed the papers on Sir Edmund Hobarte and the Royalist Rising of 1650, and on the history of Gresham's School from 1554 to 1950.

JUNE 5   Home again after most diverting week-end for years, which we spent at well-known holiday camp on the east coast of Lincolnshire. As the brochure announces, the camp "has everything". Am even able to buy garden hat for which I have searched in vain for past twelve years, though cannot see myself taking advice of salesgirl to "pin it up in front with a flower. You'll look real cute", as I feel "cute" is not the adjective Adam will use if I do, and anyway groundsel or shepherd's purse rampant so much more appropriate. Refuse to be enticed into posing for roving photographer, but fall for having our hands dabbed with lamp-black or similar stuff, then pressed to a sheet of paper; and when calling later for our readings, purr loudly at the estimate of our respective characters. (Query: Is seer too good a salesman ever to give a really bad one?) And are relieved to learn that success is coming both our ways, rapidly for

Adam, and slowly and regularly for me. Am forbidden by Adam to learn to roller-skate, but we swim, dance, and generally take advantage of whatever is going, including, somewhat rashly, an hour of organised P.T. after church service on Sunday morning. In midst of this discover from adjacent "lass" that her guardsman son will be in the musical ride at the Royal Tournament, so immediately play my Wren, and we indulge in bursts of maternal pride until recalled to the harsh reality of the immediate display by our house captain. Should love to have stayed out the week, and must certainly go again one of these years if weeds and livestock permit.

JUNE 6   Fact is stranger than fiction according to the proverb-mongers, and how right they are. But I had never realised before that this equally true of scenes from real life and Walt Disney. Scene I: Lionel's tulip bed, a posse of Clara Butts in full bloom. Enter four young sparrows. Presently Sparrow One decides to climb a tulip stem. Up he goes, claw over claw, the stem bends over further, further. Then, crash! the tulip's head strikes the ground. Exeunt all four sparrows in a panic. Interval. Re-enter four sparrows, the performance is repeated, but as the petals hit the earth this time, off hops Sparrow One, and jauntily takes a bow. Remainder of scene occupied by spectacle of four little sparrows running up and down one tulip stem after another, obviously having the most enthralling time. Scene II: A quiet country lane, in the centre of which sits a young gold-crested wren, thinking its own thoughts. Approaches juggernaut in the guise of my parent's car. Since the bird stays put, he slows down. Whereupon the wren tears across the road, trips over a stone, and turns a complete somersault just before reaching the grass verge.

JUNE 7   Builder's foreman also a beekeeper, and to-day takes a look at mine. He supposes I know, he commences, that the way those bees are flying, back over the hives and out over that fence, we're standing slap in bee-flight every time we go through the combs? It may be all right now, but as they work up to strength, they'll have something to say about it, he shouldn't wonder, if I don't move the hives. He doesn't care for the type of hive I've got, either. He prefers double-walled. And he proceeds to make a rough sketch of one on the ground with a stick. (Mr. Westgate has several answers to this last, but am unable to remember what they are just now, though William does his best by rolling happily over the sketch, and purring loudly.) Next he looks at the second brood-chambers, given yesterday, and remarks sinisterly that double brood-chambers aren't a beginner's job. After which he gives me much valuable information on bee-behaviour, and it emerges that there are several other points of beekeeping practice on which he differs from Mr. Westgate. (Can see that there are as many ways of bee-keeping as of bringing up a family, and greater possibilities of bitter arguments between the exponents of different methods.) Have no intention of changing my hives or their position. But attend to bee-flight by cutting over a couple of pear and plum boughs to encourage a forward take-off.

JUNE 9   Our gooseberries were nowhere near the picking stage at Whitsun as, traditionally, they should have been. But a few are now ready to stew. As with rhubarb, I find the best way is to put them into a saucepan with a little water, add sugar, syrup or saccharin to sweeten, bring rapidly to boil, then transfer at once to simmering oven, as this prevents them disintegrating into pulp the minute my back's turned. When cooked, fill flan case with some of the fruit, thicken juice with a little cornflour, pour this over the berries, and leave to cool, decorating the edge of the crust, etc., before serving with a mixture of 1oz. icing sugar beaten into 1 oz. margarine, put on with the help of a cake-icing syringe. Incidentally, when using short crust pastry, a flan case takes approximately 5 oz. of flour, while 1 lb. flour produces two to two and a half dozen tartlet cases.

JUNE 10   To Toftwood, to my first bee-demonstration, at end of which am staggered to find three hours have flown, as could have sworn I hadn't been there more than thirty minutes. After much thought, have decided that I'd rather face any amount of mirth from fellow apiarists than present myself as the bees' target for the afternoon. So don full armour on arrival, when am glad to find that the county instructor fully approves, the rest of the audience take it in their stride, while I am able to get almost on top of hives to watch demonstration, without fear of reprisals. Feel that at last I'm really learning something (an ounce of seeing it done is worth, at this stage, a ton of books) and that with luck I may be able to spot my queens the next time I go through hives. Though on this occasion I find it difficult to spot one until Mr. Chelford has marked its head with red paint: and of course I'm looking somewhere else in the split second during which a virgin queen pops out of her cell. Discover with relief that Mr. C. all in favour of single-walled hives and double-brood chambers. Also gather that Norfolk's climate makes it the best honey-producing county in England, and that something like twenty-two thousand hives are scattered about on its heaths and in its orchards and gardens. Whilst one is a beginner for five years at least and, as with farming, you are still learning when you lay down your hive tool for the last time. Can well believe this, but after this afternoon feel that at least I've made a start.

JUNE 12   Do I suffer from worms in wood, asks Sam? Have discovered several spots lately that the builders' men have passed by. Have also more than one article of furniture mildly afflicted in this way. Equal quantities of methylated spirit, vinegar, and turpentine, is the answer, says Sam. "A second-hand dealer give it me. But you want to put that on with a hair brush."

JUNE 13   Hear that last night's thunderstorm killed a local cow as well as causing a breakdown in our electricity supply. Traces of it still about to-day, with distinctly detrimental effect on temper of man and bees. These last decidedly uppish, and changing the direction of their flight has merely given them more scope for saying so. Our Man, using the motor hoe near the front of the hives, is soon told in unmistakable fashion to take himself elsewhere, And my first attempt to weed the asparagus bed results in my being escorted down the centre path and out of the kitchen garden, not to mention being stung on the elbow as I go. Am not particularly incommoded by the latter. But take a very poor view of being forced to remove garden hat and comb my hair for bees; and of the promptness with which I'm escorted out again when, handkerchief on head, I make a second sortie in the direction of the asparagus beds. Much more of this, and I shall work with a bonfire beside me, and they will find themselves escorted outside the three-mile limit with a view to setting up their hives in a more secluded part of the premises on their return.

Indoors turn present of dressed crab into shell-fish cups, for which prawns, lobster, etc., can also be used. (But if using tinned fish, open at least two hours before serving.) Put into bowl, cut into small pieces, squeeze on lemon juice or a little vinegar. Fill sherry glasses (or scooped-out halves of lemons) with fish, add a little cream (top off milk) and tomato ketchup to juice in bowl, pour over fish, and garnish with sliced radish, cucumber, etc. Or if you're lucky enough to have any, blobs of whipped cream sprinkled with cayenne.

JUNE 14   To market, feeling a complete female Judas, with Hepsibah's family in trailer. Feel even worse when I leave them behind in market pen, and wonder where they will be tonight. (Also hope they're not acquiring inferiority complex . . . and losing value . . . by comparison with occupants of pen next door, who look as though they've been tubbed and brushed. But Our Man says reassuringly that it's only because they've never been allowed to run out, anyone can see by the look of them that ours have, and should therefore be healthier.) Have no such qualms over Helen, who will shortly be on her way to the bacon factory. Judging by the enthusiastic comments of those who've seen her, her face and figure would launch any number of cattle-floats. But she firmly declines to launch a single litter.

JUNE 15   Have heard it said that authors should stay at home and let their books do the talking. Having rashly accepted two invitations this week involving speeches, am once more forcibly struck by the sense of this: and, (as usual,) have to use any amount of will power to prevent myself sending last-minute telegrams to say I'm seriously ill in bed. Virtue rewarded to-day by an enjoyable afternoon at Booton's garden fête, where the school provides entertainment with a P.T. display and games: and, had I been the judge in the baby show, am sure I should have followed the example of last year's adjudicator, and given every entrant a prize. Take tickets for the cake, doll (I can always save it for a grandchild if I win it, as Eve's too big, suggests the raffler!), sweets in a bottle, and similar competitions, with my usual conspicuous lack of success. But must find out who gave the coconut cookies, two of which I ate for tea, and get hold of the recipe.

II

June 16   "They're talkin' a' hainin' our wages agen", says Ben, referring to the discussion on a wage increase for farm-workers now under consideration. B.B.C. English may be the coming language. But how much poorer we shall be when it finally supersedes the colourful and expressive words provided by our dialects. When Ben ploughs at right angles to his original work, he is working "overwart": if on the skew, he is "on the sosh". If a field is badly shaped, he refers to the odd awkward corners as "scutes", whilst a small field is a "pightle". He walks home down the loke or the drift (lane), below the hedge of which runs a "holl" (ditch), and every so often a grup leading into it (a narrow cut through the grass verge to run surface water from the road into the holl). As a rule he walks briskly enough, but sometimes he's simply pampling (strolling aimlessly). Occasionally he limps a little, or "goes himpy". And though it takes a good deal to ruffle or upset him in the ordinary way, there are times when he gets into a proper puckerterry. To Ben withered or wilted vegetables are foosey or clung, a dishcloth is a dwile, a snail a dodman. A see-saw is a titter-ma-torter (his uncle made us one when we were children), sweets are cushies, a donkey a dickey, a young girl a mawther, a pigeon a dow, a finger-stall a hutkin. He's always ready for a mardle (gossip), he tizzacks if he has a slight cough, and he bops (stoops) when he wants to pick up something he's dropped. Ben is never ill, he simply feels queer. His worn-out kettles and pails don't leak, they run. A storm is never a storm, but a tempest. And when he bids me good-bye, it is always "Fare-ye-well".

June 17   Home again after a night in London which includes visit to the Royal Tournament at Earl's Court. Naturally, Event One, ninth in order of presentation on this occasion, is the one we await most eagerly, and an excellent display we see. Hadn't realised before how graceful and ballet-like P.T. can be, though Eve alleges that she's developed so much muscle in training that her arms won't go through the sleeves of any of her summer frocks. Hold our breath during the field-gun competition (am not surprised to hear that somebody was hurt in yesterday's performance), the parachute training display, and the mock raid by Royal Marine Commandos on an enemy-held coastline, which last includes the ascent of a fifty-foot concrete cliff in which the biggest foothold protrudes only one and a half inches. The pike and musket drill display given by the H.A.C., with the bright uniforms, the leisurely goose-step march, and deliberate movements, of the Civil War period, come in sharp contrast to the staccato tactics of to-day. The Musical Ride by the Household Cavalry, the Musical Drive by the King's Troop of the R.H.A., make one realise to the full the picturesqueness of the horse. (No parade of tanks could ever tug so at one's heart.) And the Gordon "cavalry" give an equally effective display, though the upholstery of one "horse" tripped its unhappy small rider and sent him rolling. We thrilled again to the massed bands and drill display of the R.A.F., wondering the while what would happen if the W.R.A.F. drum-major didn't catch her mace when she threw it into the air (she always did, however!). And cheered like nobody's business when the 1st Battalion Royal Norfolk Regiment won its tug-of-war. As the R.A.F. type sitting near us said "A wizard show".

JUNE 19   "Do all horses consider bulrush roots an especial delicacy?" asks James. Last year he was gathering some to take home to Angela for their London flat. Some massive Suffolks peacefully contemplated both James and the landscape at first. Then he accidentally pulled up some roots. Whereupon as horse they advanced and surrounding him, pushing and jostling like a herd of playful elephants. They were only interested in the roots, which they champed with the air of gourmets savouring the perfect dish. I have never heard of anything of the sort before. But am determined to have some in readiness for Brandy next time he's over. And feel he'll probably be ready for them, as the geese—nine six-week-old haughty-looking and suspicious goslings—arrived to-day, and are attacking the meadow grass like young mowing-machines.

JUNE 21   Adam back from "Strawberryland", which is well on
           the way to becoming a depressed area. And no wonder.
One grower, paying twopence ha'penny a pound for picking, had
just been advised by his agent that fourpence a pound was the
top price for berries. Whereupon he promptly presented Adam
with a chip full, and sent his pickers off to hoe potatoes. Other
growers, faced with similar prices, talk of ploughing in the crop.
The jam factories say they are full up with imported pulp, the
canners complain that most of the tin plate has gone for export,
and the housewife has no sugar worth mentioning. Yet three
years ago growers were being urged to increase their acreage. If
there is a good reason for the home producer being butchered to
make an importer's holiday, I should very much like to know
what it is.

JUNE 22   Duly planted sweet corn earlier with the idea of
           tying up the tomato plants to it later on, as these two
plants do better in company. But only one seed has come up, so
have had to stake the tomatoes in the usual way, but have composted them well, and added a straw mulch to keep the weeds
down. All seem to have settled down well. So have the two
cucumber plants in the frame, into which I have popped a toad
that incautiously crossed my path, as Sam says that's the way to
keep the frame free of woodlice and insects. (But the toad needs a
saucer or tin of water with stones in.) Ate the first new potatoes
(cooked with masses of mint, and in the saucepan within ten
minutes of lifting) last week, the first peas and beans to-day.
What a welcome the first fruits get. But how soon the garden
seems over-run, and our fickle palates tire. Rhubarb's no longer
a treat, but there is practically nothing else, so to-day stew some
in a little water, and when cooked, sprinkle liberally with ground
cinnamon, then pour over two tablespoons golden syrup, stir
gently, and leave to cool. Rhubarb fool, for which I use two-
thirds sieved fruit pulp to one-third custard, plus the juice and
finely grated rind of one lemon, and sweeten with saccharin and
golden syrup, is something else again. Am also making a dilute
syrup by melting two tablespoons golden syrup, one to two
table-spoons boiling water, just bringing it to boil, then cooling,
and using it instead of sugar to sweeten cereals, fresh fruit,
etc.

JUNE 23   Once again the tied cottage controversy is on. And,
           ironically enough, as the farm-worker fights to free
his home, banks, insurance companies, and other big concerns are
being forced to buy up properties to house their staffs, since "I
won't move unless they find me a house" is becoming an
increasingly frequent cry. Nor is the position very different where
agriculture is concerned, if the "Situations Vacant" column is
anything to go by. "Work wanted as tractor-driver and labourer
. . . cottage essential." "Cowman seeks situation . . . with
cottage" are only two taken from a recent newspaper. The fact is,
and no amount of hard cases and argument will alter it, that
certain jobs need houses to go with them. The farm-worker is not
the only one. The rector in his rectory, the farmer in his farm-
house, the police, the gatehouse-keeper, are as tied as any.
The real evil is the housing shortage. If this were done away with
the "evils" of the tied cottage would mostly vanish overnight.

JUNE 25   Could wish that Eve's leaves hadn't such a tendency
           to happen out of the blue, but this is no doubt good
for a parent too addicted to long-range planning. And anyway,
am far too delighted to have her for four days to cavil, though
should prefer trains arriving at more convenient hours. Have been
spared a 2 a.m. journey, however, and minimise awkwardness of
actual moment of arrival by taking picnic basket, whose contents
we consume on heather-purpled birch-and-fir-wooded heath on
way home. Eve not being so averse to gooseberries as Adam, have
included Gooseberry Fluff in these. One pound gooseberries
stewed, so restfully, without topping and tailing in a quarter-
pint of water, when rubbed through a sieve gives approximately
one pint pulp. Stir in two to three tablespoons golden syrup and
1 oz. of gelatine first melted in a little pulp, add one tin evaporated milk (whipped), pour into sundae glasses, and allow to set.
The same mixture, minus the gelatine, makes a good gooseberry
fool.

JUNE 29   Royal Norfolk Show at Anmer this year, by invitation
           of the King, and royal weather, warm and sunny, to
go with it. Spent nine hours on showground yesterday, and as
usual didn't see a quarter of the things we'd planned. In bee tent,
learn how long it takes to make those entertaining wax flowers
(something like three hours a bloom), and meet a beekeeper who

has been "only" sixty-nine years on the job. Then to the thought-provoking exhibit staged by the Church and Countryside Association, a look at the latest archaeological finds (including the horse-bits from Ringstead, which might almost have come out of one of to-day's stables, instead of being two thousand years old, and possibly the property of one of Queen Boadicea's chieftains), and a visit to the Rural Industries section, housed this year in a series of huts that inevitable provoke comparison with a lambing yard. At the Women's Institute tent, learn all we can about re-seating rush chairs, as three at least of ours are in the condition of Baby Bear's when Goldilocks had finished with it, and something really must be done about them this winter. In the stock yards we admire the champion Wessex boar, some of whose female relations we have booked for delivery in October. And in gossiping with friends and roaming from stand to stand, the morning speeds at Derby winner pace.

After lunch, give up all attempt to keep together. Adam departs for tour of machinery section and the Soil Association stand, whilst Marigold, Eve and I make for the grandstand and a chance to rest. Here we watch successively the heavy horse parade, the judging of harness horses (one pair of which put on some unrehearsed scenes, and are nearly sent out of the ring in disgrace), and the dressage display by Mr. Henry Wynmalen on Bascar, which last is Eve's favourite, of course, and with a course of horse-mastership behind her, she explains why, since Marigold and I quite incapable of appreciating the finer points. Then the R.H.A. repeat the musical drive we saw at Earl's Court. After which it is the cattle's turn to parade, and round the ring they go— Red Polls, Friesians, Shorthorns, Ayrshires, Guernseys, Jerseys, Lincoln Reds, Aberdeen Angus, and the rest, some proudly adorned with the coloured rosettes of prizewinners, some without, the cows and heifers patient, a little weary, the bulls tugging at their halter ropes, all suffering a little from the heat, the crowds, and the flies. There follows a long (unscheduled) interval, and then, at last the jumping, which we have to leave when only half-way through, as the delayed start has already made us an hour late for our rendezvous with Adam. We bolt a belated tea, after which Adam is all for departure. But we haven't seen the flowers. So off to the flower tent we go, emerging laden with catalogues and quite decided that all family Christmas and birthday presents must henceforth be either plants or seeds. (I also learn that the bottom inch of poppy stems should either be burnt by passing through a gas flame or similar, or seared with boiling water before putting into vases, when they'll last quite a week.)

"Next year we simply must come both days", says Adam, as we leave for home. I only wish we could do so this. But Eve has to be put on rail in the opposite direction, so we miss the—to us— event of this afternoon, when Marsham, the family's steward, is presented with a well-deserved long service premium by the King, and enjoys a chat with the Queen as well. " 'You look young for forty-seven and a half years as a steward', she say to me. 'A lot a' that I spent as a teamsman, your Majesty', I say. 'Ah, I thought there must be something of that kind', she say to me", he confides proudly later.

JUNE 30 Weather distinctly cooler this morning, a chilly breeze plucking fretfully at leaves and branches, and cottonwool clouds marring the perfection of yesterday's flawless hedgesparrow-egg-blue sky. But still, a lovely day . . . birds singing, the air full of the scent of flowers, in the fields the crops ripening once again to harvest. Life offering all its beauty and richness everywhere to man with wide open hands . . . and with it, the latest news of the fighting in Korea, new appeals for civil defence volunteers, hints of fresh evacuation plans. I think of those we know on our ships and aircraft carriers already in Far Eastern waters, of all the agony and misery that we have all so lately undergone, and cry "Surely it can't happen yet again?" At least firmness has been shown before, instead of after, Munich this time. And we can only pray that it will have the desired effect.

JULY 1 Eve having been unable to eat quite as many cucumbers as she thought she could, decide to preserve the survivors in the manner used by my luncheon hostess one day during visit to Denmark three years ago. Peel and cut cucumber lengthways, in strips two to three inches long, one inch wide, and quarter-inch thick (not using the seedy centre) with a silver knife. Sprinkle with salt, Leave for twelve hours. Next make a "marinade" with one pint each vinegar and water, and tea-spoon whole cloves, one dessert (or tablespoon. "One adds these things to taste", was Mrs. Bjornsen's opinion) whole peppers, 1 lb. sugar. Boil all together until clear (15–20 minutes), skim, then drop in a small bunch of dill. Wipe the strips of cucumber. Next, keeping the marinade boiling, drop in four pieces of cucumber at a time, whisking them straight out again, and pack them into clean jars. When all the cucumber has been dropped in the liquid, re-boil for five minutes, pour over the cucumber in the jars, and tie down. The resultant strips should be a pale clear green, and are most appetising to eat.

JULY 3   And Eve's twenty-first birthday. Family celebrations must wait for summer leave, but we have arranged to wait indoors for her to ring us between six and seven this evening. As a rule nobody rings us up at this hour. But to-night there is a positive spate of calls, including one from chimney-sweeping firm bent on relating at length the series of mischances that will prevent their keeping their date with our flues tomorrow. Deal shortly with this and other callers. And some time after eight the call from Northern Ireland comes through, and though we are cut off in mid-call, have time to voice good wishes, and exchange sundry bits of news. The Navy, it appears, has granted her a "make-and-mend" day for the occasion. The weather, unlike ours, has been fine and sunny, so she's been gliding, and while confessing that she's never been more frightened in her life, hopes to get in six more "flips" before leave, when she'll be eligible for her "A" gliding licence. And will I please send her Royal Tournament kit, as she's taking part in a Naval Air Day display.

"Oh, to be twenty-one again", sighs Adam.

"If at the same time you could know what you know now, and be free to take a different course", I qualify. For the trouble with our hard-won experience is so much of it is useless, since the opportunity to apply it seldom occurs. Personally I think to reach thirty-five and be able to stay there, would be the ideal thing.

JULY 4   Expected to find a good deal of water in the rain-gauge this morning, but quite unprepared for actual amount, which is 149 points, just on one and a half inches. This, and the accompanying gale, have wrecked the garden. Lupins and delphiniums are stretched prone upon the gravel. Chrysanthemums have been beaten down. Red currant bushes and sweet peas are torn from their moorings. Everything is weighted with water like trees after a snowfall, and the drive is strewn with petals and leaves as though it had witnessed a wedding procession. In the fields beyond our boundaries corn is flattened like a lawn. Everywhere the soil is a slippery morass. July, though wishful thinking persists in regarding it as a hot dry month, is, in fact, often one of the wettest months of the year: and if this one goes on as it has begun, I should think it will be a record. Summer distinctly disappointing so far, and am wondering if William Cat, the sure prophet of bad weather in the ordinary way, isn't predicting yet more woe in the manner of moles before a hard winter. Normally he sports a beautifully long and thick coat, with a large smoke-grey ruff to match, from September onwards, but sheds so much fur in late spring that in summer he might be taken for a short-coated cat. He has shed less than half the usual amount this year.

JULY 6   In this machine age, man's mind flies automatically to a mechanical contrivance of one sort or another when he wants a job done. We explore animal avenues, the idea being that ours should earn their livings in more ways than one. Hepsibah and Hazel, temporarily free of family cares, are now busy acting as miniature bull-dozers on ground we want cleared of turf, nettles, and so on; and not until they have dealt with every similar plot are we having them re-ringed, this time with special anti-rooting rings. The goslings are energetically mowing the meadow. And when our pullets arrive, they will thresh out their sunflower seeds, and de-bale their own straw, to say nothing of turning their deep litter into first-class compost at the end of a year. Only William Cat remains purely decorative, for which I am inclined to blame the fact that he was brought up in a town, and so never learned to fend for himself.

JULY 7   Try out recently acquired recipe for coconut buns, which takes 2 oz. margarine, 2 oz. desiccated coconut, 4 oz. self-raising flour, one tablespoon each granulated sugar and golden syrup, half teaspoon bicarbonate of soda, one teaspoon cream of tartar, one egg, a little milk. Cream fat, sugar, and syrup, beat in egg, and all dry ingredients, and enough milk to make a soft batter, put into twelve bun tins, and bake for ten minutes in fairly hot oven (400 °). Make a double mix of this, using the second half for filling tartlet cases, with and without first putting in a scraping of jam. And am well pleased with all three results.

JULY 8   Have previously suggested that Eve should give a small dinner-party "over the border" at our expense on her birthday, and her greetings telephone call has, in fact, come from there. She now rings up again to say she hates to tell us, but Buncrana has just been put out of bounds because of typhoid fever, which has apparently been rampant for at least a week, and everyone who has been "over" in the last ten days is having their first inoculation tomorrow. Directly she rings off, rush for Aunt Sarah's *Practice of Medicine* by Frederick Taylor, when I discover that typhoid and enteric are one, I have an immediate vision of Florence Nightingale in the barracks at Scutari, and practically order a wreath at once. Subsequent perusal of the fourteen-odd pages devoted to the disease do nothing to raise my spirits. And try to take comfort from Adam's reiterated "She hasn't got it yet. And if she does, medical science has advanced miles since your Aunt Sarah trained on that book". Feel no good purpose served by repeating gist of fourteen pages in the letter I now begin to Eve, either. So content myself with remarking that if she should be unlucky, the great thing is rest, I understand. And add, in an attempt to be a Spartan mother, that she'd better not catch it, as all the invitations for her home birthday party have gone out, and I cannot face the thought of cancelling this as we had to do our proposed house-warming frolic at Christmas.

JULY 10   Thought last Monday's rain a record, but the deluge that fell in the small hours of this morning has beaten it (and almost every bit of corn left standing) completely flat. Tipped out no less than two hundred and thirty-six points, which, added to the previous lot, amounts to over four inches . . . and the average yearly rainfall for Norfolk is only in the neighbourhood of twenty-six inches. Heard a curious keening noise at one moment during the storm, what time I have been watching the drive, between lightning flashes, turn into a river. And at breakfast time a gosling corpse is discovered. Everything else awash, water through the roof at several points, and has run over the doorsills in others. Whilst at Silford Father says he has never seen anything like it in England before, the yard is underwater, and Marsham, convinced all the drains were blocked, rushed for draining rods, only to find that every channel already was full to capacity, with water racing through it in full flood. The afternoon unexpectedly "blows out", however, and the women currant pickers appear on schedule. Earlier inspections have warned us that frost and wet have materially reduced the crop. But even so we are unprepared for the actual state of affairs now revealed as the pickers go from bush to bush, when it soon becomes obvious that at this year's price (half of last year's thanks to exports of tin plate and imports of overseas fruit) there won't even be enough to pay for the new pair of scales we've had to buy, as this season's consignments have to be packed in twenty-four-pound trays. It is little incidents like these that the "feather-bed" fraternity conveniently forget.

JULY 11   Heavy rain coincides with arrival of vacuum chimney-sweeps, which holds up proceedings for half an hour, during which one catches sight of my bee-suit and tools on kitchen table, and asks do I keep bees. Am trying to, I murmur modestly. It's all right if they like you, says he. A friend of his has dozens of hives, they never worry him or any of his friends, but let his sixteen-year-old son set foot in the garden, and they're after him at once. Have heard other tales to this effect, and promptly retail a few. He counters with new ones. And presently produces an eye-witness account of an unrehearsed incident that took place in January 1940, on the borders of Italian Somaliland, when he was a member of the West African Frontier Force. They had moved up a little, and the Mahomedan Sergeant-Major had settled them under a group of trees, in several of which were bees' nests. When there was time, the Sergeant-Major intended to take the honey. Meanwhile, "There we were with our cups of char, playing the concertina", when suddenly the Italians attacked. Collected, but honeyless, the Sergeant-Major organised their retreat, Then, as he prepared to follow them, he fired into one bees' nest after another. Out came a roaring, stinging cloud, and flew straight for the attackers. The Italians fled in disorder. The Sergeant-Major received a decoration. (Have heard that bees used as offensive weapons in Middle Ages, and am entranced by this instance in modern warfare.) After which, the rain easing, business proceeds, with none of the usual dust covering and dirt. They even finish by cleaning up the farm office carpet, which is suffering from a recent wall re-plastering effort on the part of the builder's men. Altogether, as Adam remarks later, I've had my money's worth.

JULY 13   Have enormous number of questions ready for county bee-keeping instructor who, in fulfilment of long-standing appointment, is calling this afternoon to go through my hives. But all catapulted from mind when, as we're hoeing near by just after lunch, Our Man points dramatic arm at fence, and there, hanging on the wire-netting we've put up to deter rabbits, is a swarm of bees. And it isn't from anyone else's hive, either, but one of mine! Having fondly supposed that, starting from nuclei only, I shall be safe from this particular manifestation this year, have no swarm box, spares, etc., feel completely panic-stricken, and spend bulk of next two and a half hours telephoning other bee-keepers for advice, rushing to see if swarm is still there, and like Sister Anne in the Bluebeard story, keeping a frantic look-out for Mr. Chelford's car. Further drama is forthcoming when the hives are opened up (the one from which the swarm has emerged to my eyes is still as full as ever) as both turn out to be queenless, although there is indisputable evidence that No. II's was there four days ago, and am sure No. I was all right last week. The latter, from which the swarm has come, also produces another virgin queen (who, like the one at last month's demonstration, pops out just as I look the other way), and several queen cells that I could swear weren't there seven days ago. Hive II also has a new array of queen cells, the best of which is now left behind to supply a new colony-mother.

In the midst of all this, the cardboard carton perched on the fence above the swarm falls to the ground with a crash, and all the bees who have crawled into it rise in a menacing cloud. Time passes. But at last most are back in their original domain (it is too late in the season to start a new colony, and anyway two are quite enough for me at present!), being returned to base by swiftly removing the brood-chambers from their floor, standing an empty super in their place, overturning the carton into it, then quickly replacing brood-chambers and roof on top, Mr. C's. original idea of showing us how to run them up a board into the hive having been abandoned when Our Man, sent to fetch an appropriate run-way, is absent for some time, and then returns with the wrong one. My knowledge of bee-behaviour is further enlarged by the sight of quantities of bees, stern uppermost, on the hive sides, sending up a scent-call to guide home their wandering relatives. Must say that I am grateful to the little wretches for so considerately staging this effort for Mr. C's. visit (cannot conceive how I should have coped if it had taken place yesterday, instead!). But am decidedly stunned to hear that we can expect a repeat performance any time within the next week. If No. I isn't out again within four days, it will probably settle down, says Mr. Chelford pensively. But it's a hundred to one against No. II not swarming, and they will probably come out with their new queen within the next few days.

JULY 14   Was always under the impression that cold water was something to be avoided in shoe-cleaning, or when washing "smalls". Eve, whom Service life has made almost as keen a washer as William Cat, says this is all wrong. She rinses everything, woollies included, in cold water, and knows somebody who regularly unshrinks her Naval Commander's husband badly felted woollen socks with it each time he comes on leave. While fellow Wrens are always asking her how she gets "that patent leather look" on her shoes. This last a relic of her horse course days, when she learned to treat them more or less like harness, first using a cold water rag (or in extreme cases, soap and water) to remove all dirt and then continuing in the orthodox way.

JULY 18   Hive I, evidently having decided that the sooner I get some first-hand experience in dealing with swarms the better, has lost no time in providing it. Saturday they fly out of the garden, and half-way across the meadow next door, then settle on the far side of the garden's north fence, where I leave them while I dash indoors for lunch. Back in twenty minutes not a bee is to be found there, and the occupants of a cottage abutting on the meadow a hundred yards or so away have a vague recollection of seeing "something" swoop down the meadow and away in the direction of the woods about a quarter of an hour ago. Spend a couple of hours searching neighbouring fences in vain, after which I take another look at hive, when I see quite a number on the front engaged in signalling operations. Cannot believe that they have gone home of own accord, but it subsequently transpires that this is exactly what has happened.

This is much too easy, of course. And Sunday afternoon (just as we are planning to go out) once again the sky is bespangled with bees. This time, with a stirrup pump in one hand and Mr. Westgate's book in the other, treat them to a miniature shower of rain, and soon they are clustering all about the branches and trunk of a small pear tree. I fetch the secateurs and a second carton. At one period I feel convinced there are three queens if not more. Well over two hours elapse before they're back in the hive at last, what time Adam gestures encouragement from behind the landing window, and William Cat, who is only too anxious to assist, is shut mewing in the kitchen.

Feel this really must be their final fling. But arrive home lunchless yesterday to learn that they came out within half an hour of my departure, and are now in the middle of a thick holly fence. A new recovery operation has to be launched at once, and for the next three hours or so, I recall with distinct bitterness one text book that speaks blithely of "simply knocking them off the bough". Later still, when bees are re-hived once more, re-visit hedge, and am horror-struck by hearing almost as much buzzing as at the start. Put on bee armour again, dive into hedge at several points, but can see nothing that resembles a new cluster, though am able to hear a good deal. Spend night vengefully planning to carry the war into the enemy's camp by lighting a straw fire at bottom of hedge, happen what may. But an early visit this morning reveals the hedge hearteningly silent. Undoubtedly experience is the only way to learn. But I should much prefer it in smaller doses. And if Hive II starts within the next twenty-four hours, shall be sorely tempted to leave them to their own devices.

12

July 20   How quickly the country scene changes colour at this time of year. The banks and fences are full of blue harebells and yellow agrimony, mauve scabious, pale violet thistles, scarlet poppies, purple veitches, dark pink "pick-cheese", pale pink and white wild roses, deep sky-blue succory, yellow orange trefoil, and a thousand others. (A vase of cut flowers competition restricted to wild flowers only would certainly make a brave show.) And in spite of the wet, dull weather, the corn turns steadily from green to gold. If you pass by a particular field after an interval of a week or so, the difference in hue is surprising. The ripening wheat ranges from pale biscuit to red-gold, according to its variety (to the great surprise of Alison, who had previously thought that wheat was just wheat, and all of one kind). The barley that has escaped being "laid" by the recent storms, still holds its bearded ears erect. In Scotland, I gather, they mostly cut it at this stage. At Silford it is never cut until the ears have drooped well over, or "knuckled right down" as Sam puts it. The weather has done a great deal of damage. But quite a few fields look as though they could pass the test for "hat" barley, as a good crop was known round about Holkham a hundred and fifty years ago, when the farmer would hurl his hat on to the standing corn to see what happened. If the hat rested on the surface, all was well. But if it fell to the ground, the crop was poor. The maltsters of those days had an equally simple test to determine the malting qualities of a sample. They would "swim" the grain in water. Good malting barley would keep afloat. The corn that sank was just barley.

The partridge and pheasant families have had a difficult season. Time after time, when driving through the lanes this morning, I slow down to let some dash to the fence, but the party seldom contains more than two youngsters. In the kitchen garden the weather has discouraged several of my "uncommon vegetables" out of existence. But the mountain orachs, which have sprung up to a height of five feet or more, are decorative patches of deep crimson, and their leaves are equally effective in salads. While another touch of colour is provided by the purple-podded peas. These last have a sweet, slightly broad-beanish flavour, and the added advantage that the birds leave the pods alone. Have also been much amused by the immunity (so far) of the white currants on the bush that grows beside a red-currant on one of the walls at the back of the house, as it appears that the sharp-beaked little thieves have taken them for unripe red ones.

JULY 21   Norah says may she have my fair button biscuit recipe, please? For these, mix together 8 oz. flour and 8 oz. sugar, rub in 6 oz. butter or margarine, mix with one egg, roll out as thin as possible, cut in rounds, and cook in medium oven about ten minutes. Equally palatable biscuits can be made by adding lemon juice, cinnamon, ginger, or other ground spices, currants, or sultanas, or substituting dry cocoa to taste for some of the flour.

JULY 22   Hive inspection yesterday afternoon starts in sunny weather. But before I lift a roof off the atmosphere becomes heavy and threatening, and it's quickly obvious that the bees have had an advance met. report, for everybody seems to be at home, and as fractious as teething babies. Hive II is our first objective, when almost at once we come on the queen cell left by Mr. Chelford looking exactly as he left it. Is she dead inside? Is she about to come out? Can she be out, and somebody have pushed the door shut? We can't guess at the answers to any of these questions. Nor can we see a virgin queen among the workers (though that is no guarantee that she isn't there, of course). Meanwhile, everybody is getting crosser and crosser, and I have been stung three times on the fingers of my right hand, and once on my left. So I hurriedly replace the last frame, and set back the roof. We ought next to remove the empty super box from below Hive I. But the air is thick with angry bees. And whilst I hesitate, Our Man yelps that two are inside his veil, and hares off down the path. I grab the tools and streak after him, followed by what seems to be a battalion of bees, and am just in time to stop him tearing off his veil to give the new attackers a chance. Presently we are in the kitchen determining the extent of the damage (he has one sting on his ear and another on the top of his head, plus one on the leg from an infuriated guard bee which has penetrated right through his flannel trousers), applying T.C.P., and imbibing cups of tea. As this has been the end of the matter with previous stings, we then scatter on our several chores, Our Man to weed the new currant bushes on the pightle over the road, whilst I take cups of tea to the currant pickers at the end of the tennis lawn, and collect any full baskets for tipping into trays and weighing ready for the fruit lorry.

At two-thirty this morning am awakened by burning right hand, and find it's swollen to about four times its usual size, and aches and itches abominably. Apply one thing after another, without the least alleviation, and wonder how Our Man is getting on. At seven his wife appears to say he's got a face like mumps, he feels "queer", and won't be at work this morning. Offer to ring their doctor, but she doesn't want to disturb him if possible. So ring up Mr. Partridge instead. No doctor can do a thing about the swelling, says he, which will last from two to three days. (One man he knew couldn't see out of his eyes, but he was all right at the end of that time. And he himself has had a leg like a horse.) The only thing for which you want a doctor, he adds cheerfully, is if the patient collapses. Do not like to scare the patient's wife unduly. But Our Man so uncomplaining in ordinary way, that am distinctly worried by his admitting to "queer". So give his wife two Veganin tablets, and say let me know by half-past eight how he feels then, and I'll ring up the doctor if necessary. Happily it isn't. But it has now painfully dawned on both of us that we are not immune to bee-poison, as we had smugly imagined . . . we merely haven't received the full charge before. And I spend half an hour and a cake of soap getting off my too-tight wedding ring ready to despatch to the jeweller's for enlarging (a job I have been putting off for months), as do not like to think what would have happened if the left-hand sting, which was on my ring finger, had blown up as well.

JULY 25   Have at last tracked down some real flan rings. Also a cake ring. Use the former at once, and fill the cooked pastry case with uncooked red and white currants, first sprinkling the case with sugar, adding fruit, then sugaring again. (Other fresh fruits are more suitable, no doubt. But currants look so very attractive raw, and so very squashed and run-over looking when cooked.) The cake ring offers several alternatives. A Victoria sandwich mixture . . . two eggs and their weight in sugar, flour, and margarine, made by creaming margarine and sugar, then adding alternate small doses of beaten egg and flour . . . can be baked in it, and the centre filled with raspberries, sliced peaches, etc. Or the cake can be iced, and extra decoration provided by standing a small vase of flowers in the centre. The ring can also be used for fruit jellies, or meat, or vegetables in aspic (left-over peas, carrots and new potatoes can be used to advantage in this way), served with salad in the centre. No doubt penny-plain food is just as good for us as tuppence-coloured, but the eye functions at meals as well as the digestive organs, and an attractive appearance makes a world of difference.

July 27   How I wish, and not for the first time, that Nature, when bestowing curls on both my female parent and child, hadn't forgotten all about me. Emerged from hairdresser's last week looking distinctly *soignée*. But an enforced three hours in a bee-veil immediately on return home not only reduces hair-set to shambles, but reveals horrid fact that hair cut has been too drastic, and base of coiffure is now a wispy fringe of curlless ends. After which hair-style rapidly degenerates into that known in family as "old English sheepdog". Cannot bear the thought of facing guests at Eve's coming-of-age party in this state, and cannot possibly spare time for rehabilitation visit to hairdressers. I suppose he wouldn't care to call in at some chemists or similar when he's out, and see if he can buy a home perm. set, then lend me a hand with it, I suggest to Adam at one point. He'll try anything once, replies Adam gallantly. So Operation Home-Perm launched to-day. Sundry hitches, technical and otherwise, soon occur, especially as my risible faculties rapidly get out of control, when Adam's patience shows signs of becoming dangerously exhausted, and is not revived when I beg him to imagine that he's getting Hepsibah and Hazel ready for a show, think how he'd linger over them, and what beautiful curls he can put in their tails after this. Spend most of evening with head swathed in elderly towel, dealing with arrears of correspondence. But am relieved to find operation has gone off WELL, as Ben would say, and I can abandon earlier idea of receiving guests clad in medieval coif.

JULY 28   All (comparatively) quiet on the bee front, and to-day's manipulation over in record time, with decidedly less wear and tear on feelings of all concerned. Though discover later in afternoon that guard bees do not care for a hoe cautiously hooked round from behind the hives to remove weeds growing in front, and that future gestures of this kind should be made in full armour, and not when wearing a short-sleeved blouse. In spite of this and earlier incidents, however, am rapidly becoming fascinated with the whole business, and am reading all available literature. Loudly quote excerpt from one book that says what a fine partnership can be achieved if both husband and wife are keen. Fail signally, however, to sell this idea to Adam, who reiterates that he never could stand things that went buzz, and after seeing what's been happening to me lately, he cares even less for them. Pigs for him every time.

AUGUST 1   Shops have lately been brimming with all sorts of nuts ready shelled for use. Gaze wistfully from time to time at the walnuts. But no conscientious housewife with a young sackful of last year's on top of the kitchen-cupboard, and a pair of nutcrackers in the silver basket would dare to buy any. Nor do I, but wonder loudly and often this morning how professional cracker manages to get them out in such neat, unmarred halves. Mine, as usual, split into all shapes and sizes. If a rolling pin is run over the fragments, however, they can be used in several ways. Beaten into three ounces of finely grated cheese and two ounces of margarine, they make a good sandwich filling or top dressing for cheese biscuits. Beaten into three ounces of icing sugar and two ounces margarine, plus a little warm water or lemon juice, they help to enliven a cake filling. By themselves they can always be included in a plain or fruit cake mixture, and they are the mainstay of walnut layer cake. This takes three eggs, their weight in castor sugar, flour, and butter (margarine), a small teaspoon of baking powder, and a dessertspoon of milk. Beat to a smooth batter, bake (preferably in a square tin) in a moderate oven for about an hour. Leave twenty-four hours, then cut in halves, fill with walnut cream mixture already mentioned, brush outside of cake with warm apricot jam, then sprinkle with the rolled walnuts, using halves as extra decoration for the top. Or the jam and rolled nuts can be used on the sides only, and the top of the cake spread with white icing ($\frac{1}{2}$ lb. icing sugar, white of one egg, lemon juice), and decorated with halved walnuts.

AUGUST 2   At least there is one thing constant about our ever-changing weather, and that is its pre-eminence as a topic of conversation. (Am willing to wager that if Mr. Gallup took a poll, the weather would be well and truly at the top of it.) To be, or not to be, fine for the August holiday, is now the query uppermost in many people's minds, ours included, as Eve's party is scheduled for the beginning of it. Am convinced that if any enterprising individual could devise a suitable canopy held aloft by barrage balloons, he would be canonised by the givers of garden fêtes, cricket matches, tennis parties, and other open-air entertainments. And couldn't our inventors, instead of concentrating on bigger and better ways of blasting us into eternity, think of something on the lines of F.I.D.O., which could be turned on to wet cornfields to dry the grain in ear. Driving into Norwich this morning the streaming landscape was dotted with sheeted binders and combine-harvesters, but singularly devoid of human figures except for an occasional sack-caped man slashing mournfully at an overgrown fence. August, if it doesn't rapidly improve, is in a fair way to becoming as wet as July has been. The official county rainfall figure for July, I see, is 4.67 inches. My rain gauge, however, has gone nearly an inch better (or worse), the month's total being 5.46 inches, with 18.6 inches for the first seven months of this year: some three inches over Norfolk's average, which itself is well above normal. Evidently we are in a rainbelt. Should like to know how much of this is attributable to the lie of the land, and how much to the fact that we are in a well-wooded area.

AUGUST 3   Eve retrieved from station, suffering somewhat from final typhoid injections, but not from actual plague, praise be. Having obtained both her A and B gliding certificates, is now bent on obtaining her C, and determined on becoming a first-class glider pilot. Her conversation bristling with references to centrifugal force, lenticular clouds, wind variations, and (to a parent) quite horrifying stories beginning "Suddenly the cable parted when I was four hundred feet up, and I nose-dived on to the runway". And how far off is Cambridge, as that's the nearest gliding club, she's afraid. Sixty-nine miles? Perhaps that is a bit far. Am I sure that Norwich hasn't started up again? Then I could come and watch. Or have a shot myself. (I might, at that. Though I have some outsize doubts.)

AUGUST 5 and Eve's coming-of-age party. Yesterday's weather was faultless, of course. This morning's sky blotted out with low cloud, William Cat exhibits a most untimely tendency to wash over his ears (said to be a certain sign of impending deluges), while Dilys reiterates at intervals that she always brings bad weather, and isn't that a spot of rain she feels now? Remind myself that anything can happen in the weather line in these parts, and a bad morning often precedes a radiant evening, the while I dash madly round on a thousand last-minute jobs, including the putting up of extra camp-beds and earmarking sofas, as telephone and telegrams announce that sundry uncertain long-distance guests can get down to Norfolk after all. Happily, although the sun remains aloof, so do the threatened downpours, by six it is fair and warm, by half-past Our Man has given up the unequal struggle to park cars in the spots we have thought out, and is letting them pile up as they please, and Roger Winterton who has come determined to tell me that the bees are swarming, has been firmly dealt with by Felicity before he can put this amiable plan into action, luckily, as I should certainly have abandoned the party at his first words, and rushed for the kitchen garden. As usual the evening races by with no time for me to indulge in the leisurely gossips I enjoy when a guest elsewhere. Eve's grandfather proposes her health, the birthday cake is cut, and I wonder in a maternal way what waits for her in the years ahead. But not for long, as some of the guests are staying on for charades and a buffet supper, the former producing a surprising amount of talent and fun.

AUGUST 6 The Wintertons coming round to suggest a picnic at Burnham Overy Staithe, we all set off directly after lunch, complete with bathing suits and towels, arriving just as thunderstorm breaks. This clears, but water cold and tide some way out, which means the long-drawn-out ordeal of walking in, instead of a clean, quick dive, so basely cry off a bathe myself. So do Felicity, Madge and Terence, so we gossip happily whilst the braver elements court frostbite. Conversation turns on old glass, when I say I'd love to meet one of those people whose laugh shatters glasses, though not in my house. Whereupon Madge retails her sister Bridget's experience when in India. Her pet wineglasses were on the table when a rather loud-voiced woman was present, and as the latter was holding forth, one glass suddenly shivered into fragments. The next time the L.V.W. called, the same thing occurred. After that, the approach of the lady in question was the signal for the family to race for the glasses and hurriedly remove them to a safe and distant spot before the visitor was allowed over the doorstep. Presently the bathers return, we pool our teas, and Felicity produces a tin packed with the most delightful ginger biscuits. Then she pounces on a bottle of water to dilute some lemonade, when either we have a relative of Bridget's acquaintance in the party, or gremlins are about, as the bottom of the bottle immediately drops out, deluging Felicity, and flooding the biscuit tin. Was lucky enough to have taken a biscuit just in time, however, and Felicity gives me the recipe to make up at home. This takes $\frac{1}{2}$ lb. self-raising flour, 4 oz. each margarine and sugar, one level dessertspoon bicarbonate of soda, two level teaspoons ground ginger, two tablespoons golden syrup, and pinch of salt. Method is to melt margarine and syrup in saucepan, then add mixed dry ingredients. Roll into small balls (each about one teaspoonful) with floured fingers, space out on flat tin, bake in medium oven ten minutes. Store in tin when cool. This makes about three dozen biscuits approximately two inches across.

AUGUST 10   Our built-in cupboards being as far from happening as ever, and Eve bent on going to a furniture sale, decide that second-hand wardrobe would probably be a good deal more expeditious, not to say cheaper, so four of us, plus picnic impedimenta, cram into small car, and set course for auction at Wrettonham Hall. Have already, on view day, marked several unnecessary items, and both Felicity and I, egged on by our offspring, pencil-tick some more in catalogue on arrival, sternly reminding one another the while that we're here only for one wardrobe and the fun of the thing, and we simply mustn't allow ourselves to be carried away. Garden seat on which I have half an eye goes for quite five times my ceiling price. So does the set of saws for which I bid, remembering that Adam says I will turn up the teeth whenever I use ours. Then we squeeze into the marquee with Marigold and Simon, when I emerge for lunch the owner of an attractive Japanese teaset, and full of resolves not to make another bid until Lot 300 (Handsome mahogany gent's wardrobe) is reached. Like so many good resolutions this soon collapses, and at the close of play Felicity finds herself the possessor of a large copper saucepan, and two lots of doubtful watercolours for which she has given five shillings and seven shillings respectively as she wants their frames, while I have acquired three aquatints of battleships in action and an enchanting trayful of junk which has something for everybody on it, not excepting the absent Adam and William Cat. It is only by the grace of providence that our collection doesn't include an oak dresser, a chest of drawers, sundry wheel-backed and arm chairs, and a carved chest. And needless to say we haven't been able to afford the wardrobe, and are now faced with the task of removing our loot. Marigold and Simon accompany us to the car, and pack us in to the roof, when we cautiously drive off, every pothole making me wince in anguish for my teaset. But everything survives the homeward journey, the teaset is suitably christened forthwith, and the day voted a great success by all. Think it as well to revert at once to idea of built-in cupboards, however, as can see these will prove considerably cheaper after all.

AUGUST 11 "We must get some sea-lavender," says Eve. So as Adam is going to Wells, we go, too. Presently we are walking past the whelk houses, which smell strongly of tar (and less salubrious things), out along the sea wall, and down on to the mud-flats beyond. The tide is in, filling the creeks waisthigh and more, washing over emerald lawns of samphire, "the asparagus of the sea", and littering them with the corpses of tiny pale crabs, and fragments of seaweed. Beyond the weathered grey wooden bridge out on the flats, acres of sea-lavender make a purple lake which melts into the cloud banks piled high against the horizon, and flings the faintest of indigo shadows up into the almost colourless sky. A warm wind is blowing in from the sea, ridden by an occasional gull or two, which drops down into the creeks, or rests for a moment or two on the surface of the small shallow pools whose mud floors are seamed and cracked like crazy paving. Now and again one utters a thin eerie wailing cry more like a peewit or a lost soul. Or a couple start a raucous quarrel over some tit-bit cast up by the tide. But such sounds seem only to deepen the silence, not destroy it. The peace, the absence of strain and fret, is almost tangible. The old harbour town, less than half a mile behind us, might be leagues away.

We splash and slip on the drowned paths, gathering handfuls of samphire, and the frail-looking bluey-mauve blossomed stalks, lured on and on by the better one that always grows two yards ahead, until our baskets are spilling over. Then we paddle back to the spot where we dropped our sandals. And as I take one last look at that rolling stretch of purple-blue, once again I think how much more fortunate is the artist than the writer. Each is for ever trying to capture, and to convey to others, the thing he sees. But whereas one works in the medium of colour, with its instantaneous appeal to the eye, the other struggles with words which so often stubbornly refuse to assume the hue he means, and to the eye alone, in any case, nothing but blotches of ink on clean white paper.

AUGUST 16 Fourteen days sounds quite a time when it lies ahead. But as always, leave has gone with the velocity of a jet-propelled aircraft. And trying to cram into it at least six times the amount of goings on that a fortnight can comfortably hold, has left us all breathless, and me suffering badly from mental indigestion. How I wanted time to stop and stare at the view of the coastline inland from Blakeney Point, to say nothing of preferring to bathe when the tide was farther in, to brood over the varying shades of purple on Kelling Heath, which no out-apiarist seems to have pounced upon yet for his bees (or is it that I have had no time to notice hives about the heather?) . . . to linger in the little shell museum in Glandford church-yard, which Eve hadn't seen before, and whose contents she longed to take home. And I have hardly spoken to Brandy, though he has spent twelve days on the premises, contrived to let out the baby pigs, left hoof-prints all over the drive, and a bottle of my salad vinegar has been purloined for running repairs to his coat. Northern Ireland seems a million miles away. And cannot say that I'm really sorry that, in view of the news from Korea and Eve's uncertainty about career-plans, we've decided to cancel the cabin reserved for her on the *Durban Castle* for October, 1951, and think about her Kenya visit another year.

Do some necessary shopping after putting Eve on train, purchases including some root ginger for marrow jam. For this, cut marrow into small cubes, put into basin with equal weight of sugar, and to each pound of marrow add half an ounce of finely chopped ginger, and (or) juice and rind of half a lemon. Add a few chillies, allow to stand twenty-four hours, then put into preserving pan and boil 45–60 minutes, when the marrow should be transparent, and should set when put on a plate. (Once, in my childhood, the family cook overboiled the jam, when it turned into the most appetising ginger toffee. But this, in spite of our pleas, was never allowed to happen again.) Am stuffing another marrow with sausage meat and various left-over meat and vegetable scraps, well-seasoned, wrapping it up in well-greased paper, putting it into a meat tin, and baking it in a medium oven, basting from time to time until cooked, as this way it has a better flavour than when steamed or boiled.

AUGUST 18   Like the lemmings of Norway, who are said to be impelled at certain seasons to swim out to a long-vanished island, my mind is full of a restless unease: and although cornfields are no longer a concern of mine, and I have more than enough to keep me busy at home, I long to be in the harvest fields. Those who are, however, are none too pleased, as the weather has followed the pattern set by June and July, and work is constantly being delayed or held up.

"No winter, no summer," quotes Ben dismally. "I knew how it would be. We'll hatta steal the corn how and where we can."

"We don't never get the summers we used to have now," mourns Sam. "That's all along a' all these engines, and this yere beggaring about with the clocks."

"There's no accounting for harvest weather," asserts Walter. "I've knowed nigh on sixty harvests, and never see two alike."

Recently I was lent some old "field" books relating to land farmed by a family connection in North Norfolk, and covering the years 1812–27 and 1852–86. I amused myself by tabulating the harvest dates and weather, to see if I could light on a formula for prophecy. But Walter is right, of course. In the fifty-one harvests recorded, no two cover exactly the same period of time, only two or three start on the same date, and the weather varies for each one. Some started late: both 1812 and 1816 began in September, and two or three in the second period at the very end of August. Several began in July. But neither a late nor an early start ensured any particular weather, for 1812 was over and done with on September 23rd, whilst 1822, starting on July 23rd, dragged on until September 25th. And more than one that made a promising beginning ended in October. 1869 was the earliest of all, beginning on July 17th, "before the turnips were up", and finishing August 8th. It might have ended even sooner but for the local fair on July 26th, for the weather was good, with only a few showers. But the entry concludes: "Did not give the men any dinner because they left their work to go to the fair."

Can one augur from one year's harvest weather what the next may be? Definitely no. Even when classifying the fifty-one harvests on the broadest of lines as good, bad, and indifferent, no pattern or rhythm emerges. The 1812–27 period produces seven of the first, four bad, and five mixed. But the thirty-five in the second period have a much higher proportion of bad and mixed seasons, the figures here being twelve good, the same number of bad, and eleven mixed. And some records from another source covering the intermediate years suggest a half and half business, with the scales tipping in favour of fickle weather, good and bad, fickle and tedious, following one another, or grouped together, without the least rhyme or reason.

The Comet year, 1858, features as The "quickest I ever remember, the days being very fine and very long, only two showers falling during the time". But the years on either side were "a very fickle time", with much wet, and a good deal of sprouted and blackened corn. The only run of good weather occurs from 1867 to 1871, though these were not entirely unallayed, '67 having a showery final week, and '71 some troublesome winds. '68 and '69, however, had hardly a shower, the latter being noteworthy, too, for the first use on the farm of reaping machines which "cut 415 out of the 509 acres, and did it beautifully". Whilst '70, beginning August 3rd and finishing August 18th, is recorded as "the shortest harvest I ever remember, and I fear, one of the shortest crops I ever had".

The longest run of really bad harvest weather is 1877–9, though if mixed is added to bad the time is extended, for only three rank in the good class in the years 1872–86. 1872 had ten beautiful days in the middle, but "fickle and tedious" weather at both ends. '73 was "catchy". '74 a very wet first week, with winds that blew the ears off the ripe barley, before it could be cut. '76 and '77 were "a very fickle and trying time". '78 was "constantly interrupted by rain". '79 was to be known as the most disastrous harvest in living memory throughout the country, the cold wet weather prolonging harvest into October, with corn in some parts still out at Christmas. The writer of the records, however, appears to have fared better than many, for though bad weather beforehand had laid the corn so badly that much of the wheat and all the barley had to be cut by hand, there were ten days when he was able to secure the wheat "in excellent trim", and most of his barley before "the weather broke, and took three weeks to do three days' work". '80 produced heavy rains but also "a splendid fortnight". '81 began hot, then turned cold and wet "the men very patient and obliging, notwithstanding the long time they were up". '82 was fine then "catchy". '83 saw all the corn in without rain except the last field of barley, which lay about while the rain poured down for thirty-six hours. But '84 was remarkable, "the most splendid harvest I ever remember", the corn "of excellent quality, and in splendid condition". The wheat was estimated at eleven coombs an acre, barley the same, oats eighteen coombs (though these were not record yields). '85 was showery, but good on the whole. '86 "rains fell at short intervals during the whole harvest".

There were three old account and labour books, too. Wheat prices touch forty-two shillings the coomb, or sack (1853), and sink to eighteen and threepence (1852) and nineteen and six (1880), but mostly they range between twenty and thirty shillings. Barley was twenty-seven shillings a coomb in 1852, thirteen and six in 1882, the average being nineteen to twenty-one shillings. Harvest men were hired in May or June, receiving a shilling as hiring money (a custom not discontinued until 1903). During the sixties men were paid two shillings a day, and six pounds to six pounds ten for harvest, the pitchers, stacker, and "Lord of the Harvest" receiving an extra half-crown. When the work was put out, wheat was cut, tied, and shocked, for seven shillings an acre. Thatching was tenpence a yard. Income tax was only a few pence in the pound.

AUGUST 22   The whole place very quiet after Eve's departure, Adam is away, and the weather is sleepy and encouraging of anything but energy and hard work. Am evidently not alone in feeling like this. William Cat shows no disposition to play, or follow me about, but sinks slothfully to sleep under the nearest shady bush. The two cockerels that survived the great party slaughter sit humped with heads under their wings. Hazel and Hepsibah, moved yesterday into a pen that enfolds a third of a lawn scheduled for digging up and reseeding, are not ripping and tearing up the turf in anything like their usual style, but spend the greater part of the daylight hours placidly dozing in the shelter at one corner of the pen. Tell them loudly at intervals that exercise is good for expectant mothers, and that there are several more plots awaiting their attention. But cannot feel that these exhortations are having much effect, and am hoping for some more enlivening weather. The only creatures that have been really busy are the spotted woodpecker who has discovered the sunflowers planted for my future fowls (and has practically stripped them of seeds) and an unidentified marauder who is pecking the outdoor tomatoes to pieces before they are ripe.

$$\underline{\qquad\qquad} \ \textbf{13} \ \underline{\qquad\qquad}$$

AUGUST 24 Have heard it said that everyone should take up a new hobby, or try something fresh, each year, and think this an excellent idea. But have rather overdone it in my own case, and started on so many new things within the last twelve months that am constantly being confronted with my appalling ignorance of each, and seem to spend half my time with a text-book in one hand and the necessary tools in the other, trying wildly to keep two inches ahead of catastrophe. Up till now I have regarded our venture in early chrysanthemums as a comparatively restful occupation, and have spent uncounted hours sitting on a stool removing side-shoots and disbudding, thinking my own thoughts the while, with no more untoward incident than an occasional slipping fingernail removing the crown bud as well, when my mental life becomes a trifle too absorbing. Now, all at once, the miniature green forest is alive with colourful blooms, boxes arrive in shoals from flower salesmen, and this morning finds me frantically consulting the Ministry bulletin for packing instructions, and wishing I'd had the sense to watch someone else at it first. The stalks seem as omnipresent as a shy man's feet and hands at his first party. And obviously nobody has yet contrived to breed crease-resisting petals. Also I manage to tear the skin off at least one finger on nails protruding from the boxes. At last they are on the train, and I return home, keeping my fingers crossed, and trying to shut out visions of radishes sent to Eve some weeks back, which reached their destination a mass of slimy leaves.

AUGUST 25 Norah asks if I've got the Booton cookie recipe yet. If so, may she have it? I have, and send it on forthwith. Line tartlet tins with pastry, add a dab of jam, then cover with a teaspoonful of the mixture, and bake in moderate oven round about twenty minutes. The mixture is composed of equal quantities sugar and desiccated coconut stirred into a beaten egg, and I find that a medium-sized egg absorbs approximately $2\frac{1}{2}$ oz. of each. It also makes a very good flan filling (serve with more desiccated coconut sprinkled on top). Have also acquired another cookie recipe, which can be flavoured with coconut or chopped nuts, fruit, spices, etc., instead. This takes 4 oz. flour, 2 oz. sugar, half-teaspoon bicarbonate of soda, pinch salt, and the desired flavouring, 2 oz. butter (margarine), one tablespoon golden syrup. Melt margarine and syrup in a saucepan, pour over the dry ingredients, form into small balls, place well apart on slightly greased tin, and bake in moderate oven for fifteen minutes.

AUGUST 27   Have been meaning to explore the State apartments at Blickling Hall ever since they were first open to the public, but not until this afternoon do I actually get there. Angela, James and I cause a minor stir by being admitted free on flourishing our Trust membership cards. (If this incident leads to a few more people joining the National Trust, and thereby supporting a most worthwhile cause, feel we shall certainly have done our good deed for to-day.) Inside we form part of the human stream that flows steadily through the Long Gallery, and eddies around the Peter the Great room (which takes its name from the eighteenth-century tapestry representing that monarch at the battle of Poltawa, presented by the Empress Catherine to Lord Buckinghamshire when Ambassador to St. Petersburg), the State bedroom with its royal bed in readiness for George II (and amongst other treasures a chest-of-drawers we long to abduct), and finally the ante-room, gallery and south drawing-room. Each has its own peculiar beauties and features of interest. But as usual, my ill-disciplined mind fastens on some of the more trivial details, such as the self-conscious cat depicted on the fine Jacobean plaster ceiling of the Long Gallery. A bird clamped in its jaws, presumably it is meant to look ferocious, but manages to give the impression that the bird is perfectly happy, and the pair are posing especially for a photograph to be reproduced in a pet magazine over the caption "Good Friends", or similar. Whilst the fragment of Anne Boleyn's bedspread underlines the uncomfortable truth that stone, wood, and even a piece of perishable fabric outlast for centuries their human owners. The grounds are lovely as ever, and make one eternally grateful to such bodies as the Trust. Nowadays few can afford to live in "stately homes". Fewer want to do so. But how satisfying it is to roam about in their environs once in a while.

Return home to a belated tea full of these and similar leisurely thoughts, to await arrival of series of evening visitors. Just as the first batch drive through the gateway, Hazel undermines the pig-netting and gallops through the bushes on to the tennis lawn. Guests, expecting polite conversation indoors, find themselves joining in pig hunt outside. It proves to be quite impossible to push Hazel back the way she came out, half the wire has to be dislocated to get her in (what time it is all we can do to prevent Hepsibah escaping), and no sooner do we think that the incident is closed, than she immediately uproots another section, and is half-way down the drive before anyone can head her off. More destapling and restapling of netting follows, holes are dug and extra posts set in. But if it occurs again, can see us buying pig-harness, and tethering her out like a bull.

AUGUST 29   Bought two boxes of peaches to-day, made peeling easy by first dropping them into a basin of boiling water for one minute, then bottled one lot in halves and the other in slices in syrup made at rate of one pint water to half-pound golden syrup, for which I have been hoarding tins of the latter. Am waiting for the Laxton Superb variety to ripen before bottling any pears, but am asked by earlier pear-bottlers how to prevent the fruit discolouring after peeling. The best way is to use a silver or stainless knife for peeling, etc., then at once drop fruit either into a weak brine ($\frac{1}{2}$ oz. salt to two pints water), or first drop them into a basin of warm water and then into one of syrup. If brine is used, wash fruit well in cold water before packing in bottles. A little sherry added to the bottling syrup improves the flavour of the pears.

SEPTEMBER 1   Spend highly entertaining evening as one of team in the "Town Forum" that Fakenham has included in its enterprising Fair Week. The debate ranges over juvenile delinquency, co-education, Service pay (the cheers that greet my suggestion that higher pay is all very well, but as Napoleon said, an army marches on its stomach, and I think more would be achieved if authority put somebody who could cook into the cookhouse, makes me sure that half the audience at least are ex-Service!), the Welfare State, featherbeds for farmers (a new slant on this last being offered by the speaker who recently spent some uncomfortable nights on one such couch), the rival attractions of Jane Austen and Jane of the cartoon strip, Victorian manners, and the person who has done most for humanity in the last hundred years. Only hope the audience enjoyed it as much as I did.

SEPTEMBER 4   Operation Potato-Lifting launched this morning, with all the moil and labour inseparable from a small acreage and inadequate tools. Console ourselves with the thought that even if we owned a spinner, we couldn't use one, as two-thirds of our crop is growing between rows of currant bushes. And thank our guardian angel that two of the family's employees (nominally on holiday, like Adam!) have nobly consented to aid us with the digging, while the currant pickers are willing to try their hands at potato picking and riddling. The weather, too, decides to be helpful in spite of the official forecasts. And something like a quarter of the crop is safely up and housed in the garage before we leave off. Our satisfaction at this, however, is considerably diminished by a few calculations based on the estimated total tonnage, the man and woman hours involved in harvesting it, plus such inescapable items as seed, planting time and labour, cultivations, and so on, all of which suggest that we'll be incredibly lucky if we break even.

Potatoes, too, as we have recently discovered, are hedged about with a positive Great Wall of China in the way of restrictions. It appears that we need a permit to feed them to our pigs, though this is the primary purpose for which we planted them. We may sell up to one ton for human consumption, in certain circumstances. But if we wish to sell more, except to the Ministry (in which case they may still be cumbering our premises until next May or June), we must have a licence, which is unlikely to be granted us. Altogether it looks as if next year we should do a great deal better to buy our pig potatoes, plant some less complicated crop like cabbages, and give ourselves time to sit luxuriously in deckchairs, doing nothing more strenuous than admire the view.

SEPTEMBER 7   "September, blow soft, till fruit be in loft", petitions Thomas Tusser in his *Five Hundred Points of Good Husbandry*. Last night's gale has sent apples flying, torn leaves and branches from every tree, flattened the tall crimson spikes of mountain orach in the kitchen garden, precipitated soot and lumps of mortar down chimneys, and blown us straight from the ragged remnants of our summer into an almost wintry autumn. Have had twenty-seven points of rain during the dark hours as well, but the ground isn't nearly as wet as we feared, and the potato offensive continues. Atmosphere is so cool that we cannot face a salad meal, however, so have baked stuffed potatoes instead. Scrub and bake these in their skins as usual, and when cooked halve them, scoop out middles, tip this into basin, and arrange empty skins on dish, with a little margarine or dripping spread inside. Then add to potato in basin some finely grated cheese, coarsely grated raw cucumber, finely chopped parsley, salt, and a little very finely chopped chilies, mix thoroughly with a fork, and fill the potato skins. Minced left-over ham, meat scraps, sausage meat (first cooked with a little chopped onion and sage), all make useful fillings. And once in a while, try a little curry powder added to the seasoning.

SEPTEMBER 12   Operation Potato now replaced by Operation Pigstye, Adam flying from one purveyor of derelict airfield scrap to another to purchase corrugated iron sheets which he and Our Man then bolt to posts for pen sides to our new concrete yard floors. Ideas of any holiday in the conventional sense recede still further as I bring up the rear, applying bitumen paint impartially to face, fingers, and rusty surfaces of iron. And though bound to admit that one pen finished so far looks much more professional than earlier wire-netting and straw partitions, question (though not in front of Adam!) whether the latter wouldn't have served our turn for the next twelve months, whilst we indulged in a little private life.

SEPTEMBER 14   Pig pens left to Our Man to-day, while we set off in holiday mood for Oxborough, where the Norwich Arts Federation is holding its summer school. The day is dullish, but promises sunshine later, a promise to be amply fulfilled. After harvest the countryside has the serene air of purpose achieved. A lovely peace informs the landscape. We are nearing Necton when suddenly there is a roar of aero engines immediately behind and to our left, followed by a hideous explosion in front of us, just over the wire fence of the adjacent field. Flames and smoke soar into the air, bullets crackle, and the road between us and two oncoming lorries is strewn with burning fragments. Four seconds later, twenty yards more, and we and the lorries would have lain below the wreckage. But this thought does not occur to us until a long time afterwards. Now, for one horrified second, we sit unmoving, unable to believe our eyes. The next we are in the field with the lorry-drivers to see if there is any hope of dragging out the pilot. But none of us can get within reach. And it is appallingly obvious that it is already too late, and that there is absolutely nothing we can do but to try helplessly to curb our imaginations. As we leave behind us the gathering crowd and the crumbling pyre of some parents' proud hopes, I have a cowardly longing to wire Eve, who is flying part of the way home next week, and beg her to stay on the ground. But we cannot keep our children in cages, and so must bear with what fortitude we can these constant wrenchings of the heart.

Oxborough Hall, that lovely example of late fifteenth-century architecture (said to resemble both Queen's College, Cambridge, and Hampton Court), to-day sunning itself among green lawns, gives an equally peaceful first impression. But Mr. John Saltmarsh quickly has us back in the turbulent period during which it was built, and its watch towers, arrow-slits, the holes through which boiling oil can be poured, and the waters of its moat, were far from being objects of curiosity and archaeological interest. Sir Henry Hake considerably enlarges our knowledge of fifteenth-century and other portraits and their painters. The Tudor singers re-create for us songs that the originals of the family portraits looking down as they sing must often have heard in life. And a tour of the house unrolls the centuries before us, the hangings of the State bed (the work of Mary Queen of Scots), giving rise to much speculation as to how much our ancestors knew of the fauna and flora of far-off continents . . . much more than we are apt to credit them with, undoubtedly, in this as in other fields. Have always loved Oxborough Church, so in a cowardly way refrained from visiting it this time (could see all and more than I wanted of the damage caused when its tower fell in 1948, from the road as we came along) and walked about the gardens instead.

Adam delighted to see that weeds are to be found in plenty here, too. But as one of the gardeners rightly said, to hoe is only to transplant them, it's been a real weed year.

SEPTEMBER 15   Dull weather, plus the activities of spotted woodpeckers and their friends, having sabotaged my plans of growing enough outdoor tomatoes for all necessary bottling, buy some greenhouse grown ones, and spend morning at work peeling, halving, packing into jars, adding teaspoon of salt to each jar, then on with tops and rubber rings, and sterilising. Then take another look at array of green tomatoes in garden. Some of these will be packed away in newspaper in a kitchen drawer to ripen, unpecked, later. Eve having sent me some sugar, I have other plans for the remainder. A family recipe for green tomato jam uses $\frac{3}{4}$ lb. sugar, juice and finely grated peel of one lemon (or 1 oz. of finely grated ginger) to each pound of tomatoes, the method being to wash tomatoes, slice, remove hard core and some of pips, add sugar, etc., and boil to setting point. My marmalade store being low, I think of trying the green tomato recipe acquired from Anthea. For this, wash and slice 3 lb. tomatoes, put into basin in layers with $2\frac{1}{4}$ lb. sugar, leave twenty-four hours. Turn into pan with juice and grated rind of one orange and two lemons, and boil to setting point (about $1\frac{1}{2}$ hours), stirring frequently.

SEPTEMBER 18   Have often wanted to take a motor tour into the blue as it were, turning at random down any lane that looks inviting, just to see where it takes me. But feel that Simon's idea of a "mystery trip", on which he recently took his family, is much more enterprising and capable of endless surprises, to say nothing of keeping the younger members of the party alert and interested throughout. "Take the first turn left after passing a woman on a bicycle, second right the moment you see a solitary pedestrian. Turn back if you meet a girl in a red hat or somebody pushing a pram, forking left at the next cross-roads. But turn right and right again should you at any time encounter a policeman." The variations are endless, and compiling those for a suitable trip offers distinct possibilities for a new parlour game, while their carrying out provides an entertaining afternoon, the cost of which is unlikely to exceed that of a visit to the cinema.

SEPTEMBER 21   Half a hundred house martins held a conference on the electricity wires running from
house to stables this morning. And to-night the mud-scale nests
outside our bedroom windows are deserted, and silence reigns
under the eaves for the first time in months, to the vast disgust
of William Cat, who has spent endless hours on the window-sills,
hoping to lay a paw on some unwary aeronaut, and cannot credit
that he has lost his chance for this year, at all events. Michaelmas
daisies, sure harbingers of autumn, are out in increasing numbers.
Mornings are appreciably darker, afternoons shorter. A fire to sit
by in the evening is not yet a vital necessity, but without it
somehow the room seems bleak, the hearth curiously desolate.
Are we sorry to say farewell to summer? Yes and no. One more
behind us is a sobering thought. Otherwise this year the ayes are
thoroughly outnumbered. Now at last we shall have a little time
for our private lives, to see our friends, to read books on which we
can sharpen our minds instead of those not requiring too much
effort. Or shall we? Are incidents and crises already lurking
round the corner, waiting to pounce on our hopes of peace? At
least we have the illusion that a quiet time lies ahead, and feel the
better for it. If it turns out to be the proverbial donkey's carrot,
it's just one of those things.

SEPTEMBER 22   Have sometimes spent half an afternoon
rolling and cutting out biscuits, begrudging
the flying seconds with every jab I give the cutter. Felicity's
"icebox cookies" are not only lovely to eat, but the method
involved does away with this lengthy chore. Take two eggs, two
cups of light brown sugar, three-quarters cup margarine
(melted), three and a half cups flour, six teaspoons baking powder,
one teaspoon vanilla essence, half teaspoon salt. Beat eggs, add
sugar, stir in cool melted margarine. Mix flour, baking powder,
salt, and sift into egg mixture a cup at a time, stirring in well.
Knead in the last cupful, form dough into long roll about two
inches thick, place in refrigerator overnight. When wanted, cut
dough into thin even slices. Put on greased tin. Bake in moderate
oven about ten minutes. This makes about five dozen biscuits.
All measurements are level, and a "cup" equals the standard
eight-ounce measure. A little less sugar can be used, and half the
margarine replaced with cooking fat. A cup of chopped walnuts
makes a good addition. Flavours can also be varied. Not having all

the correct ingredients for my first batch, I substituted self-raising flour and white sugar without ill effects. Incidentally Felicity has no "ice-box" just now, so makes hers in cold weather. Weather rules my to-day's mixture for a different reason. Gales and such permitting, Eve is getting an "airlift" as far as Hendon this afternoon, and completing the journey home by train. If she doesn't arrive, shall leave my "dough" in the frig. until next week-end, and cook it then, as it can easily be kept uncooked for a week or so.

SEPTEMBER 25   Week-end one mad rush, with Eve home for thirty-eight hours for which she has to put in an equivalent time travelling by air, rail, car, and sea. *Cloud-Reading for Pilots* makes the double journey with her, despite my suggestion that she leaves this fascinating volume behind for me. Just as well she doesn't, perhaps, as am spending every spare second with my nose in bee books, especially those chapters devoted to winter hazards. Have fixed zinc mouse guards at entrances, but have a horrid feeling that I've bungled the job, and that any really determined mouse can easily squeeze in. As woodpeckers have been at work on adjacent pear tree, am now on the look-out for three-eighths-inch wire-netting designed to keep out both pests, but so far have found it solely in catalogues from which only vast rolls are supplied. Feeding for Hive I finished to-day, they having dealt with the syrup from their 10 lb. of sugar as fast as they were given it. Hive II, always less active, still have some three pints to cope with, and are taking their time about it. Both have a really good store of honey, but the weather and swarming and re-queening activities have left them no time to store any honey in the supers for us. All things considered, however, they have done very well, according to Mr. Chelford, have built up into quite respectable colonies, and it won't be their fault, says he, if they don't produce a very nice honey surplus next season.

SEPTEMBER 27   To Swanton Novers W.I. to judge baking competition sponsored by makers of oatmeal, etc., who have presented as prize a duck-egg blue earthenware porringer and set of porridge bowls with which I should love to abscond. Judging between the entries, all of which look pretty well as appetising, is an almost hopeless task, and at one point suggest that sponsors should be asked for extra sets of bowls so that everyone (including judge) can have a prize. Since this is impracticable, finally decide on gingerbread made with four ounces each margarine, sugar, self-raising flour and oatmeal, two eggs, two dessertspoons golden syrup, one teaspoon each ginger and allspice. Cream margarine and sugar, add beaten eggs and spices, mix in flour and oatmeal, lastly add warmed syrup. Bake 30–40 minutes in moderate oven (350°, reducing to 300°). Judge's reward no mean one in this instance, as I return home with sample from each dish of exhibits, and promptly partake of second tea the minute Adam arrives home.

SEPTEMBER 28   Visits to Home Lovers Exhibitions, like those to mannequin parades, are usually fatal to my peace of mind. And to-day's no exception. So deliberately make a jet-propelled progress round most exhibits, allowing myself to linger only by the macabre "The Burglar and You" series (shall undoubtedly imagine I hear thieves breaking in every night for the next month!), and to watch the police-officer lost in contemplation of the fish in the tropical aquarium, envying, I shouldn't wonder, the ease with which they solve their traffic problems. Then into the cat show, where I could cheerfully spend the entire day. The kittens, sapphire-eyed Siamese (several sitting on hot-water bottles) cream and blue balls of fluff, a long-haired red tabby, a long-legged short-coated Abyssinian, are playful, slumbrous, or both in turn. But do the grown-up cats really enjoy it? I doubt it, and can sympathise with the aristocrat in the blue fur coat who sits with his back to the spectators, and another whose deep orange eyes and short broad face positively radiate affrontment and scorn. The marmalade sixteen-year-old Chum, who is making his first appearance at any show in the Household Pets section, takes it more philosophically. I try to imagine William's feelings if he sat in the cage next door. But the memory of the miserable object I rescued from a similar cage in the R.S.P.C.A. home would be enough to prevent me from subjecting him to an experience which I am sure he would look upon as a prelude to being lost again, if nothing worse.

From cats to ballet is a natural transition, for both are instinct with grace. And Felicity and I have seats for the matinee performance. We see "Swan Lake" again, "Blue Danube", "Capriccioso", and Anton Dolin in "Bolero". Both of us are longing to see Petrouchka and "Nutcracker". But these don't come on until to-night, and we both have husbands at home and consciences about playing truant unfortunately, though Felicity so far succumbs as to rush to the box office as we leave, and get seats for Roger and herself for Saturday. And we both decide that next time we must somehow manage to get up for the whole week's performances.

SEPTEMBER 29   "He who eats goose on Michaelmas Day, will never lack money his debts to pay", runs the old saying. The usual argument arises as to whether new or old Michaelmas Day fits the bill . . . and which is which, anyway. In this case we dine out on the family's goose to-night, and hope to eat our own in a fortnight's time, since this last is the date of our lease. Many of the customs associated with the end of the farming year have died out. But Wisbech still keeps its hiring fair on the third Wednesday in September, when agricultural workers who wish to "break fresh ground" assemble in the old market, wearing a ribbon or cord (colour immaterial) in their button-holes. This is the sign that they seek a new master, and when they have agreed with one, he gives them a shilling. This legally binds them to serve the new employer for one year, the engagement to begin at Michaelmas and should the hiree default, the hirer is entitled to sue him. In the old days the farmer moved his new employee's chattels in a farm wagon whose horses were decorated with ribbons and twinkling brasses as though ready for a show. Nowadays the removal is carried out by lorry, less picturesque, perhaps, but decidedly more expeditious.

SEPTEMBER 30   "When is Peter Worstead's sale?" inquires Adam. "I might look in. We need some more pig troughs." I turn to the back page of the local paper. Only a few weeks ago the auctioneers' advertisements were concerned mainly with the "excellent pair of brick and tile cottages", the "well-built dwelling house", the "country house of character", and sundry "desirable lots of household furniture and effects". Now they deal chiefly with the sale of "Capital Holdings", of "Live and Dead Stock", "Agricultural Carriages", "Choice In-calf cows and heifers", pedigree pigs and poultry, and useful working horses. But more is going under the hammer than the most comprehensive catalogue includes. For the farm sale is not simply a sale, but the disintegration of a community.

The herd, T.T, or Accredited in most cases, and built up over a period with endless forethought and care, is suddenly reduced to a mere collection of Neat Stock, to be dispersed to many different homes, or to the slaughter house. Some of them are near calving, but go they must, on foot or in cattle-floats, let the consequences be what they may. And nobody will know that Rosie, that rattling good milker, but nervous as so many home-breds are, doesn't really need roping at milking time, as long as she's properly handled. That no better parent than Apple Blossom can be found after a day or two, but she must be watched for the first forty-eight hours, or, like as not, she'll trample her calf to death. That Clara, good old girl, will mother everyone's calf. That the clown-faced heifer, one of Dolly's daughters, has been used to poke her soft nose into a pocket never without a "dairy nut" or two. And how will Jock, now ready to license, turn out? Will the daughters he sires approach the record of his dam? George, who has tended him since birth, will often wonder in the years to come, but he will never know.

Tom looks at his horses. Not so many as at the last sale he recollects, when old Mr. Attlebridge gave up. Only one team now. But to Tom they are personal friends. Stormer has never been no trouble with Tom. Never no trouble at all. But he want understanding. Do he don't take to you, a proper stubborn old hoss he'll prove. Captain is titchy with blacksmiths unless Tom himself is by when he's shod. The day he went barefoot, and the little old boy took him down to the shop, he wholly went on. Broke loose and come all the way home himself, at the finish. Brisk, she's a good old mare, for all she's getting on, and likely to go a bit himpy in the wet weather. Smart recognises Tom's step long before he sets foot on the stable threshold, and never fails to whinny a greeting. What will she do when she hears that step no more? The tractor driver is luckier in this respect, though not one fancies the thought of a stranger meddling with HIS engine. And with the years even the deadest of Dead Stock is apt to acquire a life of its own. It is hard to think of the implements one has used so long and so often as nothing but metal after all.

The men speculate among themselves. They know the Old Guv'nor and his ways. He knows them, and their several capabilities. Each side has developed a mutual respect for the other, and knows exactly how far he may go. But what about the new guv'nor? What will be he like? Will he want them? Will they want him? Some live in tied cottages, and with the housing shortage what it is, feel bound to answer this last question in the affirmative, or at least decide to "give it a try". Some are tied by far more than a cottage, for they have spent all their working days on this patch of earth. Its face and character are as familiar as those of their wives. They know where the boggy place lurks under an apparently sound surface of soil, which field is prone to what weeds, where are the awkward bits, the good, the medium. Their knowledge of past seasons and crops is encyclopaedic. Their calendars less a thing of dates than "the time the Horse Close had that master crop of hay" "Lambscote was barley that year, I recollect. And Silverpits was down to sugar beet", or "Thirteen weeks, and we never set a plough into the ground", and "That was the year there was corn out till nigh on Christmas". Like the trees in the fences, they are rooted in the farm, and can be transplanted as successfully. Yet supposing they and the new guv'nor don't get on? Will is seventy-five, and, matching his skill against a youngster's strength, he'll knock off a day's work with the best of them, if he's let go his own stroke. But will the new guv'nor realise it? Ted has hired a pightle, keeps a pig or two, and some fowls. Will he be allowed to keep it on? Or is the new guv'nor one of those who think of a man's pigs as a direct incentive to steal the feeding-stuffs in the barn?

Lastly, the land, patiently abiding. Will the new man be out for money, and nothing more? One to break the soil's heart, knock out a few good crops, and then move on? Or a real farmer? Or a mixture of the two?

So many questions, which only the future can answer. For the new man must start from the bottom, and build all over again. It takes time and patience, to say nothing of humanity, common sense, and good humour (with a dash of low cunning) to weld the new set of men, stock, and implements into one harmonious whole.

These and similar thoughts throng my mind as my eyes travel down the columns, for I have seen a farm sale from inside. But Peter Worstead is little more than a name to me. His sale, I see, is next Friday. "But don't buy anything with new paint on," I remind Adam. "You know what Father says. A coat of paint often covers a peck of trouble."

14

October 1 Harvest festival to-day, and one of the nicest services of the year, so am furious when I develop some kind of twenty-four-hour flu, and have to retire to bed, instead of joining in my favourite hymns. Should also like to have seen Felicity's monster pumpkin enthroned, and wonder if anyone else who saw it immediately wondered where the mice and the fairy-godmother were lurking, as I did when I first glimpsed it in her hall.

The church thanksgiving for another harvest safely gathered in has always seemed so right and fitting, and so much a part of this season, that I was surprised to learn not long ago that it is not, as I had always supposed, a custom centuries old, but dates back less than a hundred years. Brooke claims to have held the first such service in Norfolk in 1854. (Its claim to be the first parish to hold such a service in the country is disputed by a village in the south of England.) Apparently the custom of largesse, under which the harvesters made a house-to-house collection the moment harvest was done, and then spent the money in the nearest public house, had resulted in scenes and scandals of the most unlovable description. The vicar of Brooke, Dr. Beal, in an attempt to put a stop to these, decided to hold a harvest festival in his church, and afterwards entertained men, women and children to dinner on the vicarage lawn.

"The attempt to put an end to the system of public-house feasts, in which neither wives nor children can join, appears in this instance to have been eminently successful", reported *The Times* of this service and frolic. The following year a number of parishes followed Brooke's lead. But for a long time the custom was far from general. It took forty-four years to travel the sixteen or so miles to Attlebridge, for instance, where, as a boy, Uncle

Humphrey witnessed the excitement that preceded the first such service, the inhabitants enthusiastically arriving at the little flint-walled church with such laden bags and baskets, wheelbarrows and carts, gigs and traps, that when they had finished decorating inside the building, it looked less like a church than the produce section of an agricultural show.

OCTOBER 4 Letter from Angela, who writes "London is very dark, thanks to the gas strike. We are cooking with a one-burner oil stove, an electric kettle, a hay-box, and about a quarter-inch of gas. But baths are a curse." The newspapers tell of emergency operations carried out by candle-light, or sick people turned away from hospitals. "What we housewives should do is go on strike", snorts Mrs. Beetley. Personally feel that State ownership and control are, and must always be, a failure until men realise that life imposes duties and responsibilities as well as rewards, and that an agreement is equally binding on both parties to it. It is idle to condemn the late Hitler and his gang for tearing up treaties whenever it suited them, if in our working lives we are willing to do just that, no matter who suffers in the process. Not so long ago "word of an Englishman" was a synonym for probity, and an unbreakable oath in the East. I wish that I could think an Englishman's word was worth as much anywhere to-day.

OCTOBER 5 A psychiatrist would have an explanation for it, no doubt, and possibly a cure, but have a thoroughly irrational dislike of peeling apples, and always avoid this chore if I can. Wanting some swift form of apple pie to-day, side-stepped it by grating several large cooking apples (peel as well) into an oven-proof dish, with layers of blackberries in between, finishing with a layer of apple. Added a little water, sweetened with golden syrup, then sprinkled on crumble crust . . . 2 oz. margarine rubbed into 4 oz. self-raising flour and 1 oz. sugar. Baked in medium oven forty minutes, starting at bottom of oven, so that crust wasn't cooked before fruit; and result distinctly gratifying.

OCTOBER 6 Hepsibah seen striding purposefully into her stye with bundles of straw this morning, and late this evening she is proudly surveying her family of ten, who already seem as lively as month-old kittens. Our policy of making friends with our animals pays a big dividend at such times, as she appreciates our good will, and is ready at any time to allow us to approach. There are occasions, however, when I hardly appreciate the effusive fondness with which we are greeted. Presenting Hazel with a bolted cabbage this afternoon, what felt like several tons of affectionate pig immediately collapsed on me, asking to have her stomach rubbed, and pinning my left leg against a post. Managed finally to extricate myself without broken bones, but am still aching from knee to hip.

OCTOBER 7   The earliest of our chrysanthemums, the pinky-gold Sweetheart and the snowy Chastity, have practically finished blooming. But the lemon-buttercup Imperial Yellow, the bronze Carefree, and the crimson and beige Balcome Triumph are now in full flower, to the admiration of everyone who sees them.

"You haven't grown these out of doors", one florist says accusingly as he lifts some out of the box. "You've got them under cover".

"No, we haven't. They're out in the open", I assure him.

"They're lovely stuff", he tells me. Last year they would have been worth twice the money he's giving us for them. But what with the weather, which has made an abnormally long season for all the other garden flowers, and the fact that everyone is so hard-up, well, there it is.

It is, indeed! But although we've only just managed to pay for the cuttings, wire, and so forth, with nothing at all for all the hours I've spent on them, I shall grow just as many next year. For one must pay some tribute to beauty; we have had the house full of flowers, and we've had the fun of giving hundreds away into the bargain.

OCTOBER 9   Like all novice beekeepers, have been overwhelmed with advice of all sorts. The latest is in a letter received this morning from a septuagenarian friend, who suggests that one can read too much about bees. "An old hand once told me 'Keep them warm and feed them well, and that's all you need worry about'," he writes. But then the old hand knew what he was doing, and as I have noticed before, the more one knows the simpler any operation becomes. Actually my intensive reading has already simplified my methods enormously. For wintering I have had no truck with packing, inside the hives or out, but followed the example of a well-known honey farmer who has tried out practically everything, and now simply puts a couple of quarter-inch thick slats above the crown-board for ventilation. Whilst for security against gales, have fastened each hive to the stand with a piece of baling wire. Moles having elected to burrow under the back legs of the stand, both hives have acquired a slight list. So loosen the soil in front, mount the stand, and depress the front legs to match.

A wasp hovers in front of Hive I during this performance, and as I hop down, decides that this is the moment for a burglarious entry. He couldn't be more wrong, of course, as my activities have disturbed the inmates, and several guards bounce out to investigate. One grapples with the wasp at once, and a fine display of all-in wrestling begins. Quite forgetting that, unlike pigs, bees resent all intrusions, however well-meant, I foolishly attempt to reinforce my side with a small twig, and am promptly attacked in my turn. My retreat is no less expeditious, but not nearly fast enough, as a few minutes later a sharp prick on one knee reveals a guard bee attached to my linen slacks. Luckily the full charge has not got through, and I escape with nothing worse than a slight irritation, and a resolve to let them fight their battles unaided in future.

OCTOBER 12   Rabbits now in season, so must try out Angela's rabbit mould, and "conyng in gely", a fifteenth-century recipe acquired recently. For the former, cut up a rabbit, boil in vegetable soup until tender. Put meat twice through mincer, then put into saucepan, add $\frac{1}{4}$ lb. butter (margarine), a chopped onion, salt and pepper if necessary, a teaspoon paprika. Mix in a little of the liquid to which a little gelatine has been added, put in a long mould, place in frig. to set. Eat cold, cut in small slices.

Our ancestors either roasted their animal whole: or "hakked" it into joints, next fried it in "fayre freysshe grece", then put it into a "potte" with fried minced onions, some broth, wine, mace, cloves, pepper, and canella (cinnamon). When "wyl-y-boylid", powdered ginger and salt were added, and the cony served. Incidentally it seems that the creature was a rabbit for its first year, achieving cony status at the age of twelve months.

Nowadays the name seems to feature only in our local courts, when a man up before the Bench for poaching rabbits is charged with "trespassing in pursuit of conies".

OCTOBER 14 As a cat-lover with an undisciplined imagination, I have not infrequently wondered what happens if one travels abroad, acquires a cat, and then wants to bring said pet back to England. Cats, like dogs, must undergo six months quarantine in these circumstances. How do they withstand the ordeal? How well are they looked after? How much does it cost? Stella's Lalka is now providing the answers to these questions, with four months of his incarceration accomplished. He has a private residence the size of a small summerhouse, with his own grass run at the back. He is well fed, and conversed with in the manner appropriate to a lonely Siamese gentleman. On the occasion when he ran a temperature he was removed to sick-bay, and given special attention and treatment. Stella was notified at once, and rushed up to London fearing the worst. But on arrival she found a convalescent Lalka sitting on an electric blanket, and overjoyed to see her. Of course he misses her and waits for her visits. But he seems to understand that it is just one of those unavoidable things, to be borne as philosophically as may be. His board and lodging cost twelve-and-six a week, his sick-bay sojourn only being ten shillings extra.

OCTOBER 16 Have acquired a few pullets, partly for compost making . . . given the material, and run on the deep-litter system, one bird can produce five to ten cwt. per year . . . and partly for eggs. Adam mainly interested in the latter angle. But the price of eggs is such that only cracks and other misadventured specimens are allowed in the kitchen at present, everything possible going to the packing station. One thin shell in yesterday's batch, through which I manage to put a finger, so make spiced soda cake to-day, using 9 oz. flour, 4 oz. each sugar, margarine, sultanas (or currants), half a teacup of hot milk, half-teaspoon bicarbonate soda, grated nutmeg, cinnamon, and allspice to taste (approximately total of spice, one teaspoon), and said egg. Rub margarine into flour, add fruit, spice, and sugar, mix in egg, add hot milk to which bicarbonate of soda has first been added, put mixture into tin and straight into oven, baking 1–1½ hours.

OCTOBER 19   To Ketteringham with Kate this afternoon. The gardens lovely, and full of colour, despite the date. Am particularly fascinated by the display of Michaelmas daisies, especially the magenta-purple Walpole Wonder and Beechwood Beacon, and the pale blue feathery Photograph, three names I immediately add to my list of plants that I hope to acquire in the not-too-distant future. Immense bullrushes (of which, risking a ducking, I immediately acquire six) wave about the lake in front of the house, and in the river beyond where a heron, immobile as long as we watch him, waits patiently for incautious fish. Sun has dispersed the earlier mists which reduced our speed on the journey here, and irradiates the turning leaves on the trees in the park, irresistibly reminding me of the books written here not long ago, and the "Yellow Leaves" that featured in the title of one of them. Gardeners are busy about the grounds. Bees have made a home in a stone urn on a distant terrace, and are winging in and out of it. But these and other activities do nothing to disturb the peace that lurks in shrubbery and hedged about lawns, and encloses the whole.

Peace lies thick in the little church close by, where we try to decipher the writing of the remains of the brass to "Syre Thomas Grey", who built the chancel about 1492, and to "Jone, his wife". The two delightful half-timbered cottages opposite, now being turned into one, resound at the moment with the noise of tools and falling bricks. (One of the latter misses my head by a scant quarter-inch as I poke it incautiously through the door leading to the bottom of the stairs!) But peace is only just round the corner, waiting to step in and take possession the minute the workmen leave. Presently the Hall will be full of small boys, for it is to be a preparatory school. Can imagine few more gracious settings in which to acquire a love of learning and spend a happy childhood; and leave regretting that Adam and I have no son to enter for it.

OCTOBER 23   Summer has been staging a mild come-back lately, and we seem to have had more sunshine during the past fortnight than in any similar period in the more appropriate months. Signs of autumn continue to multiply, however. Russet and gold are the prevailing colours in the hedgerows. Mud-caked heaps of sugar beet, looking the last things capable of producing sweetening matter for our puddings, cakes, and tea, are stacked along the roadsides. Leaves, acorns, and the "conkers" beloved both by deer and children, if for somewhat different reasons, come showering down. Here and there the ground is littered with the green hedgehog husks of sweet chestnuts, though once again none appears below the tree half-way down our drive, leaving us to speculate on whether it can be "blind", like some of the crocuses, whether chestnuts, like willows, are male and female, or what can be the matter. Somewhat belatedly I gather sage, mint, thyme, and the rest, to dry for the winter. And all the time I keep my fingers crossed against the first frost, which can't be far off. One good frost, and we shall have seen the last of the chrysanthemums, we have been warned. So am keeping half a dozen pails full in the butler's pantry, as an insurance. And when the fatal frost comes, shall endeavour to render first aid to as many frost-bitten blooms as possible by putting them under the cold water tap before the sun touches them.

OCTOBER 24   Much affronted last night when eating nuts to find molar affectionately known in the family as my L.D.V. tooth (the result of an unfortunate incident with a gun in 1940) has broken off again, so this morning have to dash into Norwich for repairs. Give lift to an American airman I overtake on way, when conversation for next twelve miles ranges from the climate at his New Jersey home (apparently much like ours) to wars, their causes, and possible cures. Like me, he believes that the ordinary people of all countries are peaceably inclined, and when let alone by politicians and propaganda machines, get on with one another as easily as with the man and woman next door. So why must nations resort to war, which the winner loses equally with the defeated? Neither of us knows the answer. But the pale-blue flag of the United Nations floating over the City Hall to-day suggests the best if not the only way of preventing our Dark Ages from becoming darker yet.

OCTOBER 26   Variety is as necessary in meals as in any other department. But like most housewives, when over-busy, am apt to take the line of monotony and least resistance. Then something starts off a train of thought which ranges over as wide a field as a game of "That reminds me". In this case salt beef is reached via a number of things, including carrots, and serve it in the old way with dumplings . . . $\frac{1}{2}$ lb. flour, two teaspoons baking-powder, made into a dough with cold water, shaped into dumplings, which are dropped into a saucepan on the top of already boiling potatoes, and boiled for twenty minutes. On this occasion beef arrives from butcher already salted. Next time shall try salting some of my own in brine made by adding salt to water until an egg will float in it: or else follow Elspeth's example. She uses 1 lb. brown sugar, 1 lb. bay salt, 2 lb. salt, 2 oz. saltpetre, boiled in two gallons of water, putting in the meat when cool, and leaving it in for about ten days. Mutton can also be treated in this way.

OCTOBER 27　Dinner with Jean and Rodney last night, and as we step out of their door, see car roof a mass of sparkling crystals, and burst into loud wail on behalf of our chrysanthemums. Can do nothing on arrival home at midnight, and not much more this morning, though I spend an hour cutting blooms (and getting frost-bite myself), and another lengthy period in the butler's pantry, holding flowers under cold-water tap. (This appears to salvage some, but half the Carefree and all the Balcome Triumph are past help, and their petals turn blacker and blacker as the day progresses.)

Am still rendering first aid when telephone rings, and after some introductory chat, caller enquires if he may bring staff photographer, and take me at my desk for a "Women at Work" series their paper is running. They can be along in an hour. Rashly consent to this, replace receiver, then take shattered glance around. Hair, as usual, looks as if I've been turning somersaults, and ended up in a Christmas tree. My writing-table, adjacent table, window-sill, shelves (and floor), would lead the ordinary observer to conclude that I am about to embark on a paper chase, the darning basket occupies the centre of the sofa, minor debris litters the place, and pails of chrysanthemums are standing all over the hall. Spend the next sixty minutes frantic-ally trying to bring about some order in this chaos, and have just finished when my visitors arrive. The next twenty minutes are wasted cloud-watching, as the sun has arrived with the visitors, and is doing its best to confuse the lighting effects. Eventually a cloud obliges, some shots are taken, and rashness breaking out once more, I suggest including William in the finals. This pleases everybody except William, who, when at last we think we have him arranged, leaps over my pen as the camera clicks. A second is more successful, though his expression is anything but amiable. But I shall be surprised if he doesn't make the better picture at that.

OCTOBER 31   Spend most of day digging up some hundreds of the best chrysanthemum plants, secateuring stems to within six inches of stools, and removing them to glasshouse (a friendly market gardener's) and cold frame (our own) for next season's cuttings. Evening spent with family as Mother is celebrating her birthday, though not in the traditional manner. According to the ancient Celts, this was the last day of the year, and they lit enormous bonfires at night. When cold, the ashes of each were scattered in a circle, when everyone who had helped to make the fire then put a stone inside, and if next day any stone was found displaced or damaged, it was believed that its owner would die within the year. Later superstitions centre chiefly about one's future husband or wife. I have peeled apples and thrown the single coil of skin over my left shoulder in my time, though I can't in the least remember what initial resulted. (And am sure it was never Adam's!) But have never eaten a salt herring before going to bed, when one's future partner should appear with a cup of water in one's dreams. Nor have I roamed blindfold in a cabbage field, and pulled up a stalk, when a clean one presages a poverty-stricken husband, earth on the roots a rich one, a hard stalk a strong man, soft a weak-willed, a short stem a short man, a long stalk a tall, and so on. And I'm not going to try it now, either, says Adam firmly, as we pass a field on our way home, and I suggest a little scientific investigation!

NOVEMBER 2   "I'm sure I've beaten you this year. I made my Christmas cakes yesterday," says Mrs. Peacock, when we broke clear of one of those dodging matches on the pavement where each swerves the same way in an attempt to pass. "No, you haven't," I crow. "I made mine a fortnight ago." The snag in these advance preparations, however, is that they simply bristle with temptation. Have actually made four cakes of varying sizes. Of course we have to eat one, to find out how it tastes! Then I'm sending a parcel to Eve, so in goes another. A third has featured as a birthday present. And have a hideous feeling that Number Four will never stay the course. So am now saving ingredients for fresh one. Puddings and mincemeat have yet to be made, and a parcel from Eve has arrived with part of its contents (including raisins) missing. But currants still there, so the new version will consist of 9 oz. flour (I prefer wholemeal self-raising), 6 oz. each margarine and sugar, 3 eggs, 2 oz. cherries, 2 oz. mixed peel, and 4 oz. each sultanas and currants, baked $1\frac{1}{2}$–2 hours in moderate oven.

NOVEMBER 3   Lorry drives into yard this morning with four pedigree Wessex Saddleback gilts, the latest addition to our pig family, and to be known in future as Hildegarde, Henrietta, Hyacinth, and Hermione. None is anxious to leave her temporary home at first, but finally one slithers down the miniature Cresta Run that leads to earth, and makes a dash for the side-door porch. The two lorry-drivers and Our Man scatter. I seize an empty pail and bang its sides vigorously with the car-washing brush. And although they are strangers to us and our ways, a rattling bucket strikes the same chord everywhere in the pig world, and they are soon following me through the first gate. Curiosity impels them to pause at intervals, what time Hepsibah rears on her hind legs to look over the front of her stye and squeal what sound remarkably like porcine insults. Hazel, next door, is too occupied with new maternal concerns to join in. But the fattening pigs swell the eldritch chorus, and it is all I can do to make my contribution audible above the din. By rattling just in front of the newcomers' noses, however, I keep them moving, and they are soon in their new quarters. "A lovely lot", we all agree. And I find myself contemplating the view oblivious for once of the autumn pageant all around, beauty for the moment residing for me in four black and beige figures against a background of brickwork, trodden straw, mud, and fading green pasture. "Lovely," I repeat to myself, as I turn away. Though when I think of their price and the prohibitive cost of comprehensive insurance, I foresee endless alarums, excursions, and telephone calls to the vet. whenever one has a tail the least bit out of curl.

Afternoon brings proofs of "Woman at Work" photographs, in one of which I look dismal to a degree, and in the other (plus a scowling William) I am convulsed with mirth. Much prefer the latter myself, though must remember for future occasions, if any, to push under some papers the ancient tobacco tin in which I keep stamps, as this has come out best of all. The staff photographer prefers the first effort. As he points out, the idea is to catch one at work, as if I didn't know he was in the room. And am bound to admit that Number Two suggests anything but honest labour. So agree to Number One appearing, comforting myself with the thought that press photographs are usually blurred anyway.

NOVEMBER 5   What makes a day memorable down the centuries? Can think of several reasons, but must confess an abortive attempt at arson seems an odd one. Yet three hundred and forty-five years have passed since Sir Thomas Knyvett, of Ashwellthorpe, near Norwich, then Justice of the Peace for Westminster, arrested Guy Fawkes in time to thwart the plot to blow up the Houses of Parliament. Last night the official celebration and "noises off" resounded through the village, sending William Cat indoors and on to my lap at the first crack. The family have fireworks for three-year-old James this evening, which we are too late to watch, though we hear he was thrilled to the marrow. I wonder how long the "plot" would have been remembered, if it hadn't been for children? Or is it that when it comes to playing with fires and fireworks none of us ever grows up, and one excuse is as good as another?

NOVEMBER 9   Sugar (lack of) still one of my biggest housekeeping headaches, but the unrationed Dutch fondant mixture now available will at least provide icing for the Christmas cake. Have also acquired a tin of Australian mincemeat, which I am augmenting with some grated apple, suet, and a little sherry, and putting it into jam-jars until wanted, to eke out the home-made supply. Am using old family recipe for the latter, which takes 2 lb. each beef suet, apples, demarara sugar, $2\frac{1}{2}$ lb. raisins, $1\frac{1}{2}$ lb. currants, $\frac{1}{4}$ lb. mixed peel, juice and rind of three lemons, $1\frac{1}{2}$ oz. ground sweet almonds, one teaspoon mixed powdered cinnamon and mace (or pudding spice), $\frac{1}{4}$-pint brandy, $\frac{1}{4}$-pint port or home-made wine. Half this quantity made up at home in my salad days. Don't expect to have fruit enough for more than a quarter this year, and sherry must substitute for the more expensive liquids.

NOVEMBER 10   From far end of tennis court, where I am pulling up unwanted chrysanthemum stools, see poppy-seller disappearing down the drive, so follow her to the house to fetch my purse. An odd emblem to choose for remembrance in some ways, since poppies are more apt to suggest forgetfulness and sleep. And yet, perhaps, the right one after all, since none of us can afford to dwell perpetually on our losses, or on the strength of that ultimate Iron Curtain against which the loving heart must always dash itself in vain. For me, wherever my body may be on Remembrance Sunday, my thoughts will be on Danish soil, and on the verse of a Danish hymn. "Fight for all you hold dear. Die if it is necessary. Then life is not so hard. Neither is death."

NOVEMBER 12   Pedigree of the four gilts, at present referred to collectively as "the girls", now to hand, from which it appears that they are already equipped with names that are registered in the pigs' Debrett. And when I say can't we have them altered, as three of them have the same name anyway, distinguished only by different numbers, Adam tells me that it's dead against the rules of the National Pig Breeders' Association, and adds will I kindly cease referring to that august body as the "Pig Club". Second thoughts suggest that on the whole the young persons may just as well stay as they are, as the supply of names beginning with "H" is far from inexhaustible, and can foresee us descending to Halice, Hamy, and others before we've done.

NOVEMBER 14   Spend thoroughly entertaining evening as member of All Women's Brains Trust at Norwich. As a fellow member remarks (and how I agree with her!) the great thing about these is that, unlike lectures, there's no "homework" attached, as none of us have the least idea beforehand of the subjects on which we are expected to express our views. To-night they include questions on psychology versus individual responsibility (am inclined to agree with questioner that not enough stress is placed on the latter these days), should girls do a period of national service (if women are to claim equality with men in other walks, they should shoulder the responsibilities as well), the Festival of Britain, are women less bound by red tape than men (the trust unanimous in saying "Yes, and a good thing, too!"), should local government be above party politics (only one dissentient voice on this, and that emphatically not mine) and for what would the twentieth century be remembered in the centuries ahead . . . a question that was variously answered by the vote for women, television, the atom bomb, the development of a social conscience, two world wars, utility clothes, and the amazing strides made in flying.

NOVEMBER 15   Letter from Eve who, after featuring as understudy and prompter in the station play, is now apparently billed to appear as a cannibal lass, and also as a member of the *corps de ballet* in "Robinson Crusoe", the station pantomime. It has been raining every day, she reports further, with much bitterness. She'd no idea when first posted there that Northern Ireland would be so wet. At the moment I feel it has nothing on North Norfolk, or at any rate, our part of it, as so far this month there has been only one day when I have not had to record more or less points in my weather book. Fortunately the bulk has fallen at night, and there has been a certain amount of sunshine during some of the days. But underfoot everything is one vast mudpie, through which William Cat stalks with the air of an offended Queen Elizabeth before whom no Raleigh hastens to cast a cloak.

After lunch, am rung up by Felicity who, earlier in the month, has asked if she may nominate me for the committee of our W.I., and now says that I have been duly elected, and also voted into the vice-presidency. Feel that this, like Punch's definition of second marriages, is a triumph of hope over experience on the part of fellow members. As while the spirit is more than willing to help, the flesh is already fastened to so many jobs that have only managed to attend two meetings this year. And spend rest of afternoon wondering exactly how I am going to stretch my time sufficiently to cope with even a quarter of my future duties.

NOVEMBER 16   Day dull, cold and drizzly. Must do something to combat general gloom, so decide to try out Felicity's baking-powder biscuits (scones to me, as she remarked when giving me the recipe). These need two cups of sifted flour, four teaspoons baking-powder (omit this if self-raising flour used), three-quarters teaspoon salt, two to four teaspoons lard or margarine, three-quarters cupful of milk (or half and half milk and water), the cup in each case to be the standard 8 oz. measure.

Mix flour, baking-powder, salt. Add fat, mixing in lightly until the mixture is the consistency of coarse meal. Add liquid slowly to make soft dough. Knead on floured board half to two minutes. Roll to half-inch thickness, cut into rounds with small biscuit cutter (I use an egg-cup), bake in hot oven until light brown on top (approximately 10–15 minutes). When cool, store in tin. Heat through just before serving split and buttered, either singly, or with halves put together again.

November 19   Another wet depressing day. William, who hates rain, and seems convinced that I could stop it falling if only I'd give my mind to it, does nothing but jump on my writing-table and walk up and down over papers to stir me into action . . . which he does eventually, though not quite the kind he meant. Out of doors there are miniature lakes on the drive, on the stack-cover that swathes the straw bales for which there is no room in stable or shed, on the paths, and in the pig runs. Hepsibah and Hazel, confined to the yards of their styes, relieve their feelings by tossing their heavy iron food troughs about as if they were made of cottonwool. Meditate on the advantages enjoyed by the hedgehog, who sleeps comfortably through all this. And indoors once more melt two tablespoons of honey in a large glass of hot water, which I drink before once more picking up my pen. A bee-book in which I have lately been browsing recommends this for mental and physical fatigue. As at moment I am endeavouring to cram twelve months' work into three, while feeling about as wide-awake and active as a mouse when the cat's finished playing with it, am testing this out for myself. Results to date certainly encouraging. But foresee if I continue to imbibe honey syrup at present rate, shall have to quadruple the number of colonies at the bottom of the kitchen garden next season.

15

November 21   Do I realise, demands Adam, that it's less than five weeks to Christmas? I do indeed. Also that Christmas puddings and mincemeat are still only a beautiful thought, and that I mustn't put off the job of making them a second longer. Grandmother's recipe for former is 1 lb. each breadcrumbs, beef suet, currants, raisins, sultanas, brown sugar; $\frac{1}{2}$ lb. flour, $\frac{1}{2}$ lb. peeled and cored apples, $\frac{1}{4}$ lb. mixed peel, 3 oz. ground sweet almonds, $\frac{1}{4}$ oz. mixed spice, six eggs, juice and rind of one orange and one lemon, half-pint stout or ale, one teaspoon milk, a little salt if required. Her family distinctly larger than mine. Even so, cannot believe that she ever owned a basin able to cope with this quantity, which makes four good-sized puddings. Assess our needs and resources, and decide that one will be enough this year. So make up quarter quantities, using whole-meal flour, as I find this gives a much better flavour as well as more food value. Great-grandmother boiled hers eight hours. I boil mine one and a half, then leave it in the Aga simmering oven overnight. And while it's boiling, deal summarily with the mincemeat, filling six honey jars with this. Can now sit back, as main preparations are in hand, and turkey on order, though not without some trepidation as to the possible super-colossal price of the latter. Must confess my sympathies with Martin, who rears them, however. The other day, when a town acquaintance railed at the cost this year, "Have you ever reared one?" interrupted Martin. "Well, suppose you buy one day-old, and try bringing it up, especially with feeding-stuffs costing what they are to-day. That'll cost you something. And I'll bet you'll be thankful to pay my price next time".

NOVEMBER 24   Put some of Felicity's scones into oven to warm up for belated tea, when front door bell rings, and it's Mr. Chelford, who happens to be passing by, so has called in to ask after the bees. He's had his tea, so reft mine from oven again, and on my voicing grave doubts as to mouse-proofness of my zinc guard efforts, we proceed to end of kitchen garden with torch. The first thing he does is to tap each hive. Can I hear anything, he inquires? Not a sound, though I try hard enough. That's all right, he murmurs. If they'd been queenless, there'd have been a positive roar. No. I guard is right. No. II's is a trifle high. While I hold the torch, he takes out the drawing-pins and lowers it, several bees come out to reconnoitre, and more buzzing starts when we lift the roofs and take a quick look inside. Then I am invited to lever up each hive enough to estimate the weight of stores (they have ample). After which we go back to the house where I have a sheet of foolscap bristling with questions needing answers.

When he departs, leaving me considerably wiser, and minus earlier visions of hives becoming mouse barracks, I put scones back into oven, only to take them straight out again, as another unexpected visitor who has already tead arrives. Finally Adam appears. He's had his tea, too. So as it's now well after six, give up the unequal struggle, and prepare next meal instead.

NOVEMBER 25   On our way into Norwich this morning we overtake one cattle lorry after another. Passing down King Street we catch a glimpse of their animal cargoes being unloaded on the "Hill". The bedevilled beasts low and bellow, as they have always done. Men shout at those who hesitate on their way into the pens. Prospective buyers confer. But one sound is missing . . . the shrill yap–yap–yap of the drovers' dogs. In its place gears are grinding, engines labour and purr. For the old order changeth . . . To-day the farmer who wants his cattle taken to market, or brought home from a sale, reaches for his telephone, and arranges for a cattle float. Yesterday he would have sought out old "Jimma" or one of his drover brethren with a "Jimmy, I've got some cattle for Norwich Market on Saturday", or Dereham Friday, Fakenham Thursday, or wherever it might be. And at the appointed hour "Jimma" with his "ol' dorg", would be in the yard. Arrived at his next destination he would at once begin to look round for farmers wanting stock to be driven home again. Calves, heifers, cows, bullocks, sheep . . . nothing came amiss to "Jimma", and few and far between the markets and sales at which one did not catch sight of his weathered face. But clever drover as he was, he would have been lost without his "ol' dorg".

Like human beings, dogs are many and various, and the superlative stock-dog was born, not made. But as with any other calling, training is half the battle, and "Jimma" could work miracles with that inspired mongrel, the old Norfolk stock dog. His succession of dogs were practically human. At a word they would round up cattle from a distant pasture, and bring them round for the master to inspect. Another word, and one especial beast would be separated from the herd, and held aloof. Sheep would be rounded up, and in an open field would stay huddled where the dog had collected them, not daring to move until he gave the signal. On the road, a gesture from "Jimma", and every beast was pushed against the fence and held there, until the approaching traffic was safely past. And once in a while a Saturday would come when "Jimma" had no animals to drive up to the "Hill". But he was always sure of bringing some home. So on these occasions he would go into Norwich by train, taking his dog with him. One day he was offered a lift, but forgot his dog. Off went the dog alone to Foulsham station, boarded the train, and rejoined his master on the "Hill". Another time, racing for the train at Lenwade, he caught it just as it was pulling out of the station, the porter slammed the door behind him, and his dog was left on the platform. Presently "Jimma" arrived on the Hill, some ten miles farther on. Waiting for him on its paved slopes was his "ol' dorg".

So well known was "Jimma" for his skill in training dogs, that many a farmer entrusted him with promising puppies. One of these pupils was to become a legend . . . he could cow even the black-faced Suffolk ewes, who would attack and rout the ordinary stock-dog . . . and "Jimma", recognising his quality, was determined to have the animal for his own.

"About that dorg", he began, the next time he encountered the farmer in question. "I aren't a-partin' with him. I can't help him belongin' ter yore nevvy", as the farmer began to expostulate. "I'll get him another dorg. But I aren't a-partin' with this yere one." Nor did he, until the miserable day when the dog was found poisoned.

"Jimma" was broken-hearted. He was also, for the first time in history, without a dog. Generally he had at least one puppy in hand, being trained partly by himself, and partly by his "dorg". Meeting a client one day, he answered the customary "Well, Jimmy. How are you going on?" with a disconsolate, "I ain't got no dorg".

"I've a good little bitch", suggested Mr. Hemblington.

"Can't do with bitches at all", muttered "Jimma". But so broken in spirit was he that eventually he took the bitch and departed, still muttering.

Not long afterwards Mr. Hemblington encountered "Jimma" at a lamb sale.

"How's that little bitch of mine turning out? Any good?" he inquired.

"Jimma", like most of his ilk, never committed himself to a direct affirmative. But his features twisted into an expression of alarm. "What! Do someone want ter buy that bitch off on you? Don't you sell har," said he. "Do you think a partin', I ont mind har meself".

If you wanted a dog of your own, you had only to mention the matter to "Jimma", or one of his friends, the recognised price being one shilling and a pint of beer. My parent having mentioned one, with the proviso that it should be delivered to his home, was pounced on by "Jimma" on the Hill one morning with the words "I ha' got yore dorg. A right good 'un. Only he cost two-an'-a-tanner. Here t'be".

"I can't take him now", protested Father. "What am I going to do with him all day? Besides, I've got to go home by train this afternoon. And you know they won't allow dogs on trains."

"Don't you fret, guv'nor. I'll hev' him down ter City Station ter meet you." And there he was. A quick glance round, a swift swinging back of the carriage door, and the dog had disappeared under the seat at such a speed that an approaching porter noticed nothing. Nor was there a movement or a sound to be detected even by the elderly lady, scared of dogs, who was a passenger, as the train proceeded, until Father reached his destination, several stations down the line, when the dog was out of the carriage like lightning, and trotting behind his new master as if he had never known another.

George Reymerston, another large stockbreeder, was also never without a dog, some of them bred by himself, some of them

bought from "Jimma", all answering impartially to the name of
Joe, and all so highly skilled that they seldom made the slightest
mistake. If they did, the punishment was invariably the same.
"Lie you down, you mucky old dog," yelled George Reymerston
from his gig. And down would squat the culprit until such time as
his master relented, and told him to get up. Came the day when
George Reymerston, his mind on other matters, drove out of the
field without giving the accustomed sign. On reaching home he
was surprised not to see the current Joe running between the
wheels. But assuming that Joe was not far behind, he handed
over the reins to his man, reminded him to feed the dog, and
went indoors. Next day came, but no Joe. Another day passed.
The following morning Joe was still missing. All at once there
flashed into George Reymerston's mind a picture of Joe, crouch-
ing down in a field at his off-farm, several miles away. He
ordered his gig and drove straight off. Sure enough, there was Joe
in exactly the same spot where he had been told to lie down
two and a half days earlier.

November 27   Am extremely sorry to see that the Minister
               of Agriculture has ranged himself on the side of
the big battaloins, and against the part-time smallholder. In
theory, no doubt, the full-time holding he prefers, complete
with suitable buildings and house, is very nice indeed, and many
a part-time holder would be glad of one. But even the optimists
admit that it will take years before the merest fraction of the
land-hungry can be accommodated with these desirable young
estates. Meanwhile a vast reserve of potential energy, hope, and
ambition and hard work is wantonly thrown away. The part-
time holding has a number of very real advantages here and now,
whatever its place in Utopia. Not the least is the part it plays in
weeding out the triers from the stayers. To work for a master,
when much of the thinking, planning, and worrying is done for
you, is a very different thing from working a plot, however small,
unaided. And a lifetime on the soil is still too short a time to learn
all there is to know. Then there is the seasonal labour problem of
the big units. In the past some men made a comfortable liveli-
hood by combining working a part-time holding with casual
labour on a neighbouring farm. And what of the many who, by
reason of age, lack of capital, poor health, or similar causes, can
never hope to undertake a full-time holding? They are not seek-

ing the easy way. As part-time smallholders, the word "leisure" will vanish for ever from their vocabularies. But they want a deeper thrill and a more lasting satisfaction than can be found in watching a footballer score a winning goal, or the greyhound on which they have staked five shillings romp home. If part-time holders are driven off the land, the nation will be the greater loser.

NOVEMBER 29   A most interesting series of letters on field names now occupying three parts of the correspondence column in our local press. Horse Close, Sheeps Close, Church Close, and fields named for the points of the compass or their position beside woods, etc., seem a feature of practically every farm. But several are new to me. And have not seen others that are in my collection, so join in the fun myself for benefit of fellow squirrels.

At Lyng Richmond's place goes back to pre-Conquest days, when it was part of the Earl and Honour of Richmond (and in the fifteenth century it was still paying a yearly tribute of fifteen shillings to the holder of the title). Then there is the Kings Grove, said to have witnessed Edmund's last stand against the Danes. Kidholms, which may be another reminder of Viking invaders, since it is also the name of a small island off the coast of Denmark; and the "Strips", long tongues of meadow on which the paper from the long-vanished paper mill (at which Parson Woodforde was once a customer) was spread out to dry. Sparham has Lambscote, the Upper Common, Drift Field, Far Hills, Minxes, Gypsies Pit, Swains, Hall Field, Lincolns (called after the shepherd who stole the sheep, and was transported more than a hundred years ago), Pinkels, and others. Binham has a Swimmers, Upper and Lower Morphews, Fiddlers Hill, Froghill, Bishop's Hill, Hourglass, Deadman's Close, Summerways, Shovel's Pit, Clamp Lands, Greenway and Middlemoor. At Walsingham you will find Long Bullion, the Bleach, the Scrubs. At Billingford there is the Tharten Acres (which is twenty-eight acres, not thirteen, as you might guess), Hovel Breck, Cuckoo Hill, Clam Breck, Ram's Breck, Brittle and Clap Closes, Broomhills. And in other villages I know are Litesters (dyers) Piece, the Hang and Went, Gibbet Hill, Great and Little Delphs, Long Langyds (pronounced Language), Poison Piece, Castle Breck, Long Melfer, High Oaks, Ashyards, the Wongs,

Starvecrow, to mention only a few. There must be enough in our county alone to fill a volume.

NOVEMBER 30   Several out-of-reach cooking apples have now tumbled down, so turn the two largest into apple fritters. Use corer to remove core, peel apples whole, then cut horizontally in thin slices, dip in batter made from 2 oz. flour (use four if extra apples used), one egg, milk. Orange fritters are good, too, but have found these rather tasteless if cooked with ordinary batter. So for these I use one tablespoonful of vinegar instead of the egg. And if there's an egg shortage, vinegar batter is useful for other things as well. (Mix vinegar well into the flour, adding milk gradually.)

DECEMBER 2   Frosts have spoiled the last flowers in the garden, and it is too early to bring holly into the house. But was pleasantly surprised to receive a bouquet at brains trust at Costessey on which I sat last night, so this morning am able to fill three vases. Questions raised were mainly serious, most needing ten volumes, not to say two months, for an adequate answer, especially those concerned with the cost of living, the state of the world to-day, and what we should do to improve it if the power were in our hands. (Needless to say, I allow my compost-humus-soil bee to buzz out of my bonnet at this last, and only wish I could make it sting enough of those in authority to get some action.) Need no time at all, however, to make up my mind on a question concerning a Parliament composed entirely of independent members, as am all in favour of this, and do not envisage the chaos predicted by rest of team if this should ever come to pass. Meeting ends on lighter note, as final question posed is, "What makes a cat purr?" Pleasure, of course. But the questioner is obviously out for the mechanics of the action. And I feel that William is much better equipped to deal with this than I am.

DECEMBER 4   Wake to find ground buried beneath nearly four inches of snow. More covers the roofs and cascades at intervals from wind-blown boughs. Yet more descends from the sky during the morning. The pigs stamp about disconsolately, the hens refuse to venture out at all, the prospect of catching up with outside work recedes further, and the roads are unbelievably treacherous. Presently the sun comes out, tempting William Cat from chair-seat to window-sill, but no farther, though from my window I can see a stray cat turning somersaults in the snow down the drive. Recall childhood days when this sort of weather affected me in much the same manner, and sent us out on meadow and field slopes with tin trays and toboggans. But cannot say that I really care much for snow anywhere but on a Christmas card these days. And feel even less in favour of it after slithering my way down to Felicity's for a W.I. committee meeting. (Shall certainly consider visiting the nearest blacksmith and getting myself "roughed" like the horses, if the road-surface doesn't improve!)

"Is there anything the wretched stuff is good for?" demands Adam bitterly, as he finally skids the car into its lair, and relates a few of the narrow escapes he's had on his way home.

"Childblains on the feet," I tell him. "All you have to do is to run barefoot in the snow until your feet glow: about five minutes." Have not been plagued with these for years myself, as, in defiance of all the wiseacres, I make a practice of sitting with my feet in the fender whenever possible, and while writing, have them on a hot-water bottle or within scorching distance of an electric fire. But have more than once applied this drastic-sounding remedy with complete success in days gone by. And can still see myself and Brother John, having declined to go to a dull party on plea of having bad colds, chasing stocking-and-shoeless up and down the snow-covered tennis lawn on a moonlit January night!

DECEMBER 6   Cold snap still on, so am working through all available soup recipes one by one. To-day's is beetroot bortch, for which I cut up one large peeled beetroot into chunks, peel and slice two onions, and put into saucepan with one pint milk (milk and water will do). Add salt and pepper, simmer until onions are cooked (about forty minutes), then strain through colander, pressing beetroot, but not pressing it through. Thicken with one tablespoon cornflour. It should be served with blobs of whipped cream on top, but not, alas! in these days. A small knob of margarine on each plate is a help, though. Tinned soup is improved and goes further by making a stock from two bay leaves, one small sprig of thyme, the outside portions of one head of celery, one medium carrot (diced), one potato (grated), seasoning, one onion (optional), $2\frac{1}{2}$–2 pints water, simmer for 2–3 hours, then strained, the contents of the tin being added just before serving.

This is the day that Hanya, in Cracow, will be expecting Father Christmas to call, as in Poland the children have their presents on St. Nicholas Day, and sugar figures of the saint are on sale in the shops. Inga, whose family were natives of Bremen, has a delightful little St. Nicholas house, full of windows. To-day she lights a candle behind one window. And every few days she lights another, until by Christmas Day the whole tiny structure is illuminated.

DECEMBER 11   Have I made sure of seats for the pantomime on Boxing Night, writes Eve. Theirs has been a great success, and already they are lined up for a play in the New Year. She hopes that the latter won't need grass skirts, though, as it's far too cold a costume for this weather. And although gravy browning and liquid cascara are grand for "native" make-up, they're frightfully hard to get off. She's had three baths in succession, but her skin isn't back to normal yet, and the stain keeps coming off on her clothes.

DECEMBER 12   What makes a successful party? A good deal of preliminary hard work, pleasant company, a lot of laughter, among other things. We had all three and more this evening at our W.I. Christmas and birthday party (one visitor said she couldn't remember when she'd laughed so much!) and nobody could believe that the clock hadn't gained when at last it occurred to somebody to look at it. Felicity and our secretary, who have slaved throughout the year, collected well-earned cheers, bouquets, and thanks. And my only regret was that Wilfred Pickles couldn't see himself "Down our Way" as our younger members envisaged him.

DECEMBER 13   Do not really care for cold frosty weather unless I have plenty of time for brisk walks. And too much too early makes the winter seem twice as long. "If the ice'll bear a man before Christmas, it won't bear a duck after," says Ben. But so far, whenever I step hopefully on the surface of a frozen puddle, I crash straight through. Make a tour of apple and pear trees on which I optimistically plastered mistletoe berries last January, but not a trace of growth. And hurriedly cut a few holly boughs with berries on, before the birds strip the lot, as they've already done in the kitchen garden. The tree, the ivy, and the rest of the decorations will wait until Eve gets home next week. But cards and presents are already arriving, among them a box from Rhodesia that has travelled in the mail-boat's cool chamber, and unpacked, discloses a mass of Chincheringchee flowers from Sally. When open, these look something like a cross between jonquils and wild white hyacinths, and, with care, will last for months. Rosemary always strong-mindedly refuses to open a single letter or parcel until the twenty-fifth. Can never bring myself to do this, and think it's a bad idea, anyway. Christmas is such a lovely time that we might as well make it spread over as many days as possible.

DECEMBER 15   Wake to find another blanket of snow over everything, with more falling thickly, and this is the day our fat pigs have to go to market. Latter in this case is Ashington, only seven miles away in normal weather. But dare not essay the long steep hill on way, so have to make detour which more than doubles the journey. Have not been to Ashington market before, either. So of course I manage to overshoot the entrance, and have to near-skid practically all round the town before I can manoeuvre into the saleyard. Am soon entangled with a tractor and trailer, and another trailered car, as even to experts the yard isn't easy to move in, and the snow and slush makes it fifty times worse. Then a most helpful policeman takes a hand, and assists me to push the trailer round, what time I see with horror that we've forgotten to change the number-plate before setting out, so that it doesn't agree with the car's. Luckily the gallant constable doesn't notice it, and presently am on my way home at a pace not exceeding fifteen miles per hour. In due course quite a few housewives will be having bacon for break-fast. I wonder if they ever realise what adventures it goes through before it reaches their plates?

DECEMBER 17   Can I suggest some cold sweets for Christmas, asks Norah. The children aren't keen on Christmas puddings, and she has a fair hoard of jellies, tinned and bottled fruits, etc. Have been collecting a similar store for Eve's benefit, and amongst others, hope to make the following.

Pear Sundae. Put the pears into sundae glasses, melt a little red-currant jelly, pour over the pears, decorate with chopped nuts. Am also trying some with chocolate sauce instead of the red-currant jelly, melting a bar of plain chocolate for it if I have any to spare, and if I haven't, making the sauce with one dessert-spoon cornflour, one dessertspoon (more if liked) cocoa, one breakfast-cup milk, sugar to taste.

Peach or Pineapple Shortcake. Make sponge sandwich by creaming 4 oz. sugar and 4 oz. margarine, stirring in two well-beaten eggs and 4 oz. self-raising flour, bake in moderate oven approximately 30 minutes. When cool, cut in halves horizontally, fill with sliced peaches or pineapple, and put second layer of fruit on top. Decorate with mock cream, cherries, etc. Or if a peach or pineapple trifle preferred, serve it in a dish, pouring fruit juice to which a little warm water, sugar, and lemon juice have been added over the cake after the first filling has been put in, but before adding the top layer of fruit, and decorating.

Most fruits can be made into a mousse by dissolving two table-spoons gelatine in $1\frac{1}{2}$ cups boiling fruit juice (or two-thirds juice, one-third water), plus the juice of one lemon. Allow to cool, then beat until foamy, add one well-beaten egg white, then beat all together until well mixed. Pour into mould and serve with fruit concerned. With jellies, sponge, fruit, or plain, the decorations are the thing. An effective way of decorating a green jelly is to use orange-skins cut to look like water lilies, and filled with orange or lemon jelly forked up, the "flowers" flanked with angelica reeds and bulrushes made from cocktail sticks with a roll of marzipan dipped in cocoa on top.

DECEMBER 19   Have previously booked Eve a seat on the London train due to reach Norwich at twelve-twenty, and made an appointment at dentist for her in mid-afternoon. Sail on to platform just as train rumbles in, but no sign of Eve. Spend next hour sitting outside in car worsening a threatened cold, then bounce on to platform to greet the one twenty-seven, only to draw blank once more. The next isn't due for nearly two hours, so having visited Enquiries and asked them to hold any message that may come, I descend on Marjorie and family to thaw out, and ring up Adam to say that he can expect me when he sees me, as I'll probably be spending Christmas at the railway station. Report back at three o'clock to learn the three-three is running late, so take a brisk walk around Thorpe, returning just as train steams in. Platform thronged with new arrivals, but still no sign of Eve. Just as am rehearsing litany of later trains, and recalling where Marjorie has hidden their front door key, catch sight of Eve at farthest corner of platform, and thankfully retrieve her, though too late for dentist and projected last-minute shopping tour.

Home again, to find more hitches have occurred in day's programme. Owing to oversight on part of market clerk, Hepsibah's family were entered for market last week instead of this, and now they reach saleyard to find only three rabbits and four elderly hens on premises, when they have been strongly advised to retire, so there they are back again.

And she supposes that when we go to fetch Brandy to-morrow, the roads will be too bad to ride him back, and he'll have to stay at Silford, laments Eve. Why couldn't this weather have waited until after Christmas? A sentiment we echo as one mind.

DECEMBER 23   Eve only too prophetic re Brandy, our visit to Silford being for nothing, Father rightly remarking that with the roads as slippery as they are, both Eve and Brandy risk broken legs if no worse. And where does she suppose she can ride him if she gets him over in one piece, anyway? Have promised to take her over the minute the roads improve, but no sign at all of this so far, though lorry-driver who arrives unexpectedly to fetch Kate Pig just as we are embarking on late lunch, says it's quite clear round Thetford.

Kate, whom we have envisaged occupied in maternal cares as from December 8th, has followed Helen's non-productive and expensive example, and if it hadn't been for the snow, would have departed for her second honeymoon a week or more ago. At the moment she couldn't care less for the idea, and our hitherto successful technique of rattling a food bucket two feet in front of a hungry pig, is quite useless as Kate has breakfasted largely, and just lunched on a good-sized cabbage. Now she fancies some exercise. As fast as we shove her towards the lorry she charges back, we skid on the ice-covered gravel, and she capers merrily over the back lawn. Presently the lorry-driver grabs an empty pail. Put a pail over a pig's nose, and it will back away, when you can back it into the lorry, he explains. He's done it scores of times. But not this one! Kate reverses in every direction except the right one. In one of her skirmishes she pounces on a large soup bone lying below the bird board, and begins to worry it like a starving dog, the while we entertain the direst visions of choked pig, and wished we'd insured her, after all. Then she's on the flower beds again. Finally Adam fetches a wooden hurdle to bring up the rear. And whether it's a good idea, or Kate is tiring, at any rate she's in the lorry in two shakes of a duck's tail.

DECEMBER 24 As we are foregathering at Silford with the family to-morrow, have a small party on our own turkey at home to-night. Quite a few countries make much more of Christmas Eve than the Day, Denmark for one. Well in advance the Christmas pig is slaughtered, geese plucked and dressed, cakes baked. The tree is brought in, the house decorated with boughs and berries, and tulips are planted on the graves of loved ones. At 4 p.m. Lise and her family will be going to church, then home afterwards to a dinner of rice-porridge and goose, with the tree and presents to follow...

Poland, too, has its Christmas celebrations proper on Christmas Eve. In Warsaw at six o'clock public transport stops, and shops close. In Polish homes the Christmas tree, decorated with paper chains and toys made by the children throughout the year, is waiting with more presents besides those given on St. Nicholas Day. But not until the first star is seen may the tree be lighted up. Since the eve is a fast, fish is eaten (in the old days it was cooked in thirteen different ways). Then there is beetroot soup, kluski (dumpling) and cake, both sprinkled with poppy seeds: and tiny puff pastries filled with mushrooms gathered earlier in the forest, and kept till now. And wafers stamped into a picture of the Holy Mother and Child are broken and shared, when the participants kiss. Old-fashioned householders lay a spare place at the table for any stranger, lest Christ should knock at the door, and spread their tablecloth over hay ... a custom that was kept in the Polish messes in Scotland during the late war. Christmas Day in Poland is more of a grown-up's party, and includes a large luncheon of goose, ham, and sour cabbage.

CHRISTMAS DAY Surely one of the most precious gifts of Christianity is Christmas? In the endless struggle to keep alive, we have far too little time for the things that really matter. But at this season, whatever our private preoccupations, however black and cloud-banked the international sky, we know a blessed relaxation. Work can wait, worries be postponed, quarrels forgotten. To-day belongs to peace, to joy and kindliness, to goodwill and giving. Isn't everything hideously expensive, and can one really afford cards and presents this year, demands Adam. Can we afford not to afford them? Years ago I was told of an elderly couple who literally hadn't a penny to spare. But each spring the old man hunted the fields for plovers' eggs, and brought them as a gift to his wife. When he died, a neighbour remembered, and sought some for the widow, only to learn that she had always loathed the things. "But your husband always gave them to you!" "Yes. But you see, he had nothing else to give, so I let him think I loved them". There is a joy in giving that warms the giver no less than the recipient. And if we have to hoard our pennies for the remainder of the year, we can forget to be careful and cautious for a few joyful days, and take courage for the future from another Christmas.

Snow everywhere, and the roads, especially our miles of back lanes, snow-banked and ice-surfaced. But the sun comes out for an hour or more early in the afternoon, and shines through the leafless trees. Recall Ben's saying that "If the sun shines through the trees on Christmas Day, the autumn a load of fruit they will display," and hope that this applies to black currant bushes and raspberry canes as well!

DECEMBER 28 Five late nights in a row behind us, and several more in prospect. Once upon a time this my idea of the perfect Christmas. But am definitely not in training for any such programme at the moment, though am enjoying every second of it. Am scarcely in training for so much solid food, either; but this plethora, like the parties, will soon depart, and we can confront a vista of corned beef with what grace we may. Have never been a lover of this substance, and do not expect to feature as one now. So am evolving sundry disguises, not to say stretchings. Mash with a little margarine, seasoning, and centres of potatoes baked in their skins, return filling to skins, add chopped parsley, and serve. Slice thinly, dip each slice in batter, fry, and serve as fritters with slices of lemon. Cut into dice, put in piedish with a little stock, grate over a layer of raw carrot (or mix this with the diced beef), add a pastry crust, and bake in medium oven 40–60 minutes. Line pudding basin with suet crust, fill with diced beef, stock, chopped raw leeks and seasoning, cover with suet crust, steam or boil 2–3 hours, and serve with good gravy.

DECEMBER 30   Determined that to answer all letters received within a week shall be one of my new year resolves. But cannot help wondering how long I shall keep it, as although have dealt with over thirty in the past few days, have still masses to write, including some for Australia, British Columbia, Georgia, Virginia, Rhodesia and Denmark. Miss Smith, writing from Queensland, says she wishes the Post Office would produce Air Mail Christmas cards, as once again she's forgotten to get her overseas ones off early enough (so have I). And what has been happening to me, as it seems a long time since she heard? They have had the most unbelievable floods. In July the house carpets and furniture were taken up, and they nearly migrated to the shearing shed, whilst the R.A.A.F. had to drop them food and fodder. In September it dried up enough for her to be able to take a much-postponed trip to Sydney. But it was soon off again, they have been isolated for weeks, the wool clip is still on the premises, and the children are being fetched home for the holidays in a blitz wagon (army truck to me) which takes six hours to cover the fifty muddy miles. Shall hardly dare to mention our weather when answering this, as feel she'll wonder what on earth we're grumbling about.

JANUARY 1   "A happy new year," we say to everyone we meet. And as the words leave our lips, inevitably we wonder can we, dare we, be happy as things are. And ask ourselves how can we plan for any future in times like these. But could men ever? Looking from our century across those past, we see only a few mountain peaks of war, battle, and misery, and are apt to think that the valleys between were pleasant and peaceful. Closer acquaintance with the "good old days", however, reveals a daily round as full of potential difficulties and disaster as our own. Yet men created great things, built magnificent cathedrals and churches, painted great pictures, wrote great books, and dreamed their dreams. I have never cared for the advice to live as if each day may be one's last. If one followed it, one would attempt nothing, risk nothing, hope for nothing. If we are to live at all, we must have faith in the future. And so, come what may, I continue to wish for all of us, "A Happy New Year".